After qualifying as a Chartered Accountant in 1980, Julie founded Butler & Co in 1986. She is a farm and equine tax specialist and together with her team provides consultancy services to other accountants, land agents and solicitors on all areas of the equine world, farm diversification and bloodstock. She is also the author of 'Tax Planning for Farm and Land Diversification' as well as co-author of 'Stanley: Taxation of Farmers and Landowners'. In 2017 she became the editor of Farm Tax Brief and her articles are published regularly in the national accountancy and tax press. She lectures to a large variety of audiences through various organisations and to the rural community direct on a range of equine and farming issues. She has a lot of practical equine experience including riding a winner of a Point-to-Point race when she was in her early forties.

Butler's Equine Tax Planning

3rd Edition

Butler's Equine Tax Planning

3rd Edition

Julie Butler
FCA
Founder & Joint Managing Partner

Law Brief Publishing

Published 2021 by Law Brief Publishing, an imprint of Law Brief Publishing Ltd
30 The Parks
Minehead
Somerset
TA24 8BT

www.lawbriefpublishing.com

Paperback: 978-1-914608-00-1

Dedicated to my late husband for his support.

PREFACE

The equine world is complicated in itself, not least the tax treatment of the assets and the business operation. As an industry it is supported in some areas by vast wealth, in other areas with intense passion and sometimes a mix of both! Within this community exists a large number of hardworking individuals trying to secure profitability alongside the abiding desire for animal welfare, in spite of the large infrastructure costs.

Recognising these key difficulties and the need to show commerciality to achieve beneficial tax reliefs, this book explores tax planning in the context of the different areas of stud farming, racehorse ownership, training, breeding and standing stallions at stud.

With the variety of ages, wealth, motive and passion amongst the equine client base, combined with the vast array of individual sectors within the equine industry as a whole, the equine tax adviser must have full understanding of the business operation and their client. If there is concern regarding any area of the claim to tax relief together with tax return disclosure, specialist advice and help must be considered. Equine Tax Planning is the essential guide for every professional involved in an equine business to help point in the right direction. Nevertheless, with the pleasure of acting for interesting individuals in a unique yet complex equine industry comes the necessity to ensure all tax planning is tailor-made.

This book aims to provide an overview of the whole range of equestrian tax planning so as to highlight the various opportunities and pitfalls that the tax adviser may come across. Whilst it does not have the scope to consider all the tax points raised in extensive detail, it does provide the idea, guidelines and strategies to help and support the equine industry and all those involved.

The law quoted in this edition is accurate as at 30 April 2021, including coverage of all statutes, statutory instruments, court cases, tribunal decisions, online announcements/guidance, Statements of Practice, concessions, HMRC Manuals, HMRC Briefs, and other publications.

We welcome all comments and suggestions for improvement to this work.

Julie Butler
May 2021

CONTENTS

CHAPTER ONE

GROWTH OF THE EQUESTRIAN INDUSTRY

Chapter 1 explores the following subjects:

- Are horses agriculture? (1.2)
- Benefits of sole trade/partnership (1.3)
- Decision to incorporate the equine business or not (1.4)
- Making hay for horses (1.5)
- The modern farmer with liveries, haymaking and the environment (1.6)
- The impact of the *Vigne* (UT) tribunal case on liveries (1.7)
- The riding school (1.8)
- The racehorse trainer does not just train racehorses (1.9)
- Survival of the small racehorse trainer (1.10)
- The racehorse owner, the costs and prize money (1.11 to 1.18)
- Trade or a hobby (1.19)
- Breeding and owning competition horses (1.20)
- Livery yards in general (1.21)

- Employing family members in the equine industry (1.22)
- Polo (1.23)
- Showjumping (1.24)
- Eventing (1.25)
- Dressage (1.26)
- Point to Point (1.27)
- Business sponsorship and racing (1.28)
- Racing clubs (1.29)
- Bloodstock agents (1.30)

This opening chapter discusses the ever-growing equestrian industry and its diversification opportunities for farmers and landowners. We touch on the business structures and their relative benefits as well as the possible tax implications. We consider the tax benefits and pitfalls of holding an equestrian business on farmland with consideration of activities away from the farm, as a sport and a hobby.

Key issues considered are:

- The tax treatment of making hay for horses
- The impact of the *Vigne* tax tribunal on liveries
- Horse ownership can be 'tax free'

Introduction

1.1

The equine industry has grown dramatically over the last few decades. Some would call this the 'golden glow' of the 2012 Olympics and the strong results of our competitors since that date together with the need for alternative, profitable uses of farmland.

Many areas of equine activity are increasing in popularity and there are clear signs of commercial growth. There is also increased interest in the 'pony-paddock' culture whilst the need for farm diversification is also having a positive impact. Websites to consider when reviewing equine tax planning are:

- www.thehorsemensgroup.com
- www.thetba.co.uk
- www.racehorsetrainers.org
- www.weatherbys.co.uk
- www.hmrc.gov.uk
- www.butler-co.co.uk

There are many other equestrian disciplines which are also currently thriving, such as endurance riding, showing and the whole area of the sports horse generally.

The decline in the farming industry has meant the sale of a large number of 'pony paddocks' to link to houses which has the combined benefit of increasing the value of the house and letting the farmer command a very commercial price for a small area of agricultural land. It is for this reason that there are so many ponies to be seen in paddocks around the countryside whilst there has been a big move away from the riding school (see **1.8**).

There is a sports horse society and also a society for each breed of horse in the UK and they all tend to have a very enthusiastic following.

All these activities have created numerous equestrian businesses such as show yards, as well as the buying and selling of show horses and competition horses. To support all of the growth, there are a large number of freelance instructors (see **5.22**), farriers and saddlers etc, which, all together, present a picture of a thriving equine industry.

The result of all the different areas of the equestrian business means differing approaches to commerciality must be taken (see **3.2** to **3.12** and **7.2**). Each equestrian business has to be looked at on a case-by-case basis and all tax planning tailor made.

This book questions how the growth in numbers involved in this area of activity and its evident popularity can be treated tax efficiently by the commercial businesses involved in the sport. It also sets out the tax 'pitfalls' to the tax adviser and equine participant where planning has not been put in place.

Are horses agriculture? The fall back of BPR

1.2

Post the Budget 2021 and "Tax Day" 2021 the Inheritance Tax (IHT) reliefs for Agricultural Property Relief (APR) and Business Property Relief (BPR) have survived any change and consultation.

Stud farming is 'farming' for tax purposes (see **7.1**), the ordinary meaning of which is considered to be husbandry, i.e. the raising of livestock (see **2.2** and **2.9**).

In the tax case of *Wheatly v IRC (1988) STC (SCD) 60* (see **2.33** and **7.23**), the decision of which has been deemed flawed by many, it was accepted that a meadow constituted pasture for the purposes of inheritance tax. However, since the horses in question were used for leisure pursuits they could not be said to be "connected with agricultural activity or with stud farming" and they were not, therefore, involved in agriculture. This judgment is, however, at odds with the accepted tax principle that the activity of growing grass can be regarded as an act of husbandry given that it is a 'crop', and grass lettings are currently taxed as farming income, provided the 'landlord' meets certain criteria and can generally gain vacant possession within 12 months. Thus it is surely arguable that such property ought to be regarded as within the definition of agricultural property (see **1.5** and **7.1**) irrespective of the way in which the crop is exploited or utilised, i.e. grazed by horses.

Unless there is a stud activity that will qualify for agricultural property relief (APR) (see **7.17**), the equine activity will have to rely on business property relief (BPR) (see **7.21**) for inheritance tax relief (IHT) purposes.

Benefits of sole trader/partnership

1.3

The unincorporated business plays an important, if not vital, role in the equine world. Many, if not most, businesses start their life as a sole trade or partnership.

The key initial tax planning point for the equine business is that an unincorporated structure is also preferable if the early years are likely to produce trading losses. A sole trader/partner would normally be able to claim prompt repayment of income tax by making a loss relief claim against their total income. If such losses fall within a company, they could not be relieved until it generated profits.

There are no legal formalities in establishing a partnership (other than one under the Limited Partnerships Act 1907 or the Limited Liability Partnerships Act 2000) and a written agreement is not necessary, although it is advisable. The mutual rights and duties of partners, whether ascertained by agreement or defined by the Partnership Act

1890, may be varied by the consent of all the partners, such consent being either express or inferred from their actions (Partnership Act 1890 s19).

Whether or not a partnership exists is a mixed question of fact and law, and it is obviously more difficult to prove the existence of a partnership if there is no written agreement. But the mere existence of a written agreement is not proof, and it must be supported by the facts (see, for example, *Dickenson v Gross KB (1927) 11 TC 614*). HMRC may require proof that there is a partnership by requesting sight of contracts, agreements, VAT registration details and bank accounts. On the other hand, a partnership may be regarded as existing even though the individuals considered they were not partners (*Fenston v Johnstone (1940) 23 TC 29*). There are many cases in which the existence of a partnership has been reviewed by the courts.

Many equine businesses – and some accountants – do not understand the legal difference between 'jointly owned property' and 'partnership property'. The former is where the equine owners own the property together in joint names. The latter is where the legal owners hold this in trust for the partnership. The key tax point here is that partnership property achieves 100% BPR for IHT, whereas non-partnership property achieves only 50% BPR. To consider the tax position of the farm in more detail, it is important to identify and distinguish between the land and other assets, and how they are being used in a partnership. The research here can be from Land Registry, a review of the legal title, and a consideration of the partnership accounts, together with understanding the intent of the partners.

If the equine business is partnership property, it should be reflected in the value of the business itself as an entry on the balance sheet allocated to the specific partners who own it in their specific proportion. Partnership property will achieve BPR at the rate of 100% (see s104(1)(a) and s105(1)(a) of the Inheritance Act 1984 (IHTA 1984)).

Decision to incorporate or not

1.4

The decision to incorporate must not be undertaken lightly. Once a company is formed, for the decision to be reversed it has to be sold, wound up or 'struck-off'. Trading through a company is looked at in Chapter 8 (see **8.17**).

Accounts have to be filed at Companies House and there are administrative concerns that should be given consideration, as well as the tax advantages and disadvantages. In some cases for equine businesses the tax disadvantages can be punishing.

Over the last decade, many professional practices such as equine vets have incorporated their partnerships subject to their professional body's approval. Likewise, with farriers and other successful equestrian establishments. Once a certain level of profit has been achieved, a company may now offer many clear advantages over a sole trade or partnership, but the equestrian world must not be unduly influenced by this incorporation fever. Some influence will come from the new "super deduction" of 130% for qualifying expenditure which is restricted to companies (see **2.17**).

Making hay for horses

1.5

It might be thought that the treatment of hay for tax purposes is of minimal importance. However, we should bear in mind environmental encouragement of subsidies that "enhance the natural environment", which could include cultivating wildflower meadows (see **1.6**). Fields used for hay cover a substantial part of the UK landscape and are of importance to the equine industry. HMRC could therefore use this change from production to environmental activity to its advantage. Such a move might become an issue, for instance, on the death of a farmer who has perhaps diversified from traditional farming in later years to haymaking with other letting activities. Increasingly, the department is taking a negative approach to 'horse haymaking', arguing that such activity does not qualify for agricultural property relief. Such action has worrying consequences for the farming community on the claiming of future tax reliefs.

The consensus has always been that a 'farmer who makes hay is a farmer', regardless of whether they are growing a crop to be consumed by livestock or horses. The potentially negative response to such an assumption might now arrive as a shock to many beneficiaries of estates that include haymaking for horses and whose inheritances are under attack from HMRC.

If the hay is sold for consumption by horses, HMRC may incorrectly argue that the sale is *not* an agricultural activity under IHTA 1984, s115 (see **1.2** and **7.17**). The department contends that, unless the hay is sold under s115(4) for 'the breeding and rearing of horses', it does not qualify for agricultural property relief. Likewise, HMRC allows hay sold for working horses or horses used in the food chain to qualify for the relief. Many farm advisers and family members who are denied the relief due to the sale of horse hay would certainly argue that such an approach is wrong.

To qualify for agricultural property relief (APR – see **7.1**), property must be occupied for 'agricultural purposes'. Agriculture is not defined in IHTA 1984, but HMRC's Inheritance Tax Manual provides some useful guidance on land uses that would fall within this category. For example, the fact that energy crops qualify as agriculture is promoted by many influential sources in the tax and farming worlds. Indeed, it is supported by the guidance at IHTM 24062. HMRC also agreed that the relief would be given for growing and selling turf in *Assessor for Lothian Region v Rolawn Ltd [1990] SLT 433.*

Notably, *Assessor for Tayside Region v Reedways Ltd (1982, unreported)* illustrates the basic requirement of cultivation. In this instance, the absence of tilling, sowing and cultivating precluded reed beds from being agricultural. Therefore, in light of the above, hay that is grown and harvested for consumption by horses used for pleasure should attract the relief. If HMRC attacks horse haymaking, the problem for those in need of inheritance tax reliefs is twofold:

- The possible loss of agricultural property relief on the farmhouse for stud; and

- The possible reduction of this relief to 50% on land if it is used in a partnership but is not partnership property.

Although in *The Estate of Maureen W Vigne (Deceased) v HMRC [2017] UKFTT 632 (TC)* (see **1.7**) (this case was won at Upper Tribunal) the focus was mainly on business property relief and livery customers, the tribunal also decided that an agricultural property relief claim under IHTA 1984, s115 and s116 for the hay field would have failed. This was because no hay crop had been taken by the business in the two years before Maureen Vigne died. This apparent 'failure' is increasingly raised by HMRC, which quotes the tribunal's reasoning that *"Equine activities are not usually characterised as agricultural."* Certainly, the hay was used to provide the livery horses with feed during the winter, yet it is arguably a misconception that the ultimate consumer of the hay was the reason for denying the relief. The tribunal stated:

> *"It fails because the evidence given by Mr Vigne was that, although from time to time a hay crop is taken from the 'hayfield', that had not happened in the two years prior to the deceased's death."*

However, this should not affect the position if there is substantial and continuous haymaking. This must qualify under the normal definition of agriculture, which is the cultivation of the soil to grow crops. For the *Vigne* business, there were only 30 acres and an occasional hay crop. If haymaking is substantial, advisers must continue to argue that this is agriculture.

The modern farmer with liveries, haymaking and the environment

1.6

It is a common occurrence in the farming industry for a 'traditional' agricultural farmer to move to letting agricultural buildings, providing livery and supplying hay as they grow older and become less physically able to undertake other farming activities. Unfortunately, this carries the risk of losing inheritance tax reliefs from all directions and APR and BPR on livery operations (see **2.2**, **7.1** and **7.24**) and haymaking are clearly under attack. It seems that animals used in the food chain can provide and protect excellent tax reliefs yet moves away from pure husbandry to horses could be punishing in tax terms for the farming and rural community.

When undertaking inheritance tax planning for farmers and equestrian businesses in advance of death, the question of to whom the hay is sold must be forensically analysed. Likewise, when completing form IHT400 after death, the raising and growing of animals, grass and hay must also be understood. Further, HMRC is likely to give the matter serious consideration. With greater emphasis on the cultivation of wildflower meadows under Mr Gove's original promotion of a green Brexit and the priority of stewardship, the tax position must be reviewed. If HMRC is being unduly aggressive about haymaking for horses, strong, solid arguments must be presented and defended.

Natural capital refers to all the elements of the natural environment – soil, water, wildlife species and habitats, forests etc. Farmers can be paid for creating environmental benefits or maintaining natural resources that provide value to wider society. By identifying and evaluating the amount of natural assets (such as clean water, carbon-capturing plants and healthy soils) on a holding, the equine business can include this capital within a business model. When well-managed, natural assets provide many benefits to humans, from food and drinking water to recreational spaces and carbon storage by measuring and valuing these natural capital assets they can be managed to maximise the environmental benefits.

The impact of the *Vigne* UT tax tribunal case on liveries

1.7

Much tax planning attention has been given to the positive First-Tier Tribunal result in the IHT case of *Vigne v HMRC [2017] UK FTT 0632.* The case has since been won at Upper Tribunal *HMRC v The Personal Representative of Maureen Vigne (Deceased) [2018] UK UT 0357.* The primary question being debated in this case was whether the horse livery activity under consideration was "mainly holding investments" (see **7.21**) and therefore would fail in the claim for business property relief (BPR) (see **1.2**) by the executors. Whilst this claim was successful, it may have been somewhat overlooked that the claim for APR was denied (see **1.5**). The key BPR point in *Vigne* was that the FTT considered that the Upper Tribunal judgement in *Pawson (HMRC v Pawson* [2013] UKUT50) was flawed:

> *"The critical question however is whether these services were of such a nature and extent that they prevented the business from being one of holding Fairhaven as an investment".*

The judge in the FTT in *Vigne* recorded that the decision in *Pawson* was flawed. The judge in *Vigne* considered that it was wrong to start on the preconceived idea that the business is wholly or mainly holding investments and *then* ask whether there were factors indicating to the contrary. The judge in *Vigne* considered that the proper starting point is to make no assumptions one way or another and to determine the facts.

The business in question was a livery but argued that *"A hay crop was grown on part of the land referred to as the hayfield".* This hay was used to provide the horses with feed during the winter months, one of the 'enhanced services' offered by the livery operator. However, whilst it was noted that a hay crop was occasionally taken, the fact this had not happened in the two years prior to the deceased's death forced the Tribunal to question its qualification for APR.

> *"**48.** The appeal was also put on the basis that agricultural property relief should be available. In that regard, the appeal fails. It fails*

> *because the evidence given by Mr Vigne was that although, from time to time, a hay crop is taken from the "hayfield" that had not happened in the two years prior to the deceased's death. Again, the task of the Tribunal is to look at the matter realistically, and ask whether an objective observer, on the basis of the factual situation as we have found it to be, would properly consider agricultural activities to be carried on at or on the land. It is our judgement that if that question is asked, it must be answered against the appellant. Equine activities are not usually characterised as agricultural."*

As noted in **1.5**, this passing comment by the Tribunal and reference to the enactment of s115(4) of the 1984 Act regarding breeding and rearing of horses on a stud farm have already opened 'a can of worms' for the average ageing farmer who starts reducing his selling of livestock and then takes on a few liveries and makes hay. If HMRC is to attack the sale of hay for the consumption by horses as a non-agricultural activity in accordance with s115, this farmer's IHT planning may well be lost, despite having worked 80% of his life as a 'farmer' in the traditional sense.

Notably, the 'objective observer' that denied APR in this case was also the viewpoint taken when reviewing the evidence of the 'enhanced services' provided by the business for BPR.

> *"45. …We are satisfied that any objective observer who had visited the site 2008-2012 would have concluded that a business was being run from and on the land which did provide services to those who kept their horses on the land and that no properly informed observer could or would have said that the deceased was in the business of 'holding investments'."*

The 'common sense' approach taken by the Tribunal with regards to the BPR claim has been noted by many, no doubt attributable to the quality of evidence provided by the executors. For example, it was acknowledged that the various yard managers over the years were remunerated and this was reflected in the accounts, with evidence showing they worked circa 20 hours a week (paragraph 30). Furthermore, in paragraph 36 it notes *"the Yard Manager would have (or be expected to have) a BHS stage 4 (or similar) qualification in equine management, which, we are satisfied, would not be necessary for grass or DIY livery provision".*

The existence of a business plan (see **1.15**) and the following through of this with an application for planning permission, albeit unsuccessful, was deemed indicative of *"expansion of the business and the perceived need for the Yard Manager to be resident on site"* (paragraph 32). Moreover, the Tribunal stated in para 43 that *"the accounts do not bear the hallmark of the Accounts of a purely investment business."* and indeed rejected HMRC's claims that, for example, the inclusion of the removal of manure, fencing and pasture maintenance under the heading 'property maintenance' should not be seen as having a duality of purpose as clearly no such costs can be referable *"entirely to the running of the livery business or to holding the land as an investment."*

The case of *HMRC v The Personal Representative of Maureen Vigne (Deceased) [2018] UK UT 0357* turned on whether the operation of livery stables was a business (thus qualifying for BPR) or consisted 'wholly or mainly of...making or holding investments' (IHTA 1984, s 105(3)) and serves as welcome pony paddock guidance.

The Upper Tribunal confirmed that the correct test had been applied to the case by the lower tribunal and emphasised that HMRC's view – that there was a presumption that land constituted an investment unless it was proved otherwise – was incorrect. The open-minded starting point advocated by the First-tier Tribunal in its decision was held to be correct. Further, the intention of the business owner was deemed to be useful as an indicator if cases fall within the grey area on the 'spectrum of holding investments or trading' and therefore qualifying for BPR.

The case highlighted the nature of the extra services, as well as the intention of the business owner or landowner. However, many argue that the decision has not made satisfying the BPR test of s 105(3) any clearer. There is a spectrum of land exploitation with clear investment and clear trade at either end, and this is referred to by the tribunals.

All of the above, along with the strip grazing, carrying out of the worming service for the customers, providing hay, and undertaking a daily check of the general health of each horse, were seen as services that go beyond 'holding investments' and resulted in a successful BPR claim. Yet, the evidence to support an APR claim was comparably lacking.

The rejection of the APR claim (see **1.2** and **7.1**) on *Vigne* is arguably a further blow to the potential IHT burden of traditional farm diversification into liveries. However, equine and farm advisers must look at all livery operations, and indeed any diversified activities, in terms of both the BPR (see **7.21**) and APR implications. Whilst on a practical level farm tax advisers are frequently finding that HMRC is raising the 'failure' of the APR claim in the *Vigne* case, it is important to recall that in *Vigne* the activity was only for occasional haymaking, with no haymaking in the past two years, on only 30 acres of land. Where a farming operation involves substantial haymaking activity combined with liveries, we must continue to argue that growing and harvesting a crop of grass is agriculture, irrespective of which animal species eats the hay or the grass. In addition, advisers must be sure to have sufficient supporting evidence of the activities undertaken. As many commentators have observed *Vigne* will prove to be a very important case and all advisers must follow developments on the case.

The riding school

1.8

Riding schools generally offer a wide range of equine-related activities and training, including lessons and tuition (see **5.22**) at all levels, holiday accommodation, trekking and hacking, show jumping tuition, dressage, etc. They may also offer ancillary facilities such as all-weather or indoor sand schools, full, part or do-it-yourself livery, holiday accommodation and tack and equine supplies. Some riding schools are small-scale and offer only basic facilities, whilst at the other extreme, they may have a whole team of British Horse Society (BHS) qualified instructors and quality horses/ponies. Once the VAT registration limit has been exceeded, however, the VAT-registered business will often have to charge VAT inclusive prices roughly equal to its non-registered competitors (see Chapter 5 generally for VAT). This means that margins are often reduced, with the effect that larger organisations often have a lower gross profit than smaller ones. Apart from the relatively few cases where a customer is VAT registered and can recover the extra money, prices have to remain competitive.

Proprietors of such businesses often have to be willing to work long hours, since many people, particularly in spring/summer, prefer to take their riding lessons in the evenings. Whilst courses of lessons may be paid for by cheque, individual lessons are usually paid for in cash, making this business an ideal target for HMRC's compliance teams who historically mistrust 'mainly cash' businesses.

Any riding school will come under the BHS licensing provisions and although historically, most livery operations did not come within the operation of the licensing provisions of riding schools they are now being encouraged to join the scheme set out at **1.21** below.

The chief objective of the licensing provisions is to ensure that horses are properly fed, accommodated and cared for. However, there are also provisions about the supervision by responsible persons of horses which are hired out for riding unless a rider is competent to ride without supervision. The licence holder must hold an insurance policy covering him for liability for injury suffered by persons hiring horses for riding. The licence holder must also keep a register of all horses up to the age of three which are kept on the premises, and these horses must not be hired out for riding or used for riding instruction on payment.

The combination of the costs of the compliance with the BHS licensing provisions, business rates and the insurance costs associated with protecting against risk have caused a decline in the traditional riding school. Many have been making a loss and are unable to compete on price with the smaller unlicensed operations.

The structure of the equine business world has moved away from riding schools over the last 30 years. The casual rider has almost disappeared as there are so many other forms of leisure activities available. There has been a growth in general ownership, with many horses being kept at home or at a small livery yard. Lessons are now often given by freelance instructors and generally everything is dealt with below the VAT-registration limit. The collapse of farming has resulted in paddocks being sold at high prices to large houses in order to facilitate the keeping of horses. Small farms have been sold as potential equine establishments.

In short, the riding school is not necessarily where the pupils learn to ride. There has been a restructuring of the industry.

A racehorse trainer does not just train racehorses

1.9

Trainers fall into three basic categories, those training their own horses, those of relatives under a permit, and those training horses for the general public. A trainer may have any number of horses, from one to two hundred, in his yard. Many trainers operate as a sole trader; however, some are salaried employees of an individual or employees/directors of a company.

A trainer's income mainly consists of training fees, although some trainers operate racing clubs in which individuals pay an annual subscription for a share in a syndicate owning one of the trainer's horses, together with other benefits such as hospitality at the racecourse on race days. Trainers incur large overheads, notably in payment of staff and the purchase of feed, hay and tack. Other expenses such as veterinary costs and the costs of transporting horses to and from the races may be charged to the individual owner or may be borne by the trainer and then charged in an all-inclusive training fee.

A racehorse trainer does not just train horses. A racehorse trainer needs a skill base at least equal to and arguably greater than the average small business owner. So what skills are required for training?

Marketing: Attracting owners, requiring charm, confidence, previous winners and entertaining are essential.

Public relations:	Keeping owners happy. Having a positive profile together with press and possibly TV coverage. Role models such as Jenny Pitman come to mind.
Debt collection:	Historically, owners do not pay bills unless subjected to heavy persuasion. Positive debt collection can conflict with good marketing skills.
Financial controller:	Budgets, forecasts, keeping bank managers happy and trying to cover excessive overheads are an everyday need.
Bloodstock historian:	The thoroughbred's antecedents and potential must be known in detail (i.e. its progeny and form) by the trainer. Reference to any form of reference book can be seen as a weakness.
Fitness expert:	A total understanding of; equine fitness, build up, recovery and responses to pressure.
Handicap expert:	Total understanding of all handicaps and maximising benefits for the owners.
Choosing the right race:	Placing the horse and finding the 'right race' are a necessity. This requires a total understanding of the whole racing calendar by the trainer.
Motor vehicle buyer:	The business miles required of the average racehorse trainer can easily exceed a motivated sales representative. There is a need to combine speed with durability and the safety of livestock.

Geography:	The trainer must have a total knowledge of the location of all racecourses, combining visits to prospective owners, current and past owners.
Human resources:	Staff. Racing is labour intensive. The trainer probably needs the skills and expertise of a psychologist, team motivator, employment law specialist and, even on occasion, a marriage counsellor!
Bloodstock buyer:	Ability to have full 'crystal ball' facilities to buy right and be able to judge the right stamp. The trainer needs an 'Alex Ferguson' knack for introducing young raw talent.
Bloodstock seller:	Ability to always sell at a profit and at the right time, ideally foreseeing all future injuries.
Veterinary skills:	Many trainers would claim that they are expected to know more than a qualified vet but are unable to charge for this skill.
Catering supremo:	Owners expect full English breakfast after watching horses work and various forms of amazing entertaining all included in their standard training fees.
Post-race analyst:	Stating 'he/she will win a race' with confidence is not sufficient. Winning a race will be necessary. Each owner requires explanations, charm, drinks in the bar and positive observations on actual and future performance. This generally has to be conducted whilst saddling the next three runners or when the trainer arrives home wanting to collapse in peace and quiet.
24-hour chemist	One national newspaper is quoted as saying that trainers would all need chemists on a 24-hour shift to analyse all the ingredients that go to making a horse fit. They also

> state 'one wonders how trainers can sleep at night'. The responsibility they must take for the welfare of their charges is constantly being undermined by developments beyond their control.

Larger trainers have more financial resources to provide the above infrastructure. Perhaps financial training and serious profit projections before commencing would be a positive direction as opposed to just introducing some lower quality races.

Survival of the small racehorse trainer

1.10

The tax treatment of a trainer is largely dependent on whether HMRC consider that the operation is run on a commercial basis as a trade, or as a hobby. As the distinction affects the availability of losses for offset against an individual's other income, it is particularly relevant for the permit holder and the smaller trainer, who may be more likely to make losses.

Where HMRC regard racing as a hobby, any costs incurred by a trainer in connection with training a horse they own should not be deductible for tax purposes. On the same basis any trainer's prize money received in relation to a horse he owns should not be taxable. It is, however, understood that some trainers do claim deductions for such costs and presumably tax any trainer's prize money and in these circumstances it should be ensured that details of all horses owned by the trainer are fully disclosed to HMRC. This is important for both a permit holder training his own horses and the commercial trainer, many of whom buy a horse at a sale without a specific order from an owner and may subsequently be unable to sell all or part of the horse.

HMRC accept that where a trainer buys a horse without an order, he may claim the costs associated with the horse provided that it is clear that he is making genuine efforts to pass the horse on to an owner. The trainer should keep evidence of his efforts to sell the horse. Any HMRC enquiry will consider this point.

Horse ownership can be "tax free" (outside the scope of tax)

1.11

The main taxation issue facing anyone involved in the racing of horses (and ownership of competition horses) is whether this constitutes a taxable activity (see **4.3**). In order for an activity to be treated as a separate taxable trade, it must be managed on a commercial basis with a view to the realisation of profits. As far as racing is concerned, the majority of horses in training are not profitable as only a relatively small number win enough to cover the cost of their training. S30 ITTOIA 2005 specifically states that animals kept wholly or mainly for racing or other competitive purposes should not be treated as trading stock and thus the racing activity cannot constitute a taxable activity. In the main, the income and expenses incurred for the purposes of that activity should be confined to a separate racing account and be excluded from any tax calculation. There are limited exceptions to the rule that racing activities do not form part of a trade.

Following the principle in *Sharkey v Wernher [1955] 36 TC 275* (see **3.21**, **4.12**, **6.11** and **7.13**) horseracing, i.e. owning racehorses, is outside the scope of tax, i.e. not taxable. This is generally because HMRC regard the prospect of profit from racing to be so remote, it is not a taxable activity.

HMRC may attempt to combine the breeding and racing activities (see **7.14**). The argument would be that the breeding of horses is a hobby and ancillary to the racing activities and therefore disallow the expenses of the breeding operation and to bring this outside the scope of tax. The profit from the sale of a successful racehorse to a stallion syndicate is potentially tax free (see **4.14**) but how many profitable racehorses are there?

Background of the small breeder

1.12

The Thoroughbred Breeders Association's (TBA) statistics show that the average member only has a few mares or, perhaps, part of one stallion (see **6.16**). Most horses racing on the flat are fillies or colts that will have some life after they have finished their time on the racetrack. Some horses will retire to stud at their prime before there can be possible loss of value. The problem is that a breeder who does not occupy a stud farm may find it more difficult to convince HMRC that he is operating a bona-fide trade.

For most tax advisers the biggest possible impact on their client base is the entry into horse ownership and/or breeding by a client. This activity is often viewed by client and tax adviser alike as 'tax free' (see **1.11**) and therefore irrelevant. However, it is suggested that all practitioners need to be fully aware of their client's racing/equine interests, especially with regard to tax planning or during any future HMRC enquiry on their clients' affairs generally. The whole question of late registration of a taxable 'business' is dealt with later in this book (chapter **3.13** below).

Stallions and broodmares

1.13

Stallions feature throughout this book as they integrate with every angle of tax planning. It is stallions which normally provide the greatest financial rewards for owners since they will generate fees for nominations, i.e. the right of owners to have their mares covered by the stallion. A stallion will normally cover at least forty mares in a season. For this reason, stallion syndicates are often established in which each syndicate member (usually a mare owner) owns one-fortieth interest, which gives the right to nominate at least one mare each year to the stallion.

Broodmares do not generate income until they produce progeny. Before they can do this they require a nomination, which can cost tens of thousands of pounds for the right to visit a successful stallion. This is a very high-risk investment, since there is no guarantee that the mare will conceive, and even when she does, it may take up to five years before the owner knows whether he has a profitable animal on his hands, or just an expensive pet! For progeny bred for national hunt racing this period may be even longer.

The thoroughbred and the non-thoroughbred

1.14

The UK thoroughbred horse is registered with Weatherbys. Only thoroughbreds can race. The term 'bloodstock' refers to the thoroughbred racehorse. Many tax cases, particularly those dealing with stud farming refer to the thoroughbred. The HMRC Internal Manuals on such subjects as agricultural property relief (APR) for inheritance tax (IHT) refer to horses as opposed to thoroughbred horses whereas the legislation does not. It is assumed that the tax principles relate to thoroughbred and non-thoroughbred equally, although again, each case must be tested on its own merits. This is looked at further throughout the book. The key objective is to always prove commerciality.

The equine business – the need for the business plan

1.15

It is well known that it can be difficult to be profitable with businesses involving horses. See cases *Murray (TC03474)* (see **3.20** and **8.11**), *Thorne (TC03851)* (see **8.21**) and *McMorris (TC04204)* (see 4.3). The quality end of industry is profitable, the bottom struggles. A business plan must be produced to prove profitability. The infrastructure costs are high, and areas of the sport are not as geared up commercially as they might be at a generic level. There are profits to be made from a well-run equine business. A livery, for example, must always try and control costs below livery charges; and a stud business must be able to sell stock above production costs.

An essential part of income tax protection is that every proposed equine enterprise has a business plan. There would be income tax losses (a stud has the first eleven years to produce a profit) and in order to protect this claim, there must be proof of commerciality. Dealing and 'making' of horses can be very profitable.

It has been said that there are three things certain in life – death, taxes and that on the question of commerciality, HMRC will always ask for the original business plan and how this is adjusted and reviewed as the business progresses. Income tax aside, equine businesses, apart from studs, also have to rely on BPR (business property relief) for inheritance tax relief (see **1.2** and **7.21**) and therefore must be seen as a business carried on for a gain in line with s103(3) IHTA 1984. How can it ever be proven that an unprofitable business was to be of commercial design if there was no original business plan demonstrating this?

The importance of accounts and legal agreements

1.16

Should the equine accounts show too much investment activity, this must be flagged up in the same way as problems over legal ownership and protection. Professional advisers can help structure greater trading activity, while accountants and tax advisers can flag up the tax problems so that they can action improvements to trading. Both accountants and solicitors can flag up the lack of legal agreements. Working as a team means there is greater chance of maximising future IHT reliefs, and indeed, protecting all tax reliefs. Strong legal agreements will help protect against disputes and tax confusion.

The racing and breeding cycle

1.17

As the breeding cycle often involves a transfer of the yearling from the stud into racing, and its return to the stud after its racing career to produce bloodstock of its own, there is considerable merit in the view that that racing is actually an integral part of a stud farm's activities and ought to be included as part of the taxable trading activity.

The racing activity can arguably be regarded as an essential part of the breeding process as a horse will need to be tested through its success in racing for its speed, stamina and courage in order to determine whether it is likely to have a successful breeding career. If a breeder's racing activities were to be regarded as an integral part of his breeding trade, then the expenses of racing would be an allowable deduction for tax purposes and any winnings would be taxable.

In order for any activity to be treated as a taxable trade (see **8.2**), it must be managed on a commercial basis with a view to the realisation of profits. As far as racing is concerned, the majority of horses are not profitable as only a small number win more than the cost of training. **CHAPTER 3** deals with the 'trade or hobby?' problem in more detail.

Combining racing and breeding

1.18

In general, HMRC currently regards the prospect of profits from horse-racing to be too remote and so do not accept that it is a taxable trade. It is regarded as a hobby or recreational activity or, in the case of a company, a non-taxable activity. This means that the costs of training are not tax deductible but, conversely, any winnings and capital profit are tax-free. Nonetheless, there have been cases where the taxpayer (normally a company or a breeder who personally trains and races progeny) has been treated as carrying on a taxable activity but these have been extremely rare.

There is one other occasion when HMRC may attempt to combine the breeding and racing activities. This is when they consider the breeding of horses to be a hobby, and merely ancillary to the racing activity. In this situation, they would not allow relief for the breeding expenses since these expenses would be considered to have arisen from a non-taxable activity.

Although the hobby breeder is not trading, the taxpayer may, in certain circumstances, still need to consider declaration of the occasional profit which he may make. HMRC does not need to establish that there is any continuity of trade in order to do so. If a hobby breeder achieves a very successful sale, there is a fair chance that he will be able to persuade HMRC that his losses from the past years should be taken into account, in which case, the amount of income tax payable will be reduced or eliminated. Again, the hobby element is looked at in **CHAPTER 3**.

The tax adviser must encourage clients to notify them of large one-off profits so they can determine what correspondence with HMRC should take place. At **1.20** this subject extends to the breeding and owning of competition horses.

Trade or hobby

1.19

One of the major taxation issues facing the equine industry is whether HMRC consider it to be a commercial business and tax it as a trade rather than a hobby (see **Chapter 3**). If the business is considered to be a hobby, this will result in a denial of loss relief against other taxable profits if a loss arises but could still lead to a potential tax charge if the business becomes profitable. The VAT registration angle is considered at **5.4**.

The breeder who occupies a stud farm (see **Chapter** 7), whether leased or owned, is more likely to be regarded as carrying on a trade and therefore taxed in the same way as a farmer breeding, for example, cattle or sheep. The starting point when considering the taxation of the bloodstock breeder is section 9, Income Tax (Trading and Other Income) Act 2005 (ITTOIA), which states that the profits of a farming trade will be taxed as trading income. Farming is defined for tax purposes as the occupation of land wholly or mainly for the purposes of husbandry. Husbandry includes "the breeding and rearing of horses in connection with those activities". (see 7.1).

If the trade is treated as 'farming', then it will be covered by s9 ITTOIA 2005. Should the equine trade (for example dealing) not be held to be farming then it may be covered by s10 ITTOIA 2005. This sub-section gives further guidance on the way in which the trade will be taxed and states that if land is occupied for a purpose other than farming but is managed on a commercial basis with a view to the realisation of profits, the profits will also be taxed as trading income.

The equine breeder who does not occupy a stud farm may also be treated as if carrying on a bona fide trade under the general charging provisions of s5 ITTOIA 2005 but not 'farming' for tax purposes.

Breeding v owning competition horses

1.20

If, in general, breeding horses is a taxable activity and racing (including ownership of competition horses) is a separate non-taxable activity then the transfer of horses from the stud to racing and from racing back to the stud will be accorded special tax treatment. This matter was considered in the 1995 case *Sharkey v Wernher (36 TC 275)* (see **1.11**, **3.21**, **4.12** and **6.11**) and the principles from the case were later enacted by Finance Act 2008 Schedule 15 Part 1 which inserted the rules in ITTOIA 2005 Part 2, s172 A-F and CTA 2009 s156-161. The case established that a horse must be valued when it leaves the stud to go into training for racing (and competing). The market value of the horse at that time will determine the profit or loss realised by the stud from breeding and this will be reflected in the bloodstock accounts. Therefore, even though the horse has not been sold, any profit or loss from breeding is taxable or allowable when it leaves the stud to commence its racing career. Such profit or loss will have been realised 'in kind' rather than in cash so that tax will be payable on any profit even though the breeder will not yet have received any proceeds from the sale of the horse to meet the tax liability.

The whole issue of 'owning' horses for competition (racing, eventing, dressage, show jumping or polo) as opposed to a direct trading operation is looked at throughout the book and specifically in **Chapter 4**.

Livery yards in general

1.21

In the UK over the last few decades there has been a large increase in the number of livery/DIY yards for horses as a consequence of an expanding equine leisure industry. The recent need for agricultural diversification will probably increase the number of new livery yards even further. The legal and tax angles of livery yards feature throughout the book. With lockdowns and problems of travelling abroad during Covid-19 ironically the livery businesses have been thriving as UK recreation.

At present, all cat and dog boarding kennels have to be inspected and licensed by law as do riding schools, whilst livery yards currently fall outside the licensing requirements. There is no control over the standards of care offered or the experience of the staff in charge of these yards.

It is of concern to British Equine Veterinary Association (BEVA) that if there is no registration system for livery yards and no control over the standards of care then the ability to maintain proper disease control within the horse population in the UK is inadequate.

The tax position and planning around livery yards is looked at in **1.7** with regard to *Vigne* and the VAT position is looked at in **5.21**.

Employing family members in the equine industry

1.22

The world of equestrianism is forever growing and following closely in the footsteps of their successful parents are the offspring of livery yard owners, trainers and profitable competitors from a contrasting array of equine disciplines. It can be a smart move to employ family members, particularly the younger generation, within an equine business due to the added security and trust one would have with their own son or daughter, as well as the potential for tax savings on reduced profits.

However, being a member of the family does not eliminate any employment laws or bypass the minimum wage requirements. The worker must be at least 14 years of age and fulfil a role that is required by the business. If the family member is to be employed the employer must register with HMRC and make provisions for the correct reporting of PAYE and National Insurance liabilities. There are certain situations whereby if the individual is employed only part time (a Student in the summer holidays for example) and certain other criteria are met, the employer may be able to apply for special rules which negate the need to register as an employer with HMRC.

Often family members and children are paid a sum just below the Primary and Secondary Threshold for National Insurance contributions (set at £184 per week for 2021/22) but above the Lower Earnings Limit (£120 per week for 2021/22) to enable the employee to gain the benefits of National Insurance contributions, such as contributing years toward their state pension, without either the employee or employer becoming liable for National Insurance contributions on the wages. The wages must also be paid on a 'Real Time' compliant basis.

Real time information, most commonly known as RTI, is a reporting requirement designed to make pay as you earn (PAYE) submissions more efficient. It requires an employer to make an electronic submission to HMRC every time a payment is made to an employee in order to provide HMRC with wages information in 'real time', enabling an up to date record to be kept by HMRC which can be viewed by the employee at any time. There are a number of different software services available to make RTI submissions through, the most cost effective at the time of writing being HMRC's Basic PAYE Tools which is free for businesses with up to ten employees.

There are some key points to be aware of before setting up a PAYE scheme and paying a family member through RTI in the equine business;

1. Employees must be paid at least the national minimum wage or the agricultural minimum wage where applicable.

2. Employees will be entitled to sick pay, holiday pay and all other statutory payments.

3. Depending on the employee's salary and age, they may be required to be entered into a work place pension scheme as a result of auto enrolment.

It is certainly worth considering the above points to avoid unnecessarily burdening yourself with extra administration or payroll costs.

As mentioned above, payments to family members must be within the guidelines of the minimum wages applicable but equally must be comparable with commercial rates and akin to a wage any other person could expect to achieve for performing the same tasks. For example, it may prove somewhat difficult to justify to HMRC why your 18 year-old daughter was paid £40 per hour to muck out and bring in horses, conversely, if she had designed you an outstanding website this may be another story.

Amongst the most important points to consider is that the family member must actually be working in order for the total amount of their wages to be valid in their use as a business deduction for taxation purposes. The payments cannot be a 'disguise' as pocket money paid to the business owners' children. All payments must meet the 'wholly and exclusively' test, meaning there must be no duality of purpose to any payments made to the family member, as with any other member of staff.

There are a lot of tangible tasks that can be carried out by family members as part of an equine trade, but as always payments must be made in a compliant and disciplined manner with strong documentation to support them which must be based on fact and evidence.

This was put to test in the case of *Alan Nicholson v HMRC (2018) TC06293*. In *Alan Nicholson v HMRC*, the tribunal disallowed a sole trader's payments made as wages to his son whilst at university, concluding that the expenditure was not wholly and exclusively incurred in the interest of the trade being carried out by the father. See **5.4** for business expenses and VAT.

The First-Tier tribunal (FTT) found that the self-employed taxpayer could not deduct the 'wages' he paid to his son as an expense against his self-employment income, as there was a dual purpose to the payments. It was considered that the taxpayer was helping to support his son at university and there was no methodology or keeping of records in relation to hours worked or payments made.

The point at issue was whether or not an amount of £7,400 claimed to be wages paid to the taxpayer's son, was incurred wholly and exclusively for the purpose of the taxpayer's trade, and hence deductible against his self-employment income.

Many family members are employed in the family equestrian business in very genuine conditions. However, it is of upmost importance for accurate records to be kept of all duties carried out by the family member, as with any employee, to defend an attack by HMRC.

It is contended, in the case of *Alan Nicholson*, that the payments made were of dual purpose. They were "natural parental love and affection" and/or 'personal benefit' purposes rather than solely a business purpose. As a dual-purpose expense, the payments made to the son of the appellant failed to meet the legal conditions of s. 34 TMA and therefore were not deductible from his self-employed income. See **7.15** for equine competition expenses for business purposes.

The FTT noted, howbeit, that it is likely that the expense would have met the wholly and exclusively test if he had paid his son on a more time recorded basis or had there been some form of methodology in calculating the amount payable and an accurate record maintained of the number of hours his son worked.

The wages claimed were based on 15 hours per week at £10 per hour for the "promotion of the business through internet and leaflet distribution and computer work" which the son carried out whilst at university.

However, there was no evidence to support these actions. The wages were paid partly in cash (a bank statement evidenced payment of £1,850) and partly in food and drink, which the taxpayer paid for whilst visiting his son and paying for his weekly shop.

Details that the equine industry can take from this case are the upmost need for accurate keeping of records of labour and services provided by family members, being just as important (perhaps even more so) as with any other employee. Details of hours worked should be kept along with the duties carried out as well as a structured way of calculating the employee's pay in line with their terms of employment. The wages owed should then be made payable as cleanly as possible to the employee to avoid any blurring of the lines between the employer and employee, a payment in full via bank transfer would be the preferred way of doing so to enable clear reconciliation for the business accounts.

If an accurate and methodical approach is taken to the employment and calculation of a family member's salary, along with evidence of the work carried out, the conditions of *Section 34 (1) TMA 1970* will be adhered to and therefore the wages deductible as expenses from the business or trade. See **Chapter 4** for more details on allowable expenses within horse ownership. For specific advertising expenses see **3.14** detailing HMRC's BIMs on Advertising Expenses: Sponsorship.

Equine industries lend themselves to family employment. If the equine business is considering employing a relative, there are five simple steps which if in place will make it very difficult for HMRC to challenge any payments made:

1. Make a simple agreement with the employee covering as a minimum; the duties to be performed, the hours to be worked, the rate of pay and how they will be paid.

2. Keep evidence of the work they have performed, along with timesheets to assist in the calculation of wages due.

3. Pay your relative in full directly into their bank account to avoid 'payments in kind'.

4. The wages must also be paid on a real time compliance basis.
5. Keep a payroll record, contemporaneous with other business records.

Polo

1.23

Polo has been a growth industry. It has benefited from exceptionally good marketing and PR aimed at the 'glamour' market, not necessarily just those traditionally involved in equine pursuits themselves. Many supporters and participants might be categorised as those who attend Royal Ascot – they enjoy the glamour, the clamour and the entertaining.

As a result of this, the leading polo organisations seem to have attracted excellent sponsorship deals (see **3.15**) and have television coverage of all the big games on the leading television sports channel.

The sport has also concentrated on its grass roots, i.e. encouraging a revival of pony club polo for several decades and a big interest in club level polo, encouraging courses for beginners and a significant social element to activities.

Every player has a handicap starting at –2 and going up to 10. Generally, most of the players rated 10 originate from Argentina, whilst there are many UK professionals with handicaps of only 3 or 4 goals. The handicap system works so that when two teams of four line up against each other, the handicaps of each player in each team are added together so that the teams can be balanced by the aggregate handicap of the whole team.

There are expressions such as 'low goal' and 'high goal' polo and this is based on the aggregate handicaps of the teams. A low goal team is one which by definition has a relatively low goal handicap. A new professional polo player with a low goal rating can be very attractive to a team wishing to keep their handicap down.

The polo industry creates a large number of businesses and associated tax problems and need for planning. There has been a trend for polo clubs to be owned by individuals with a passion for polo but sometimes coming from very commercial backgrounds and who operate these activities in a very commercial manner. There are a number of polo schools which offer tuition (see **5.22**) for people wanting to be introduced into the game of polo and there are a number of polo livery yards which will keep polo ponies for their customers. Many of these polo livery yards will also buy and sell polo ponies, as well as hire polo ponies for those players who do not want the all-year round responsibility, but nevertheless enjoy the game. This can also be very useful for those who have injured ponies etc.

In order for the UK professional polo player to survive, it has been said that they 'need a very large trust fund income'. However, there are those who can make a living from the sport and in addition to appearance fees and fees for playing certain teams, they generally support their income through buying and selling polo ponies and also 'making' a polo pony which will often involve re-training, for example, a small failed racehorse or breeding their own polo ponies which in turn leaves them operating stud farms. It is often the dealing side that can produce the largest contribution to profit.

A lot of the stud farms that produce polo ponies are based in Argentina, Ireland and other countries but there has recently been a growth of the UK polo pony stud. Tax planning in relation to these activities is covered in **CHAPTER 7: TAX PLANNING FOR STUD FARMS**. In the UK polo is a summer game and in the winter the horses are grazed at grass liveries. In this context it is worth considering the recent case of *Gill* (see **2.9**).

Show jumping

1.24

Show jumping in the UK has seen a meteoric rise over the last decade and more. Horses used in show jumping have been sold for more than £1 million on a regular basis. The "golden glow" of the 2012 London Olympics has been a positive.

At grass roots this remains a buoyant industry. Everyone who learns to ride wants to progress by trotting over a coloured pole and then jumping multiple coloured poles and then entering a show jumping class at the local show and enthusiasm for this does not seem to have diminished in any way.

As the standard of show jumping improves so the cost of an experienced show jumper increases dramatically and, despite relatively small prize money, the horses command very high prices. Many tax advisers see this as merely a way for their successful clients to indulge the interests of their sons and daughters, but there are still some very important tax and commercial angles which ought to be considered.

In particular, there are important questions to be considered regarding the tax status of sponsorship payments, competition yards and the boundary line between a commercial business and a hobby (see **CHAPTER 3**). There are also a large number of professional show jumpers who buy and sell horses (see **5.11** for details on the margin scheme) to support their profession and also give freelance instruction (see **5.22**).

The European and world show jumping scene has been particularly commercial and strong with huge development at every level, especially with high prices being achieved for quality horses. Many famous names have entered the sport which has pushed up horse prices and the glamour image in equal proportions. Sales to daughters of 'super-rich' popstars and Russian billionaires post London 2012 have broken previous records set for sales of show jumping horses, further increasing the sport's image and popularity.

Eventing

1.25

The eventing industry can probably be seen as possibly the least commercial of all equestrian disciplines. Competitors require all three skills of dressage, show jumping and cross country. They need to possess boldness to ride cross country, technical competence to perform dressage and superior technical riding skills and judgement for show jumping. Likewise, the horse needs to have all these skills. A good eventing horse commands a considerable price premium in the same way that a good polo pony or show jumper does. Eventing still achieves some television coverage at Badminton and Burghley Horse Trials and the attendance figures for spectators at three-day events, such as Badminton, Blenheim or Gatcombe, remain very strong. Eventing also provides a commercial outlet for a large number of other related businesses such as equine clothing retailers and refreshment providers.

Eventing does not have the benefit of the glamour and, therefore, does not attract the valuable sponsorship deals seen in polo or the horse racing world. As a result, it is extremely difficult for a professional 'eventer' to survive commercially and again they frequently have to involve themselves in other equestrian activities, such as developing and selling young event horses in addition to giving instruction and trying to attract suitable sponsorship deals. The industry does, however, have a commercial infrastructure with successful eventing yards, and freelance eventing instructors etc.

Dressage

1.26

The dressage industry is another area of growth and, like polo, attracts glamour and potential sponsorship (see **3.15**). It is, perhaps, rather cynically perceived by the outside world as just a beautiful and elegant way to spend a lot of money on a hobby activity. However, there are some core elements of commerciality with top horses being sold for large sums. There are strong commercial aspects involved in being able to either breed or produce a top dressage horse and success in the competitive world of dressage goes hand in hand with this.

As a result, there are studs which focus purely on breeding dressage horses and there are some studs which breed horses for the dual disciplines of, say, dressage or eventing or show jumping. There are a relatively large number of good freelance dressage instructors, there are dressage livery yards and the sport has a very dedicated and committed support structure.

Point to Point

1.27

The Point to Point industry is amateur racing which runs from November to June annually and is another very thriving and popular sport. All the riders have to be amateur jockeys, although they can earn their living from other equestrian pursuits (there was a time when they had to be entirely amateur) and each Point to Point is, in the main, run by a local hunt.

Each Point to Point horse has to have been fairly and regularly hunted with a local pack of hounds (which does include blood hounds and drag hounds). Prize money is very small whilst enthusiasm levels can be exceptionally large.

The sport includes a large number of activities, not only fund raising for local hunts but offering a second chance for retired racehorses that are perhaps no longer good enough to support full training fees in a proper training yard, but can provide a keen amateur with a lot of fun. Point to Point also offers an alternative for young racehorses to race without too much financial outlay. There have been many successful Cheltenham Gold Cup or Grand National winners who have originated from the world of Point to Pointing.

Those who own and ride Point to Pointers find it an exceptionally enjoyable and thrilling way to spend their hard-earned money. When compared to keeping a racehorse in training or some of the other equestrian disciplines, it is also relatively cost effective.

However, point to pointing has been hard hit by COVID and racing has survived very well. The result is that at the time of writing there has been a large swing away from running horses in point to points towards the larger prize money and overall support of mainstream racing. The next 2021 / 2022 season will be interesting to see the long-term impact.

Point to Point also attracts a large number of spectators and, within its structure, it supports a large number of equine businesses, such as point to point livery yards (which often double as hunter livery yards) and small training yards.

Point to Point horses can cost only around £2,000 to £5,000 to purchase. A good place to purchase potential Point to Pointers will be Ascot bloodstock sales or direct from the trainers. The jump trainers who love their racehorses and want to see them going to good homes are very keen to try and sell them to a good Point to Point yard for relatively small sums, which they could probably justify under the heading 'equine welfare' rather than 'commercial reality'.

Business sponsorship and racing

1.28

Sponsorship is looked at in more detail in **Chapter 3**.

Horse racing is a high-profile sport and one of the most televised. Many companies are using racing to promote their products through advertising and sponsorship. It is important to consider the tax treatment of expenses incurred in connection with racing by businesses which do not operate a racing or breeding trade. Common examples of such expenditure include owning and running a racehorse, sponsorship and advertising. There is no doubt that racing has proved to be a very successful marketing tool for a number of businesses. The key is being able to provide the detail and evidence marketing success to HMRC.

Successfully claiming a deduction for racing expenditure will be more difficult when the owners/managers of the business themselves have a known interest in racing, particularly where the company is a private company. HMRC will probably seek to argue that the expenditure has been incurred because of the personal interest of the owners rather than for the benefit of the trade.

The general rule for deductibility of expenses is in s54 CTA 2009 and s34 ITTOIA 2005. These sections state that expenditure will be deductible if it is wholly and exclusively incurred for the benefit of the trade of the business. Therefore, in general, a business will be able to obtain tax relief for racing expenses, and conversely will be taxed on any race winnings, where it can satisfy HMRC that the expenditure is incurred to promote the trade, for example by increasing awareness of its location, products and brands. Advertising and sponsorship may satisfy this criterion. When HMRC question the tax allowability of the expenditure, the business should be able to support all the arguments with evidence and statistics (see **3.17**).

There is the risk that there may be a taxable benefit on the employee or owner where HMRC regard the business's racing expenditure as a perk for that person. This is particularly likely to be the case where the business in question is a close company as defined by s439 CTA 2010 – that is, very broadly, where five or fewer persons control the company – where it is more likely that a director shareholder will be able to influence the spending of the company. BIM 42555: *"sponsorship is often a form of advertising. A business tries to obtain benefits for its products, goodwill or reputation and public image by association with a popular or successful event or person"* (see **3.18**).

Racing club

1.29

Increasingly the ownership of racehorses is open to a wider group of people through the establishment of racing clubs, where individuals pay a subscription for a share in horses owned by the club and usually for hospitality at the racecourse when the club's horses are running. Many trainers are now starting their own clubs as a means of introducing people to the experience of owning a racehorse.

A racing club organised by a trainer may be regarded as a separate trade but there is the possibility that HMRC might seek to challenge the tax deduction of the provision of hospitality for the club members on the grounds that this represents entertaining potential and existing clients. The possibility of an HMRC challenge would be reduced if the members of the club paid a specific charge for the provision of hospitality rather than this being included in their annual subscription.

Bloodstock agents

1.30

The industry of the purchase and sale of horses is vibrant in the UK. The VAT position is considered at **5.27**. There is currently a large increase in agents working in the commercial areas of show jumping, polo, eventing and dressage.

Conclusion

The equine industry is energetic and the opportunities and passions to succeed are strong. There is a fine line between the hobby operation and the commercial business and it is therefore essential that there is a business plan for all diverse choices. The difference between commercial ownership and the trade must be defined. There must be robust evidence of the commercial operation. The choice of business structure needs careful review and planning. With HMRC's attacks on the DIY livery yard as an investment and haymaking for horses not seen as an agricultural activity there must be a full understanding of the industry and the specific operation. With the variety of different interests, e.g. racing, competition, hacking and tourism, each operation must be looked at on a case-by-case basis.

CHAPTER TWO

TAXATION AND THE EQUINE INDUSTRY

Chapter 2 explores in more depth the taxation surrounding equine activities. Exploring losses and the benefits of a stud farm, protecting tax reliefs and planning for the future. Key issues considered are:

- Tax planning for a passion (2.1)
- Stud farming is farming for IHT (2.2)
- 11 year loss rule for stud farmers (2.3)
- Protection of equine land and buildings from CGT (2.4)
- The equine house (2.5)
- Equine cottages (2.6)
- Horse racing is "tax free" – are other equine activities (2.7)
- Integrated stud and racing (2.8)
- The studs, farm and grazing for leisure pursuits and grazing agreements (2.9)
- Stock valuation (2.10)
- VAT registration (2.11)
- Stallion and other equine income missing from tax returns (2.12)
- Enterprise Investment Scheme and equine activity (2.13)

- Equestrian landlord and grazing rights (2.14)
- Protecting future IHT and CGT reliefs (2.15)
- Are stallions farming? (2.16)
- Capital allowances (2.17)
- Stud farm – the APR/BPR basics (2.18)
- APR – how long will it stay (2.19)
- APR – agricultural value, the period of ownership (2.20)
- The importance of a structured Will (2.21)
- Will planning – deed of variation (2.22)
- Will planning – identifying tax efficient assets (2.23)
- Making lifetime gifts of equestrian businesses (2.24)
- Holdover election (2.25)
- Potentially exempt transfers (2.26)
- Rollover and reinvestment into new qualifying asset (2.27)
- Thoroughbred and non-thoroughbred stud (2.28)
- Commercial or hobby – the HMRC fight (2.29)
- Stock transferred to "equestrian sport" (2.30)
- Retiring from the equestrian business (2.31)
- The importance of the equine property valuation for IHT (2.32)

- The significance of the IHT400 (2.33)
- The evidence of the *Graham* case on services (2.34)
- Principal private residence – *Longson v Baker* (2.35)
- The big garden – *Phillips* (2.36)
- The new CGT return from 6 April 2020 (2.37)
- Stamp Duty Land Tax (SDLT) and "mixed use" (2.38)
- *Foster* probate valuation – impact on equine (2.39)
- Debts, loans and lifetime gifts within the equine industry (2.40)
- Lifetime gifting and relievable chargeable transfer (2.41)

Tax planning for a passion

2.1

The current UK tax regime offers a large number of beneficial tax reliefs to the agricultural and business sectors and the equine industry needs to take full advantage of these. The aim of this book is to highlight the benefits and help avoid the tax pitfalls.

In the author's experience, many practitioners and taxpayers ignore the equine elements of their and their clients' affairs as 'outside the scope of tax' and of no consequence for the tax return or tax planning. There are many examples where this is not the case and where it will be necessary to consider tax recording, compliance or planning aspects. For example:

- breeding and stud activities could be a taxable trade. There is also the potential for income tax relief on any losses and the protection of valuable inheritance and capital gains tax reliefs on stud property (see **Chapter** 7);

- stallion nomination fee income will be taxable (see **6.4** to **6.9**);

- leasing income received in respect of a racehorse can be taxable (see **6.2**);

- owning a racehorse can result in some tax efficiencies that can be taken advantage of to lower the cost of this activity, through utilisation of such things as the specific VAT scheme (see **5.6** and **5.28**).

CHAPTER 3: HMRC ATTACK ON THE NON-COMMERCIAL EQUINE BUSINESS is devoted to trying to differentiate between business and hobby activities and to the task of defining the business element.

Stud farming will normally be regarded as farming and should, therefore, qualify for all the beneficial tax advantages currently associated with farming. The tax planner can also encounter some pitfalls here – see CHAPTER 7: TAX PLANNING FOR STUD FARMS.

The tax affairs of those involved in the equine industry can become complex as a direct result of the tendency of those involved to allow their passion for the sport to lead them into its many different areas, such that a small initial interest can expand considerably and cause unexpected complexity.

Some specific tax points are as follows:

- stud farming is classed as farming (see **2.2**);

- racing itself is generally 'tax free' – it is generally *not* a taxable activity (see **2.7**);

- stud farm losses attract special loss relief treatment (see **Chapter 8**);

- stallion nomination fees are assessed under other income unless the stallion is integrated in a stud farm (*Malcom v Lockhart (Surveyor of Taxes) 1919 7 TC 99*) (see **6.8**);
- horses are not subject to capital gains tax;
- when horses move from stud to racing or racing to stud they are transferred at market value – *Sharkey v Wernher (1955) 36 TC 275* (see **2.31**);
- stock is valued at the lower of cost and net realisable value on an item-by-item basis (see **2.10** and **7.9**);
- gambling is tax free, i.e. not assessable to income tax;
- the special Racehorse Owners VAT scheme, administered by Weatherbys, allows owners to claim back their input VAT (see **5.6**).

Stud farming is farming for tax

2.2

Agriculture equates to husbandry; and therefore there is need to demonstrate that the farming activity is both 'active' and commercial, with the appropriate badges of trade. 'Husbandry' is specifically said to include crop-growing, the breeding and rearing of horses, and the grazing of horses in connection with those activities (s996(s) of the ITA 2007), together with short rotation coppices and energy crops. Stud farming is, for tax purposes (see **1.20** and **7.1**), farming, where there is occupation of land; however, general equine diversification, such as the activities of horse liveries, horse racing, eventing etc, are not considered as such.

Where the mares are boarded at stud by the owner of the horses in return for a keep fee, the mare owner is not carrying out an agricultural activity (see **1.19**), as he or she is <u>not</u> occupying land; however, this activity can qualify for EIS (Enterprise Investment Scheme) relief provided conditions are met (see **7.16**).

IHTM 24068 sets out HMRC's understanding of the stud for agriculture: "*it is considered that an essential requirement is for an element of horse breeding carried on in a systematic manner, with proper record keeping*".

IHTM Manuals also state:

> "*You should usually decide whether a stud farm qualifies for agricultural relief by reference to:*
>
> - *The information on the file;*
> - *Supplemented as necessary from other HMRC sources, such as the tax papers for the business or SAV (livestock);*
> - *Business accounts for the five years preceding death.*"

For a stud farm to be considered farming, there must be the associated ownership and occupation of land and not just boarding out mares.

11-year loss rule for stud farms

2.3

The subject of losses and how to maximise tax relief is always a subject of great interest to tax adviser and taxpayer alike. **CHAPTER 8: PLANNING FOR EQUINE TAX LOSSES** devotes itself entirely to this subject. As part of the introduction, it is important to highlight the 11-year loss rule specifically applicable to stud farms only as agreed by HMRC with the Thoroughbred Breeders' Association and also that a specific 'sting in the tail' is associated with this (see **8.13**).

Thus, current year losses can be offset against dividends, employment income and profits from a trade. Losses can also be offset against capital gains (see **8.7**). The major difference between a stud farm and a farm is the ability to claim tax relief for losses for the first 11 years (see **8.13**) instead of this being restricted to six for a regular farm. This is in recognition that the stud farm takes significantly longer to develop horses for the equine market than the average farm develops crops and livestock products. The 11-year loss extension is part of the hobby farming rules.

Many equine businesses trade at a loss. Horses are expensive to keep and infrastructure costs such as compliance with riding school regulations and employment law can turn a potential profit into a loss. However, a profit must be obtained eventually and at all times it must be shown that the enterprise is commercially viable, should any losses be claimed against other income streams.

Protection of equine land and buildings from capital gains tax (CGT) including rollover relief

2.4

The March 2021 Budget and "Tax Day" 2021 did not alter the basic CGT reliefs and so the opportunity for large CGT planning still exists.

We are constantly asked by clients to explain the tax consequences when an equine landowner sells a small parcel of land that has potential for housing development, or an equine client wants to raise funds from selling land to 'live the good life'. All situations and operations must be reviewed on a case-by-case basis and full tax planning put in place well in advance to maximise any tax efficiencies that may be obtainable. A review for tax planning can also look at the question of commerciality, i.e. whether assets sold are genuinely used in an equine business prior to sale.

There are a variety of types of disposal by equine landowners for the development of projects such as houses, an outright sale of the whole property or part of the land to a developer. Increasingly, we are seeing an option over the land being granted and exercisable if planning permission is achieved. Another arrangement that has seen growth in recent years is the promotion agreement – where, for a down payment, the developer usually obtains the planning permission and shares in the sale proceeds arising from the end development with the landowner.

The latter two arrangements allow the tax practitioner time to organise matters so that business asset disposal relief (BADR) formerly entrepreneurs' relief (ER) is available on sale. The developers generally do not enter into promotion agreements unless there is a realistic chance of obtaining planning permission, so even at this stage it is worth evaluating appropriate tax planning strategies to maximise the tax reliefs available.

The March 2020 Budget and the reduction of the lifetime limit for ER for capital gains tax (CGT) from £10m to £1m has placed more focus on the advantages of rollover relief. ER has been renamed business asset disposal relief (BADR).

However, rollover relief (see **2.27**) was already increasing in popularity prior to this, to the extent that it has created a class of buyer in the business property market – the rollover buyer, especially in the stud farm market. The COVID-19 pandemic had an initial negative effect on the residential property market, however, the equine property market is still relatively active and rollover deadlines of 36 months after exchange have to be achieved.

The land agents and farm property press classify rollover buyers as those purchasing farms and seeking rollover relief for CGT from development gains. The gain from the development of houses on the whole or part of a farm can be rolled over into another qualifying business asset, which is often a stud farm or equine property.

The tax adviser acting for the rollover buyer has to be careful that the sale does indeed qualify for rollover relief and does not become caught in any income tax traps such as slice of the action schemes (e.g. where the landowner benefits from the developer's profits, a deal involving the landowner taking houses as part of the deal which can vary in value, and so on). Rollover buyers can also be those seeking to shelter any business gains into the purchase of a stud farm or equine property.

Many tax advisers consider that it is a combination of the positive general tax reliefs on a farm purchase, (e.g. the potential inheritance tax (IHT) relief and possible option for claiming input VAT and income tax losses), combined with the strong role of rollover buyers that had been keeping stud farm sales prices strong at the time of writing.

More difficult capital gains issues arise if the land is held outside the stud farming partnership. To obtain BADR and reduce the tax burden on the transaction, the landowner would need to take advantage of the 'associated disposal' rules, whereby the land disposal needs to be linked to their "withdrawal from participation in the business" concerned (s169K, Taxation of Chargeable Gains Act 1992 (TCGA 1992)). Following changes in s41, Finance Act 2015, it is generally the case that the landowner needs only reduce ownership by a minimum of 5% of the total business to trigger the application of these rules, although usually withdrawal is higher than this.

The equine house

2.5

The inheritance tax advantages of farming have always been that the farmhouse and farm cottages are potentially business assets and eligible for agricultural property relief (APR) (see **2.19** and **7.17**) for inheritance tax, as well as the specific land and buildings used by the horses themselves.

The tax status of the 'equine' farmhouse can thus be a very complex issue for the adviser (see **7.34** – **7.36**). Care must be taken to ensure that, for capital gains tax purposes, optimum use is made of the private residence relief (PRR), whilst trying to ensure that the farmhouse does, potentially, qualify for APR.

Although for APR purposes (see **7.24**) this only applies to studs, the ability to claim 'the equine house' as a business asset for inheritance tax relief should not be overlooked. IHT is looked at in detail in **CHAPTER 7: TAX PLANNING FOR STUD FARMS**. The income tax implications of commerciality are considered at **8.2**. The VAT position of the stud farmhouse is reviewed at **7.34**.

For income tax purposes, tax allowable expenditure on an equine house may be apportioned rather similarly to the method commonly used for farmhouses. The claim for expenses will be proportionate to the scale and nature of the business, for example:

- does it provide holiday accommodation for those on riding holidays;
- does it include an office or staff accommodation;
- does it include a place for staff and client meetings etc;
- is it the stud farmhouse? (see **7.24** to **7.30** and **7.34** to **7.36**)

As mentioned in chapter **1.1** above the CGT position of houses with stables, particularly in relation to private residence exemption, was looked at in *Longson v Baker* [2001] *STC 6 73 TC 415* (see **2.34**).

Equine cottages – Farmer and Balfour

2.6

Most stud farms employ staff who need accommodation on the premises so that they can deal with problems 'on site' as and when they arise. The case of *Revenue & Customs Commissioners v AM Brander (as Executor of the Will of the late fourth Earl of Balfour) (2010) UKUT 300 (TCC) and Farmer (Farmer's Executors) v IRC (1999) STC (SCD) 321* (see **7.31**) has given some hope for stud cottages – which were previously part of the stud operation and now let out – qualifying for business property relief (BPR) (see **1.2** and **7.21**) and therefore a lower inheritance tax liability being generated. Some of the disputed accommodation in the case mentioned above was in converted buildings and the guidance given by the ruling can be utilised (see **7.31**). However, the capital gains tax eligibility of each property has to be looked at on an individual basis, and the tax practitioner should review this regularly to maximise the possibility of BPR being obtained.

Horse racing is "tax-free" – are other equine activities?

2.7

On the principle that HMRC has sought to collect tax on profitable activities whilst simultaneously attempting to deny relief on those that are loss making, HMRC has traditionally viewed the ownership of racehorses and associated activities as 'tax free' due to their general inherent loss-making nature.

Guidance is given in HMRC's BIM 55701 which states:

> *"Horse racing, however, is not a taxable activity. Where, as is often the case, a stud farmer also races horses, considerable care may therefore be needed to ensure that the division between the two activities has been correctly made.*
>
> *In particular, attention should be given to any transfers of animals from the stud farm to training (that is, being kept for the purpose of racing) or vice versa."*

As racing is not taxable – any prize money won or proceeds from sales of horses-in-training is also not taxable; and therefore any associated racing expenses are also not allowable.

Clearly, this means that the taxpayer cannot claim tax relief (in principle) on the losses or the cost of owning a racehorse.

A frequently asked question is: can the tax-free status of racing be extended to other equine pursuits, particularly where carried on by the same individual? For example, is the ownership of dressage, show jumping, show and general competition horses also tax free? The answer is that it depends on the particular circumstances of each individual case. The motive behind ownership has to be looked at and carefully examined. Clearly, a professional trainer of horses is trading and will exhibit the commercial badges of trade.

Integrated studs and racing

2.8

Problems may arise when a stud owner also races horses. What is the taxable element and what part is tax-free? The tax advice is often complex.

Paragraph BIM 55701 of the HMRC Business Income Manual sets out the overview as follows:

"*Stud farming, which…is taken to mean the occupation of land for the purpose of breeding thoroughbred horses, is a very expensive and high-risk activity. In some cases, it may be carried on by wealthy individuals essentially as an adjunct to their racing activities. Nevertheless, for tax purposes it is treated as farming and thus as the carrying on of a trade…*" [assuming the stud meets the definition of commercial viability]. One of the key practical tax planning points here is to encourage the taxpayer/stud owner to keep records which differentiate between the activity of racing and stud ownership, to help the correct recording and apportionment of cost information.

If a breeder transfers an animal to training which is then subsequently returned to stud at a higher value after a successful racing career, the uplift in the market value achieved whilst it was in training is effectively enjoyed tax free.

Furthermore, the value at which the animal is returned to stud is relieved over the rest of its life. The valuations of animals at the dates of transfer to or from training are, therefore, significant.

The whole subject of integrated equine activities features throughout the industry. The equine taxpayer rarely just owns a horse or trains or competes or breeds. They normally undertake some or all these disciplines at the same time.

The stud farm v grazing for leisure pursuits and grazing agreements

2.9

In principle it is the stud farm that qualifies for APR and not other equine pursuits – other than specific working horses.

IHTM 24068 provides direction:

> "*With any other horses, there will need to be a link with agricultural use, for example, where horses are used as draught animals on a working farm, the grazing of such horses will constitute agricultural use. This will also be the case where the horses being grazed are declared to be part of the food chain under the horse passport scheme introduced at the end of November 2003. The grazing of horses used for leisure pursuits will not constitute occupation for agricultural purposes… Where horses are grazed in connection with, for example, a livery business run by the deceased/transferor, business relief may apply as an alternative.*"

For details on BPR see **1.2**, **7.20** and **7.21**. For the definition of agriculture see **2.2** and **7.1**.

The case of *Charnley & Another (Estate of Gill) v HMRC* [2019] UKFTT 650 (TC) has been causing quite a stir in the world of agricultural tax. The case concerned the application of agricultural property relief (APR) and business property relief (BPR) on the farmhouse and land at Woodlands Farm, and the taxpayer won, despite the fact that the majority was held under a grazing licence.

Following on from the success of *Vigne* at UT (see **1.7**), and *Graham (The Personal Representatives of Graham Deceased v HMRC* [2018] UKFTT 306 (TC)), which concerned BPR on enhanced liveries and serviced holiday accommodation, respectively, similar arguments have now been used in *Gill* such that a grazing licence with a sufficient level of farming "services" can also be deemed to be a trading business. For many, the result was seen to be the right decision given the hard work put into these businesses by the individuals concerned. Whilst this was a cattle grazing case, it has implications for grazing agreements for horses. See also *Wheatley* **1.2**, **2.17** and **7.23**).

Stock valuation

2.10

Stud Stock is valued at the lower of cost and net realisable value on an individual animal basis. The herd basis can be used – see **CHAPTER 7: TAX PLANNING FOR STUD FARMS**.

Horses treated as stock are to be included in the accounts individually at the lower of cost and market value (see HMRC BIM 55710), with the valuation being made at each year end. Mares will usually have been either purchased or transferred from training, although it is not uncommon for them to go to stud without having been raced. Horses purchased will be brought in at cost (unless market value is lower), while those transferred from training will be brought in at the market value on the date of the transfer. Where a horse has been bred and reared by the breeder and never raced, it should be brought in at the cost of rearing and keeping the horse (again, unless market value is lower). The accounts will reflect these amounts in stock unless, as mentioned, the current market value of the animal is lower, in which case this lower figure will be substituted.

The net movement in the value of stock is included in the profit and loss account and hence stock values can significantly affect the taxation position. HMRC therefore tend to examine such values in detail and it will often be worth seeking a written independent valuation in certain cases. There is a specialist bloodstock section in the Shares and Assets Valuation Division of HMRC (see BIM 55705). Requests for advice should include:

- The name of the horse to be valued
- The valuation dates
- Any opinion of the open market value together with the reasoning behind the valuation.

When establishing the correct tax position of any equine business the valuation of stock must be given serious attention (see **7.9** to **7.11**).

VAT registration

2.11

The question of VAT is complex and warrants its own chapter (**CHAPTER 5: PLANNING FOR VAT**). Sooner or later the equestrian taxpayer will have to consider whether or not they can register for VAT and, if so, should they register?

HMRC give the following direction on acceptance for VAT registration in respect of stud farms:

> *'Breeding is a long-term activity. A mare will not produce a foal every year, and the average may not be better than one in every two years. A breeder therefore will normally need to own several mares before supplies (sale of offspring) can be made with any degree of regularity. However, there will be exceptions to this, e.g. it is becoming more common to acquire one or two well bred mares, cover them by an expensive stallion and sell the offspring for considerable amounts of money. In these circumstances we would accept there was a business activity and registration may be permitted. In cases of doubt the trader should be requested to submit written details of their business*

> *intentions. Where subsequently a trader is registered it should be as an intending trader'.*

In order to achieve VAT registration, however, there must again be the clear 'intention' of making a profit – it *must* be a business. In *C & E v Lord Fisher, QB [1981] STC 238*, the courts set down the principle that an activity pursued for pleasure and social enjoyment is not business even if undertaken in an efficient and business-like manner. *The Turnbull v Foster (Surveyor of Taxes) (1904) 6 TC 206* case ruled that although there was an element of hobby there was the simple commercial objective of achieving a good bloodline, which could produce profit, and was therefore a business.

In order to claim input VAT, the goods or services would have to have been purchased in the course, or furthering, of the business of stud farming.

There must be a business and there must be an intention of making a profit in order for a VAT registration application to be entertained by HMRC.

Stallion fees and other equine income missing from the tax return

2.12

As has already been stressed, horse-racing is generally treated as tax-free so that HMRC can deny tax relief for activities which are habitually loss making. They will, however, seek to collect tax on profitable activities such as the breeding of stallions, one-off breeding successes, successful horse dealing and other similar activities.

Owning a racehorse can be viewed as 'chasing a dream' but, generally, if a horse is successful enough to stand as a stallion, it may be argued that it must be potentially financially rewarding, and this will alter the narrative from a hobby to a profit-making venture, at least in the eyes of HMRC. A large number of equestrian taxpayers omit this source of stallion income from the information supplied to their accountant. Generally, stallion fee income is taxable as other income, but – as described above – if integrated with a stud farm will be regarded as trading income.

HMRC will, therefore, try to tax success and not give relief on the failures. It is for this reason that the racehorses tax status changes on becoming a stallion and entering the bloodstock industry. In broad terms, it changes from being 'tax free' to taxable.

Enterprise Investment Scheme and the equine activity

2.13

The Enterprise Investment Scheme (EIS) is a government-backed tax investment scheme aimed at entrepreneurs willing to risk their own funds in what are regarded as higher risk commercial companies. The conditions for obtaining the relief are often complex and are generally beyond the scope of this book. However, the EIS can be incorporated into equine tax planning, subject to the relevant conditions applying, thus allowing a start-up company the ability to raise up to £5,000,000 a year (with a maximum of £12,000,000 over the lifetime of the company) from investors in a very tax efficient manner. Farming is specifically an excluded trade for the purposes of the EIS and, as stud farms are deemed to be farming for APR for inheritance tax, it is unlikely that they can qualify for this status. However, whilst a stud farm is treated as agricultural activity and hence within the definition of 'farming', some sections of the stud farming activity may perhaps escape the definition of farming for this purpose. Likewise, other equestrian activities which are neither studs nor farms may qualify for the tax relief.

EIS is available on an investment in shares in a qualifying unquoted trading company. Up front income tax relief at 30% on the net amount invested in qualifying shares is available to the investor and, in some cases, there may also be the chance of CGT deferral in respect of other capital gains arising in the same or an earlier tax year.

If the EIS investment is held for more than three years any gain generated on the subsequent disposal of the EIS shares will be tax-free.

With the post Brexit move away from farm subsidies and the apparent efforts to revive the rural economy, it is perhaps arguable that there should be more encouragement to convert traditional farms to equestrian activities, and utilisation of the EIS could provide funding for such projects. However, there can be planning permission problems standing in the way of such development – things such as providing quality accommodation for staff, or conversions of existing buildings to meet the needs of the equine activity – are often questioned in detail; it would be encouraging if such applications could be met more favourably by the planning authorities. The engagement of good planning consultants here should help greatly in achieving the conversion aims.

Whilst there will be problems, a combination of the available tax reliefs and the efficiency that the share structure it offers could mean that the EIS may represent a useful means of funding the capital requirement of developing equine projects, such as the farm conversions discussed above.

The equestrian landlord and grazing rights

2.14

It is essential that a grazier's agreement is properly drafted and maintained for tax and legal purposes. The key point is that the landlord must remain the paramount occupier with regard to grazing rights granted to the equine business. Only in this manner will entitlement to valuable capital taxation reliefs be retained by the landowner, and thus any tax efficiencies achieved.

A well drafted, properly constructed grazing arrangement will give the landowner the ability to show that they are the paramount occupier and therefore bring them within IHTA 1984 s117(a). The result is that the minimum period of occupation or ownership required to be eligible for agricultural property relief is reduced to two years rather than seven.

The following functions will have to be carried out, in order to qualify the grazing agreement as correctly drafted:

- the owner cultivates, sows and establishes the grass crop;
- the owner harrows and rolls the grass as necessary;
- the owner fertilizes the grass crop in spring and through the season as necessary.
- it is important that the owner should cut or spray all weeds to prevent seeding and the owner must do any mowing that may be required for whatever reason.

The grazier must also covenant not to mow or cut the grass and the owner must maintain any hedging, fencing and ditching needed and any other work of a proprietary nature.

If the landowner manages to achieve the above, he should then be deemed to be trading with paramount occupancy and, therefore, eligible for not only the APR on the land, but also the APR on the farmhouse. The period of occupancy could then be reduced whilst greater potential to claim business expenses and qualify for capital gains tax relief will arise.

Protecting future IHT and CGT reliefs

2.15

The principal short-term approach to tax planning in the equine industry is the concern to maximise income tax relief and claim maximum relief for VAT. In concentrating on these important aspects, however, the CGT and IHT positions can sometimes be overlooked, although they are featured throughout the book. It is imperative to understand the principal benefits of all the available tax reliefs at all times, to maximise overall tax efficiencies.

CGT is chargeable on the disposals of assets and is generally based on the difference between sale proceeds and the original cost of the asset, or its March 1982 market value if this produces a smaller gain or loss.

The advantage of business status in the equine world is that such enterprises now have access to enhanced capital gains reliefs. These reliefs enable a large amount of increase in value in the land and buildings to either escape tax or achieve minimum penalty to tax, e.g. rollover relief (see **2.27**).

The genuine equine business may perhaps also be used as a means of sheltering future development profits (see **2.39**). Most equine businesses incorporate the use of business land and buildings which at some time might be developed for residential or other use with a large potential capital gain.

Are stallions farming?

2.16

This chapter has already looked at how easy it may be for some advisers to omit stallion fees from a tax return due to lack of understanding. Every equine client is different and tax planning must be tailored to meet the specific individual needs on each occasion – the same strategies that work in one place will not also be appropriate for another enterprise.

The advantage of operating an activity as a 'trade' and, in particular, achieving qualifying status as a 'farm'; is the availability of the business tax reliefs flowing from the ownership of the land and buildings where a stallion stands. This subject is looked at in more detail in chapter 6.8 below.

Stud farms in the past have caused difficulties. As long ago as 1933, the House of Lords held that stud fees were taxable as farming profits (see *Lord Glanely v Wightman (HM Inspector of Taxes) (1933) 17 TC 634*) (see **6.1**) and the provision was restricted to animals used on the farm. However, the case of *Malcolm v Lockhart (1919) AC 463, 7 TC 99* held that stallion fees should be taxed under the relevant rules of the time, Schedule D Case VI. This highlighted the fact that every equine establishment and every equine taxpayer will be unique. For inheritance tax, this decision may not be of relevance because of a specific statutory direction in IHTA 1984 s115(4) that:

> *"The breeding and rearing of horses on a stud farm and the grazing of horses in connection with those activities shall be taken to be agriculture and any buildings used in connection with those activities to be farm buildings".*

The case of *Wheatley v IRC (1998) STC SCD 60* (see **1.2**, **2.33** and **7.23**) before the Special Commissioners decided that the grazing of land by horses is not an agricultural activity, unless the horses have been used for the purpose of agriculture or are held as part of a stud farm business.

Capital allowances

2.17

The tax legislation does allow a deduction known as capital allowances, which is available to breeders, trainers and all equine businesses operating a commercial business. Allowances are given on certain qualifying assets, with different rates of allowance applying to different classes of asset. The tax legislation covering capital allowances is set out in the Capital Allowances Act (CAA 2001), with important updates made to this legislation by the Finance Act 2008, and subsequent Finance Acts.

Items such as equine swimming pools, horse walkers, solariums and box heaters should be regarded as plant, and therefore these qualify for capital allowances. However, items such as a ménage, arenas and gallops may be questioned by HMRC. Recent case law has also established that a moveable item would also be regarded as plant, and therefore portable schooling fences would also qualify for capital allowances.

All weather surfaces are now integral to training racehorses. The case of *Shove v Lingfield Park (1991) Limited [2004] EWLA CIV 391* held that the all-weather surface was not plant and therefore could not quality for capital allowances. The case of *Anchor International V IRC [2003] VIXSC SP00354* held the opposite in relation to artificial sports surfaces, which has somewhat muddied the waters. Broadly, if the surface has an identity of its own and is not part of a structure, capital allowances should be available. The issue is set out at HMRC manuals CA 21260.

There is some positive news for companies looking to make significant capital investment over the next two years with the announcement of a new super-deduction of 130% for qualifying capital expenditure. Currently a company spending £10m would achieve tax relief of £2.6m in the year of expenditure, whereas they would achieve tax relief on £13m under the new rules.

It had been predicted that there may be further allowances available for green investment and forecasts of a rise in corporate tax rates, and there is now a real focus designed to stimulate business investment.

The new measure is only being introduced temporarily for two years for expenditure from 1 April 2021 to 31 March 2023. This will allow a 130% deduction for investments which would normally qualify for 18% plant and machinery writing down allowances. The new rules also allow for a first year allowance of 50% on special rate pool expenditure (which normally only attracts 6% writing down allowances).

The change is therefore a significant increase and acceleration of tax relief for many companies that would currently achieve 100% tax relief on only the first £1m of spend. This could be particularly beneficial for those companies now benefitting from an extended loss carry-back period and generating significant corporation tax refunds. For the equine industry it would only apply to those trading as a limited company.

There will be a number of exclusions including contracts entered into before 3 March 2021 even if expenditure is incurred after 1 April 2021.

The new super-deduction is only available to equine companies within the charge to corporation tax. Unincorporated businesses cannot benefit under this new rule and will continue to be able to claim the capital allowances at 100% of up to £1m under the annual investment allowance. The annual investment allowance had previously been extended for another year until 31 December 2021 when it is due to revert back to £200,000. This is when some unincorporated businesses may notice a wide gap in the timing of tax relief as expenditure in excess of this would only achieve relief at either 18% or 6%.

Stud farms – the APR/BPR basics

2.18

As stud farms should qualify as agricultural farms, they can benefit from the tax advantages of Agricultural Property Relief (APR) for inheritance tax (see **2.2** and **7.17**).

To attract the relief two conditions must be satisfied:

- the land must be 'occupied for the purpose of agriculture' – this incorporates general farming, rearing of animals (including horses on a stud farm), and using land for grazing, providing the owner is responsible for the upkeep of the land; and
- it must be 'agricultural property' as defined by s115(2) IHTA 1984 (see **7.1**).

Agricultural property includes UK land, buildings used as farm buildings and cottages and farmhouses of a character appropriate to the land. Land outside the UK will not attract the relief but should be eligible for Business Property Relief (BPR). The availability of the APR on farmhouses can be complex (see **7.24** to **7.29**).

APR: how long will it stay?

2.19

With IHT relief being of such potential value to a stud farm, the tax planner might seek to consider the history and origins of APR as well as the future, i.e. how long will it stay.

Despite the findings, the considerations of the All-Party Parliamentary Group (APPG) and the Office of Tax Simplification (OTS) were not implemented in either the Budget 2021 or "Tax Day" 2021. One suggestion of the APPG was removing APR and BPR and replacing the 40% rate of IHT with a lower rate between 10% and 20%. Both the APPG and OTS also suggested scrapping the CGT uplift on death.

There has been a review of inheritance tax (IHT) by the OTS, the outcome of which may result in significant changes to the current reliefs offered. Tax practitioners should take advantage of the lack of change as in due course existing tax planning strategies may have to be redrawn if any significant changes to IHT occur. Lifetime transfers have been suggested (see **2.24**).

Many advisers are looking to serious succession planning, including through lifetime transfers (see **2.25** to **2.27**). Before this can happen, the legal advisers and accountant must fully understand the ownership of the equine property (see **1.16**).

APR: agricultural value – the period of ownership

2.20

APR is available only against the agricultural value of the property, which in many cases – especially farmhouses – can be very different to open market value. The value of agricultural property is often lower than the open market value as the agricultural value assumes use is restricted to agricultural occupancy only.

'Agricultural value' is set out in IHTA 1984 s115(3) as:

> *'the value which would be the value of the property, if the property were subjected to a perpetual covenant prohibiting its use otherwise than as agricultural property'.*

This subject is an important tax planning consideration for equine stud farms with very high values.

Many equine tax advisers trying to protect the future inheritance tax liabilities of their clients might look to the ownership of a stud for IHT protection but what is the minimum period of ownership?

To obtain APR the property must be held for a minimum period. There are two periods of ownership relevant to the 100% relief:

- a minimum two-year period for the owner farmer; or
- a seven-year period for the owner of the property let out on tenancy.

The period required to qualify for full relief differs in certain circumstances where property is received on death and subsequently transferred, or when an individual who has recently received an agricultural property by gift or inheritance dies.

Importance of a structured will

2.21

If a will is not structured correctly and does not specify to whom the business property is to be left, this will invariably cause significant problems. Examples of this include a stud farmer and a trainer. There is often a batch of assets which could be divided between the children, e.g. the training yard, the gallop and the house; and it would be a big problem if these were just divided between children as opposed to allocated between the family in a business-friendly manner – as well as with an eye on the tax position.

The 100% relief on the assets will be spread over the whole estate in whatever proportion the property is split, regardless of whether part of the estate is exempt. For example, if the relief was apportioned onto assets passing to the spouse the relief would be wasted, as the transfer would already be exempt.

Will planning – deed of variation

2.22

Whether or not lifetime planning has been implemented (see **2.26**), there are opportunities to structure the will tax efficiently. If the will is not tax efficient, the executors and beneficiaries may consider using a 'Deed of Variation' to rewrite the will.

Will variation provides a useful mechanism for deferring and in many cases mitigating the inheritance tax liability arising on death.

As the law currently stands, it is open to any adult beneficiary under a will to vary the terms of the gift to that beneficiary. Such a variation can be made up to two years after the date of death of the person who made the will provided all the other beneficiaries agree. Failing this, a beneficiary may 'disclaim' their individual bequest, in which case, the assets simply fall back into the residue of the estate of the deceased.

The two most common forms of variation are to either effect a redirection of the gift to the beneficiary's children (which will avoid inheritance tax on the beneficiary's death), or to redirect the gift to the surviving spouse. The surviving spouse may then make subsequent lifetime gifts, which benefit from tax relief as Potentially Exempt Transfers, (i.e. exempt so long as the donor survives seven years from making the gift) (see **2.27**). Furthermore, the redirection of gifts to registered charities will avoid tax altogether.

Post-death will variation is effected by means of a formal Deed of Variation, which must be executed within two years of the date of death. It is perhaps surprising that the Government has so far overlooked this useful mechanism for avoiding or mitigating liability to Inheritance Tax and the benefits of using a Deed of Variation should always be considered. This can be a very efficient way of passing the equine business tax efficiently through the generations.

Will planning – identifying tax efficient assets

2.23

Will planning should help the owner to verify the tax efficiency of his/her assets. For example, does the equestrian business qualify for BPR (see **7.21**)? Where there is a mix of taxable and exempt equestrian activities it will be important to take account of the interaction of the nil rate band (see **7.35**), surviving spouse exemption and business relief.

Ideally, any individual holding agricultural land that qualifies for APR (see **7.1**) or a business which qualifies for BPR (see **7.21**) should ensure their will takes advantage of APR and BPR and that the benefit of these valuable reliefs is not wasted by passing those assets qualifying for the relief to the exempt surviving spouse.

The surviving spouse may wish to control the business after the death of his or her spouse. Instead of leaving assets direct to the spouse, those attracting APR could perhaps be bequeathed to a nil rate band discretionary will trust, from which the spouse can benefit.

Making lifetime gifts of equestrian businesses

2.24

Some high-profile trainers have attracted publicity by passing on their businesses to the next generation via lifetime gifts. This can bring significant IHT advantages, but there are potential pitfalls that advisers need to be aware of.

Where assets which do not qualify for business or agricultural reliefs are concerned, it will also be important to ensure that gifts are made without a 'reservation of benefit' (GROB).

If 100% APR (see 7.17) or BPR (see 7.21) is anticipated on the agricultural or business property on the death of an individual, a simple planning strategy might, of course, be to retain the property, ensuring it remains under current qualifying conditions. No tax should arise on death and the beneficiaries would inherit at market value.

On the other hand, there are also those who consider that the favourable relief will not last forever and that action should be taken now (or at least before death).

Additionally, it is not inconceivable that the current benign regime for APR and BPR might change, and perhaps become more restrictive. A lifetime gift may, therefore, be desirable to take advantage of the 100% exemption. The capital gains tax consequences of any gift must not be ignored but with entrepreneurs' relief (now BADR) and also the possibility of rollover relief, there are strong incentives to consider lifetime transfers.

Also, practically it may be impossible to hold the property under the same conditions to ensure the relief is available. For example, where the trainer, equine business or stud owner are becoming old and are unable to work there may be strong consideration to pass the business down a generation.

Holdover election

2.25

Holdover relief under s165 of the Taxation of Chargeable Gains Act 1992 (TCGA 1992) is available on the gift of an eligible asset (e.g. an equine business), from one UK resident individual to another. The relief given is the amount of the chargeable gain that would have accrued to the transferor on the disposal of the whole or part of the equine business. This gain is deducted from the cost of acquisition of the transferee, which is deemed to be market value under s17 of the TCGA 1992. Such an election has the impact of passing the asset at the capital gains tax (CGT) base cost of the transferor; thus, there will be no 'tax-free' uplift on death.

Normally, holdover relief is limited to assets used in a trade, profession or vocation carried on by the donor or their personal company or group. But paragraph 1 of s7 TCGA 1992 extends the relief to gifts of agricultural property (see **7.1**) that qualify for APR, even if these have not been used in a trade, i.e. let farmland.

Potentially exempt transfers

2.26

Problems arise where the person making the transfer of the equine business does not survive the seven-year period and the availability of APR/BPR becomes important. Where gifts are made during the lifetime into a discretionary trust, such a transfer would be a 'chargeable transfer' and tax would be calculated and payable at the time the gift was made. Provided the gift attracts 100% APR/BPR, no tax will be payable at the time of the gift and the chargeable value of the gift, i.e. £Nil (after 100% APR/BPR), will be fixed for the purpose of calculating the cumulative value of gifts made before death.

Should the APR/BPR not be available at the date of death, the tax would still be payable on the gift made under the claw-back rules. The only difference between a chargeable transfer and potentially exempt transfer (PET) in these circumstances is the fixing of the value of the gift.

Equine succession planning must review the interaction of CGT and IHT; any gift that potentially reduces future IHT has the risk of incurring a CGT liability. If the transferee sells within seven years and the transferor does not survive the seven years, the potentially exempt transfer (PET) may fail. If the asset gifted still qualifies for relief at the time of gift and time of death, then relief is still granted despite the potentially failed PET. The risk is, of course, that in this time, either part of the farm has been sold for development or the whole of the farm has been sold, which will result in an IHT clawback.

Rollover and reinvestment into new qualifying asset

2.27

When a lifetime equine business gift is to be reinvested (or replaced) into another qualifying business asset, then this must take place within three years of the sale of the original asset. Rollover relief for CGT (see **2.4**) can also have the IHT advantage of "replacement property" relief for IHT. With the reduction in the lifetime allowance for business assets disposal relief (BADR) down to £1m, rollover relief is becoming more and more important. This reduction of the lifetime allowance is regarded by some as simply a 'development tax' by another route. However, this reduction is not just affecting development gains but sales of farms in general as less of the gain can achieve the more favourable 10% rate, thus "rollover" is becoming more attractive to equine businesses. Farm development gains can currently be 'rolled over' for capital gains tax (CGT). The rollover into farmland/equine property is a frequent event, however the farmland can be difficult to find and there are worries over the uncertainties facing farming, particularly profitability. The reinvestment can be made in stages – provided all purchases fall within the three-year period of sale and all the proceeds are invested. If anything less than the whole of the proceeds are reinvested, the whole of the APR/BPR will be clawed back. Also, only one rollover of the proceeds is allowed, and the replacement asset must be held at the death of the transferor to attract the relief. These conditions are often totally overlooked by those making gifts of equine business assets.

It may be possible to reinvest the proceeds in an asset qualifying for BPR instead of APR and effectively swap the APR on the original gift for BPR. This is provided the original agricultural asset would have attracted BPR in its own right, due to it being a business asset. APR is always given in priority over BPR if both reliefs are available.

BPR is available for trading businesses only. Where land is held as an investment, BPR in general is not available. This would apply to tenanted land. See CHAPTER 1: THE GROWTH OF THE EQUESTRIAN INDUSTRY.

It could be, therefore, that a farm or stud is gifted to the next generation. If they wish to re-invest the proceeds into a dedicated equestrian business that qualifies for BPR, then the replacement of business asset rules must be taken into consideration.

See *Stanley: Taxation of Farmers and Landowners* (1995) LexisNexis UK for an in-depth review of all areas of agricultural property ownership.

Thoroughbred and non-thoroughbred studs

2.28

This subject was first looked at in chapter **1.14**.

There are no reasons to assume that the non-thoroughbred stud or other equestrian activity will be treated any differently to thoroughbred studs for tax purposes. The legislation refers to the breeding and rearing of horses with no discrimination to the thoroughbred. The same principle for all taxes should therefore apply. It is assumed that in view of the fact that racing preceded other equine activities such as eventing and show jumping it was considered first. Racing has been involved with high financial rewards and, therefore, high-value tax liabilities are at stake. It has been the focus of many cases.

The HMRC Manuals quoted do refer throughout to thoroughbred horses, especially the 11-year loss rule principle (see **8.13**) that was agreed with the TBA in 1982. The author takes a strong approach to protecting the tax relief on non-thoroughbred operations, however, the tax principles are very similar for all activities, e.g. the stud is a farm, stock is valued at the lower of cost and net realisable value and the 11-year loss rule for studs also applies.

As with all tax problems, it is the specific facts of the individual case that are important and great store will rest on demonstrating and providing evidence of the commerciality and bona fide trading motives of a business activity, together with proof of commercial design. It is worth quoting direct from the HMRC manuals for the inheritance tax relief on business property and agricultural property relief. This guidance can be found on the HMRC Website which states: *"Stud farms engaged in the breeding and rearing of horses and to land used for grazing associated with those activities (IHTA s115(4))"*. Note that no reference is made to the thoroughbred at all here; there is no exclusivity. This legislation refers to the horse and not just the thoroughbred breed; and this should be the basis for treating thoroughbred and non- thoroughbred equally for tax. This is looked at in further in chapter **7.15**. See also the impact of transfer to equestrian sport in chapter **2.31**.

Proof and evidence of commerciality is of far greater importance than the type of horse.

Commercial or hobby – the HMRC fight

2.29

The question of whether participation in a sport is to be regarded as a taxable activity (see **3.1**) will depend largely on what the individual's motives are. Is it amateur or professional? Is it commercial or hobby? Guidance can be given from points raised in **CHAPTER 3**. Each case will have to be looked at on its own merits. (The cynic will simply point out that, to HMRC, a hobby becomes a taxable trade when it turns from loss into profit!)

It must be remembered that it is only the owning and racing of racehorses that is generally regarded as tax free by HMRC.

If a professional horseman approaches their business with commerciality and all the 'badges of trade' (see **3.3**), HMRC will generally accept that the business is taxable. As mentioned at **2.7** above, HMRC have sought to collect tax on profitable activities whilst at the same time attempting to deny relief on any activity that can be deemed loss making (see **8.1**). All those in the industry must therefore be prepared for a challenge from HMRC.

Stock transferred to 'equestrian sport'

2.30

As set out in HMRC's BIM 55715, where stock is transferred by an owner to carry out sporting activities, this must be effected for book and tax purposes at open market value. The leading case here is *Sharkey v Wernher (1955) 36 TC 275* (see **1.11**, **3.2**, **4.12**, **6.11** and **7.13**). Lady Zina Wernher undertook a variety of activities away from her stud farm. The judge said that such *"other activities, namely, those of racing and training horses 'are neither farming nor any other kind of trading but are purely recreational in character, not giving rise to any liability to tax"*.

The important issue therefore, is whether or not equestrian sport is deemed recreational or commercial? Is it business or pleasure? If the sport is an integral part of the stud, then problems over market value need not be apparent. There are those cynics who argue that the tax adviser to the non-thoroughbred horse activity is the best placed of all. The tax adviser can use the racing/thoroughbred rules when it benefits the client and adjust as appropriate provided that the decision is consistent based on facts and capable of being argued with HMRC. Where circumstances are unique, complex or the taxpayer foresees problems with HMRC, the practical approach may be to seek to obtain a ruling from them.

Retiring from the equestrian business

2.31

Many see equestrian businesses as something that clients retire into, not from, whilst others may consider that once the equine passion enters the bloodstream there is no escape and no retirement. Many elements of the equine world can be enjoyed beyond standard retirement age and potential inheritance tax reliefs can be looked forward to in future years.

The importance of the equine property valuation for IHT

2.32

Many owners of equine property will die owning the property and the probate valuation is key to maximising APR (see **7.17** and **7.20**) and BPR (see **1.2** and **7.1**).

Recent tax case law has put more pressure on the probate valuer for the equine business. Most qualified farm probate valuers have been trained in depth in all farming matters and probably enjoyed a dedicated learning time at agricultural college. However, the valuers might not have gained much experience on the diversified activities of all farms. It is therefore very difficult to arrive at the correct valuation for those alternative use activities of storage, liveries, and other commercial occupations. Experience and understanding is particularly important where there is the complication of horse livery and the large impact on taxation.

When considering the livery position, a starting point is will the livery qualify for inheritance tax relief (see **1.7**)? This will depend on the level of services carried out by the deceased, who carried out any additional services for business property relief (BPR), and what the integrated agricultural activity is for agricultural property relief (APR). An early question should also be have the owners obtained planning permission for any on-site developments not yet undertaken? Local Authority enforcement action against unlawful equestrian use of agricultural land is a threat that should be understood by landowners whilst they are operating the trade and the probate valuers need to be aware for s160 IHTA 1984 purposes.

Many agricultural landowners are unaware of the distinction between 'agricultural use' of land and 'equestrian use' of land for tax purposes (see **1.2**). 'Agriculture' is defined for these purposes as: "*horticulture, fruit growing, seed growing, dairy farming, the breeding and keeping of livestock (including any creature kept for the production of food, wool, skins or fur, or for the purpose of its use in gardens and nursery grounds and the use of land for woodlands where that use is ancillary to the farming of land for other* *agricultural purposes.*" (see **2.2** and **7.1**). The only equestrian 'use' that falls within the agricultural definition is producing horses for slaughter, working horses on the land (e.g. ploughing with horses which is a rare sight today), and grazing for breeding horses only. The context is important with regard to the eligibility for agricultural property relief (APR) and business property relief (BPR) for inheritance tax (IHT) purposes.

In the tax tribunal case of *Wheatley (Wheatley's Executors v CIR (SpC 149) [1998])* (see **1.2**, **2.17** and **7.23**) it was found that the grazing of horses did not qualify for APR. Many consider this decision flawed. The more recent case of *Vigne Deceased, Personal Representative of The Estate of v Revenue and Customs [2017] UKFTT 632* (see **1.7**) has now emphasised the need for 'enhanced services'. Liveries could therefore be at risk of achieving neither APR nor BPR and the information contained within the valuation, together with the evidence of the equestrian planning permission for use of horses on the land will be vital.

The most common form of 'agricultural equine' use for local planning permission purposes is grazing horses on the land (see **1.2**). However, as soon as more is being done to the horses than merely allowing them to graze, for example, additional feeding on the land, rugging the horses and/or riding them on the land, falls within 'equestrian use' (see **1.7**); the landowner must then apply to his/her local planning department for a change of use from agriculture to equestrian. This is where the complexity of the services come in as part of integrated tax planning. In order to qualify for BPR under 'enhanced livery', as in *Vigne* (see **1.7**), or part/full livery, there must be planning permission.

With regard to local authority planning and the interaction of the IHT reporting, the correct planning permission and the valuation could conflict. It is interesting to look at the *Palliser* case in the context of farm valuations. This Upper Tribunal (UT) (Lands Chamber) decision has brought to the limelight the question of probate valuation and the issue of 'hope value'. The valuer here did not consider hope value and thus the probate value (IHTA s160) in August 2012 was much lower when compared to the sales price for the shared property in March 2014. The reasons that the valuer presented for not incorporating hope value were because the property had a number of negatives and had been previously developed. The Tribunal did not agree with the valuer who acted for the taxpayer that there was "no hope value", especially given that the property was marketed as having "great potential" and in need of modernisation. The Tribunal calculated Mr Palliser's share of 'hope value'.

In stud farming hope value is the difference between the probate market value (s160 IHTA 1984) and the agricultural value (s115(3)) (see **7.20** and **7.29**). The position on hope value is explored in more detail in the case of *Foster* (see **2.38**).

The significance of the IHT400

2.33

There are many ways that an equine property probate valuation can be presented depending on who is providing the valuer with the information to carry out the valuation under s60. Some farming family members have different views and interpretation on the facts surrounding the equine property and some might actually want a different 'image' for appropriate tax planning. It could be that some members of the equine property are trying to protect the inheritance tax relief and their share of the inheritance by providing overstated details on services etc.

If the equine property is to be sold the next key point will be to ensure that how the farm is marketed is taken into account. Where equestrian planning permission has not been obtained, e.g. there might be planning for a few stables BUT not agreed change of use from agricultural use to equestrian, a strategy will have to be considered by the buyer for how they deal with any lack of planning permission.

The buyer might ask the seller to sign statutory declarations that the land has been used for equestrian activities for 'x' number of years. A statutory declaration is a document that is prepared with a view that once it has been sworn it becomes a document of evidence as to the facts recited in the declaration. Statutory declarations must be factual evidence. It is key to look at the elements of the declaration included on the IHT400.

It is imperative that the information included on the probate valuation is to a high quality, for example, it must:

- Be factually correct
- Correlate with the IHT400 which is submitted with the probate oath
- Tie into any statutory declarations

The timeline of activity might confuse matters as events after death can differ to those pre-death with regard to refurbishment and trading operation. The information provided to the valuer must be accurate. See *Foster* case – valuation and development **2.38**.

The evidence of the Graham case on 'services'

2.34

DIY livery yards (see **1.7**) are currently under attack from HMRC, with BPR claims being denied in some cases.

The recent release of the judgement in the case of *Grace Joyce Graham (Deceased)* again draws attention to the need for enhanced services for BPR, albeit for holiday lets rather than specific horse liveries, in order to achieve those favourable IHT reliefs. The conclusion at paragraph 93 of the case concisely demonstrates this:

> "*Overall, we conclude that Carnwethers was an exceptional case which does, just, fall on the non-mainly-investment side of the line. The pool, the sauna, the bikes, and in particular the personal care lavished upon guests by Louise Graham distinguished it from other 'normal' actively managed holiday letting businesses; and the services provided in the package more than balanced the mere provision of a place to stay. An intelligent businessman would in our view regard it as more like a family run hotel than a second home let out in the holidays.*"

Where the equine business is based on tourism with accommodation and livery, it is necessary to look at the *Graham* case. From the DIY livery viewpoint, the level of additional services could be seen as key to obtaining BPR for IHT purposes off the back of this ruling.

How would a valuer treat this "exceptional" Graham case? When cases only just fall into the eligibility for BPR, the slightest misunderstanding could result in an incorrect notation on the diversified activities in the valuation and the IHT400 (see **2.34**), with huge sums of tax at stake. A broad understanding of valuations and diversified activities is therefore required.

As the *Palliser* case (see **2.33**) makes clear, it is important where possible to look to future sales details of the equine property and the price hoped to be achieved. Everyone realises that sales prices achieved for equine property are currently volatile and therefore such valuations have a large range of values that could be applied, and these thus must be considered on a case-by-case basis. However, there should be no volatility in the information supplied to the valuer and contained within the valuation. Such detail, no matter how unusual due to beneficial ownerships, trading status and history, should be extremely well-researched. There is an oath being signed in respect of the details of the valuation and the District Valuer can be very critical of attempts to manipulate the value and descriptions.

Principal private residence – Longson v Baker

2.35

The subject of PPR, also known as a main residence relief, was introduced in chapter **1.1** and **2.5** above.

It would be impossible for an equine tax book to ignore the case of *Longson v Baker (HM Inspector of Taxes) [2001] STC 6, 73 TC 415*. Many equine enthusiasts would dispute the judge's key statement of *Longson Baker*:

> *"it is not objectively required, i.e. necessary to keep horses at a house in order to enjoy it as a residence".*

A review of the case will be essential to the reader's understanding of its implications.

From 1979, Longson ('L') and his wife owned and occupied – as their only or main residence – a property ('VF'). VF comprised a Grade II listed, five-bedroom dwelling-house, with a range of stables, sufficient for 12 or 13 horses, and an enclosed exercise yard. The land comprised 7.56 hectares and included grazing sufficient for 8 horses. L's family was interested in horses and further developed the site of the house for that purpose.

In 1990 L moved out of VF following the failure of the marriage. As a consequence of divorce proceedings, L made a disposal of his interest in VF. Under an Extra-Statutory Concession (ESC D6), L was treated as having resided at VF until 15 December 1995, the date of the disposal. L was, however, assessed to capital gains tax on the footing that only 1.054 hectares was, with regard being had to the size and character of the dwelling-house, required for the 'reasonable enjoyment' of it as a residence within the Taxation of Chargeable Gains Act 1992 s222(3). L appealed on the grounds that the whole 7.56 hectares were so required. The Special Commissioners (SpC0238) dismissed the appeal. L appealed.

Dismissing the appeal, the appeal court found that the Commissioners had not erred in law in failing to take into account the equestrian aspect of the dwelling-house; to have done so would have been to disregard the inclusion in s222(3) of the words 'as a residence' when it states '*regard being had to the size and character of the dwelling-house, that area is required for the reasonable enjoyment of it … as a residence*'. The test under s222(3) is objective; it is not objectively required, i.e. necessary to keep horses at a house in order to enjoy it as a residence; the Commissioners had been engaged in an enquiry as to fact and their conclusion was not reviewable on appeal.

The tax adviser will often be asked for an opinion on the availability of the relief for private residence relief from CGT (PRR) and this will clearly henceforward represent a need for careful review where the property has adjacent to it a large 'equestrian garden or grounds'.

The big garden – Phillips

2.36

As a follow on to *Longson Baker* we look at a 2020 case. The First-tier Tax Tribunal (FTT) has voided a capital gains tax (CGT) assessment imposed by HMRC on the sale of Mr and Mrs Phillips' home and garden. The reason for the assessment was because HMRC considered the garden to be larger than necessary for the owners' 'reasonable enjoyment' of the property.

The case is very interesting in the light of much attention being placed on development – as a result of proposed changes to the planning system many taxpayers with large gardens and pony paddocks are looking to develop. The Government's consultation on planning law reform proposes the biggest change to the system in 70 years and has massive implications for farmers and the countryside and those with opportunities of developing their garden.

There will be some capital gains tax (CGT) relief through main residence relief on the garden, but potentially there will be CGT payable on the pony paddock where it does not qualify as garden. The question raised by the tribunal is the size of the garden.

The proposed changes to the planning laws require primary legislation and will not necessarily have a smooth ride, but getting involved in the consultation is important. If anyone is in doubt about the intention or extent of the reforms, then the Prime Minister's words that 'the time has come to…tear it down and start again', in the foreword to the consultation, should be enough to dispel that misconception. The opportunities for commercial development cannot be overlooked.

The facts were that Mr and Mrs Phillips bought their house in 1997. The property included five bedrooms, three bathrooms, a garage for three cars, a one-bedroom cottage and a swimming pool, with grounds amounting to 2.3 acres, or just under one hectare. At that time, it was surrounded by fields, but by 2014 a housing developer had acquired all the adjoining land and was preparing to build on it. The couple reluctantly decided to move, and sold their home to the developer.

They did not declare the sale for CGT purposes as it was their principal private residence in their understanding. This is a mistake often made by taxpayers with large gardens – they are unaware of the restrictions. However, HMRC investigated the disposal by Mr and Mrs Phillips while it was checking stamp duty records in March 2017. HMRC considered that the size of the plot exceeded the threshold beyond which CGT relief for the main residence can be available, the relevant provision being TCGA 1992, s 222(3).

As a result they issued discovery assessments to both Mr and Mrs Phillips for £162,820, representing CGT on the part of the purchase price attributable to the balance of 0.44 of a hectare (i.e. 0.94 hectare less the allowed 0.5 hectare).

Mr and Mrs Phillips appealed against those assessments on the basis that the whole of their plot was in fact required for the reasonable enjoyment of the property and thus qualified for principal private residence (PPR) relief, as indeed would any taxpayers faced with the same situation. This could be a sale not just of the large garden for development, but also large gardens needed to cope with the Covid lockdown.

As a result of the wording of TCGA 1992, s 222(3), the FTT had to rely on previous case law, especially the 2001 case of *Longson v Baker [2001] STC 6* and the 1938 case of *Newhill Compulsory Purchase Order [1938] 2 AII ER 163* for the meaning of 'required'. It also had to consider whether the 'enjoyment' of the house was to be measured at the date of disposal or over the whole period of ownership.

Many equine enthusiasts would dispute the judge's key statement in *Longson v Baker*, although it does give clarity on the tax position:

> *'it is not objectively required, i.e. necessary, to keep horses at a house in order to enjoy it as a residence'.*

Considering *Longson v Baker* in more detail, the appeal court found that the Commissioners had not erred in law in failing to take into account the equestrian aspect of the dwelling-house; to have done so would have been to disregard the inclusion in TCGA 1992, s 222(3) of the words 'as a residence' when it states:

> *'...regard being had to the size and character of the dwelling-house, that larger area is required for the reasonable enjoyment of it...as a residence'.*

The fact that the Phillips' house was large and was set in a rural area suggested that it would appeal to somebody who was looking for a larger house and more space around it for privacy and other reasons. The FTT found as follows:

> *'We accept that the whole of the area of 0.94 of a hectare comprising the garden and grounds of Mr and Mrs Phillips' property was required for the reasonable enjoyment of the dwelling-house and so falls within the permitted area qualifying for PPR relief.'*

As a warning to those with large gardens, this is still a marginal area of what is and is not allowed and professional tax advice must be taken. What happened to Mr and Mrs Phillips could happen to any taxpayer with a large garden. This is also important in the light of the increased garden space that has become 'fashionable' under Covid.

The recommendation of the Office of Tax Simplification (OTS) to align CGT and income tax rates raises the possibility that future disposals of large gardens could be taxed at much higher rates at some future date than the current CGT levels, so the result could be very punishing. Small businesses and individuals are faced with a large amount of uncertainty and change at the moment.

A large number of equine properties have large gardens and perhaps this case is a positive for equine clients who realise that the stables cannot be allowed per *Longson v Baker* but a large garden can AND there are generous reliefs regarding the business.

The new CGT Return from 6 April 2020

2.37

Examples of use of the new CGT Returns include those residences with big gardens (outside the normal half hectare/reasonable enjoyment rules), horse paddocks included as part of the residence and garden, equine properties e.g. stud houses, those individuals with a lack of evidenced quality occupation, property caught in divorce disputes, and more. The CGT Return on residences will be due within 30 days of completion. Any CGT on the sale of the residence will also be due within 30 days.

Recent tribunal decisions have shown HMRC's enthusiasm to 'hunt down' main residence relief non-compliance. Farmers could possibly be caught by the need to sell let cottages to reduce the investment element of their trading operation for business property relief (BPR) for inheritance tax (IHT) purposes. Client communication is key.

Stamp Duty Land Tax (SDLT) and "mixed use"

2.38

The pony paddock used for business could ensure that the purchaser can apply the "mixed use" rate of SDLT. Such use has come under attack by HMRC in a number of tribunals, e.g. *Dr David Hyman and another v HMRC* [2019] UKFTT 469 (TC), *Pensfold v HMRC* [2020] UKFTT 116 (TC) and *Myles-Till v HMRC* [2020] UKFTT 127 (TC). It is important to show that the pony paddock had a business use at the time of purchase; or, that business plans were in place from the time of purchase. It is very easy for the taxpayer to forget the paddock when they sell and for tax advisers to omit to provide warnings of both the tax advantages and disadvantages. These cases were appealed in the Upper Tribunal and lost.

Foster Probate Valuation – impact on equine

2.39

The case of *Foster v Revenue and Customs* [2019] UKUT 251 (LC) explored the idea of "hope" value and how the expectation of getting planning permission for development on such land *should* be included when valuing land for inheritance tax (IHT) purposes which includes land used in an equine business. It is fair to say that farms and equine property have proved to be very desirable to property developers and this has been reflected in the consistently high land values over the past years. While this is certainly a positive for those looking to sell, it can have negative tax consequences when it comes to obtaining a valuation for probate. Under s160 of the Inheritance Tax Act (IHTA) 1984, the value of a property at any time is taken to be "the price which the property might reasonably be expected to fetch if sold in the open market at that time".

Susan Foster died in August 2013, owning an estate which included 6.39 acres of unregistered freehold agricultural land. Simon Foster, her executor, valued this land at £191,700 after taking independent professional advice while HMRC and the Valuation Office Agency (VOA) valued it at £850,000. Mr Foster, therefore, made an appeal against this determination under s222 IHTA 1984.

The tribunal identified two issues concerning the assessment of the open market value of the site, namely:

- Its residential development potential at the valuation date; and
- The correct valuation approach.

Understanding the land's history in the planning application process was, therefore, key to determining the amount of development potential and thus the amount of hope value which could have been attributed to it at Mrs Foster's death.

It is first important to note that the land was outside the local plan for development and "safeguarded" until after 2026:

> **9.** "The Site is shown as 'safeguarded land', i.e. land removed from the Green Belt and identified as having the potential to meet future development needs beyond the plan period (i.e. beyond 2026) if required. Within the plan period safeguarded land is protected from built development as though it were in the Green Belt."

Chances of development may, therefore, be thought to be relatively slim in 2013. However, two planning applications had been submitted for the land at the valuation date and permission had been recently given to other "safeguarded" land outside of the plan. Furthermore, Mrs Foster had been actively seeking development for some time having first entered into a six-year joint venture agreement (JVA) with her husband and a construction company in 2004, and later renewing this in April 2010. The purpose of the JVA as stated in the recitals was for the parties:

> "...to jointly promote the Development Site and use all reasonable endeavours to obtain planning permission for residential and ancillary uses and either procure development of the Development Site in their own right or sell the same for development."

Other issues with the Foster site listed by the appellant included: the presence of great crested newts, which are a European Protected Species; the fact the site had poor vehicular access and was effectively "landlocked"; and strong opposition from the Town Council and local community following an influx of residential planning applications at the same time.

HMRC countered these arguments, enlisting an expert planning witness in the form of Ms Howie. She noted, for example, that the presence of great crested newts could be mitigated given that they were also present on the neighbouring land approved for development; all that was required was for a survey and a mitigation planning process to be put in place. HMRC also pointed out that whilst the safeguarded land had not been identified as a preferred housing option under the initial two consultations of the Site Allocations and Management of Development

Plan (SAMDev), it was in the third, albeit not retained in the Pre-submission Draft (Final Plan) published in March 2014. This, it was argued, would have encouraged a hypothetical purchaser.

Whilst we go into a lot of detail on the *Foster* case, it is very important for probate and equine clients with development potential.

The judge sided with HMRC with regard to the development potential at the valuation date:

> **59.** "I am satisfied that at the valuation date a hypothetical purchaser would have considered there to be a reasonable prospect of obtaining planning permission for the residential development of the Site in the short term."

Given this, it is interesting to note that the judge described Ms Howie's evidence about the prospects of the Site obtaining planning permission for housing as being ambiguous and confusing, despite the fact that he ultimately agreed with her. Her written evidence and oral evidence conflicted, one moment stating there would be "reasonable expectation" of getting consent but later stating it was "highly likely to be forthcoming". During the hearing she explained that a hypothetical purchaser was likely to be more optimistic than a planning consultant, though she finally reverted to her original opinion of there being a "reasonable expectation".

The judge acknowledged the appellant's points and noted there were problems with the land, predominantly down to the fact that they restricted a hypothetical buyer to a limited window to fall in line with the Council's housing plans. However, the reliance on third parties for vehicular access, the "oversubscription" of sites for planning applications at the time, and the need to put in place a mitigation strategy to protect the great crested newts did not mean there was no development potential, simply that the value would need to be adjusted accordingly.

Whilst looking at *Foster* in detail it is important to consider the correct valuation approach for equines.

Given the tribunal's agreement with HMRC that there was a reasonable prospect of planning permission being granted on the site, it follows that HMRC's "top-down" valuation approach was taken to be the appropriate starting point rather than the "bottom-up" approach proposed by the appellant which was described as being "unduly pessimistic". The judge criticised some of the comparable land transactions used by the appellant's valuer and stated:

> **69.** "In the circumstances of this case I prefer the respondent's 'top down' valuation approach. Mr Beer criticises this approach as being remote from direct market evidence and for its reliance on subjective judgements about the nature and levels of risk. These are valid points but Mr Beer's market evidence, whether of local comparables or as contained in his schedule of strategic land sales, does not provide a sound basis for the estimation of the open market value of a site which has a reasonable prospect of obtaining planning permission in the short term".

Whilst the appellant's claim that there is no evidence that the market pays high rates of hope value in such circumstances was acknowledged, the judge interestingly noted that "the statutory requirement is to assess the open market value and that means assuming an unconditional sale" rather than taking into account that most purchasers would typically manage risk by entering into a conditional contract or an option. All these considerations must be understood by the equine business with potential development.

The tribunal then went on to take a slightly different approach from HMRC in arriving at their ultimate valuation of £590,000. Firstly, they valued the land based on the residential density per acre, using the sale of the neighbouring site as a comparable. HMRC assumed residential planning permission for 50 dwellings but the tribunal reduced this to 46 possible dwellings and, at £53,000 per dwelling, they deemed the value of the site with planning permission to be £2,438,000. The tribunal then reviewed the discounts to be applied for the restricted access and planning risk. HMRC proposed a discount of 40% for restricted access and, once combined with a discount for planning risk at 50%, the overall effective discount they proposed was 70%. In contrast, the Tribunal accepted the

50% discount proposed by the appellant for the restricted access and 60% for all other planning risks compared to HMRC's 50% and the appellant's 62.5%. The result of this was a total discount of 80%, thus giving a market value of £590,000 – a half-way house between the two initial valuations, as often seems to be the way with Land Tribunal cases of this genre.

Whilst the *Foster* case doesn't directly touch on the tax treatment, it does highlight how important business property relief (BPR) is for equine land with hope value when it comes to IHT planning. With a "top-down" valuation approach deemed the most appropriate for land with potential development, agricultural property relief (APR) will not suffice as this only covers the agricultural value and not any element of hope value.

Ironically, if 100% BPR is to be achieved, the higher value would be more beneficial from a capital gains tax (CGT) perspective, given that this would become the uplifted base cost for the beneficiaries in the future on the basis that the current provisions have not yet been altered following the Budget 2021 and "Tax Day" 2021 despite the Office of Tax Simplification (OTS)'s recent IHT report and subsequent recommendations from the All-Party Parliamentary Group (APPG). However, while recent cases such as *Vigne* (see **1.7**) and *Graham* have given hope to landowners and tax advisers alike in the availability of BPR, it is by no means guaranteed. Many still feel more clarification is needed as to what counts as an investment and what counts as trading to satisfy s105(3), IHTA 1984, and, therefore, it is key to ensure there is a sufficient provision of services on the equine property and, perhaps even more importantly, that there is evidence of them.

There is speculation as to what impact the Coronavirus crisis will have on valuations.

Debts, Loans and Lifetime Gifts within the equine industry

2.40

There can be confusion as to whether a "gift was a loan" for example, and such misunderstandings can not only lead to disputes between family members within the equine business/equine property as to whether they have received their rightful share, but also have different IHT treatment.

From a starting point, there are considerations around whether the donor survived seven years since the date of the gift. A debt may exist where the deceased lends money or indeed with increased expensive diversification projects where they borrow money. Securities for the borrowings must be understood. The basic rule for what constitutes the death estate is found in s5(1) of the Inheritance Tax Act (IHTA) 1984, which confirms "For the purposes of this act a person's estate is the aggregate of all the property to which he is beneficially entitled..." And, at IHTA 1984, s5(3): "In determining the value of a person's estate at any time his liabilities at that time shall be taken into account..."

With regard to borrowings: "A liability incurred by a transferor shall be taken into account only to the extent that it was incurred for a consideration in money or money's worth." The definition is found in IHTA 1984 s5(5). This broadly means a debt is allowable for IHT purposes as long as the deceased received something equivalent in value to the debt during their lifetime. Equine businesses can involve confused definition of debts.

It follows, therefore, that any debts created under a moral obligation (promising or intending to make a gift, for example) or that are legally unenforceable because there is no supporting paperwork are unlikely to be allowable deductions for IHT purposes. This is something that equine businesses must be careful to comply with. In these difficult times of Coronavirus, it could be that "cash-rich" equine businesses might lend money for family members to non-business members. It could be a gift is given. These will need very careful recording and advice. The Office of Tax Simplification (OTS) did suggest that the lifetime gift rules are reduced from seven years to five years. There were no changes to IHT and CGT in Budget 2021.

Statute barred debts – where the passage of time means that the debt is no longer enforceable – are the exception to this rule as long as they are actually settled from the death estate. The legislation also allows an IHT deduction for taxes due as a result of death, excluding the tax that arises on death.

Typical debts encountered by executors when dealing with a death of a typical equine estate and which are allowable for these purposes include:

- Mortgages;
- Overdrafts;
- Credit card bills;
- Home utility costs or care home fees; and
- Income tax and capital gains tax due for lifetime tax.

It could well be that as a result of the Coronavirus pandemic, borrowings will be increased to push the businesses through to the other end of the pandemic.

Although they are not debts as such, reasonable funeral costs and associated costs involved with obtaining foreign probate and realising foreign assets (limited to 5% of the value of the foreign asset) are also allowable deductions from the death estate. The standard UK estate administration costs and the costs of UK probate are not allowable for IHT purposes.

Where the deceased operated in partnership, it must be understood whether the debt belongs to the partnership or is a debt of the individual. In the same way that the loan and security must be understood, so must the underlying equine asset. We have shown time and time again that in a farming partnership whether or not the farm is owned as partnership property needs to be forensically understood. The same applies to an equine operation. Likewise, whether the loan is a partnership or individual liability needs to be understood. As always, partnership agreements, notes of partners meetings and accounts that reflect the correct legal position of assets and liabilities are important. When producing farm accounts, copies of the loan agreement should be inspected and retained. The details of the purpose of the loan, the security and exact borrower should be understood.

The general rule for estates is that liabilities are deducted from the free estate that does not qualify for the instalment option of IHT. For example, an unsecured overdraft might be set against a positive bank account balance before it is set against the residential property in the death estate. There are some specific rules as follows:

- Secured loans such as mortgages should, as far as possible, be set against the value of the asset against which it is secured.
- Business debts should be deducted firstly from business property.
- Foreign debts should be set against the foreign property.

These rules are a useful starting point but, in practice, the debts can exceed the value of the security or business property. The rules for the offset of the deficit are complex, particularly where there are both UK and foreign assets and debts.

A question might be asked: how did the debt exceed the value in the 2021 world of strict bank lending? The reality is that the debt can, especially with a country in crisis and the complexity of the equine world.

The Act provides for anti-avoidance legislation, the operation of which completely changes the basis of how debts are allowed or relieved in an IHT computation. Anti-avoidance legislation was introduced through Finance Act (FA) 2013 and applies if a death estate has a liability and the funds borrowed were used to acquire, maintain or enhance:

(1) "excluded property" (IHTA 1984, s162A);

(2) "excluded property" in the form of a foreign currency bank account (IHTA 1984, s162AA added by FA 2014);

(3) property attracting agricultural property relief (APR), business property relief (BPR) or woodlands relief (s162B, IHTA 1984); or

(4) liabilities that are not actually repaid after death (s175A, IHTA 1984).

If the borrowed funds have been used directly or indirectly for these purposes, the liability is deduced from the relievable property, irrespective of the security for the debt. If the funds borrowed were used for a purpose falling within items (1) or (2) above, the date of the loan is not relevant; the funds are caught by the anti-avoidance if there is a transfer of value after July 2013, the date of royal assent.

If the funds borrowed fall within item (3) above, the date of the loan is pertinent. If the loan was taken out before 6 April 2013 and the terms remain unchanged, the inheritance tax (IHT) treatment of the liability is to deduct the debt from the value of the asset upon which it is secured. However, if the loan is first secured or renegotiated after 5 April 2013, the anti-avoidance legislation will make a mark and the liability will be deducted depending on the use of the funds. Care must be taken in any circumstances when a loan was agreed and secured before 6 April 2013 to ensure it is not inadvertently flipped into the post-2013 regime for deductibility of debt.

They are not within IHTA 1984, but advisers should bear in mind the anti-avoidance provisions at FA 1986, s103. These are designed to prevent the artificial creation of liabilities. If the consideration given by the creditor represents or is derived from property previously gifted by the deceased, the liability is disallowed. This prevents, for example, settling funds into a trust and the trustees then lending money back to the settlor to create a debt in their death estate. A practical tip is to take care if the borrowed funds have been used for mixed purposes. By mixed purposes, it means checking if they have been used for business/agricultural purposes *and* some non-business personal purposes. It is important to retain the supporting documentation for the use of funds to support a deduction against non-relievable property. Retention of documentation and evidence is key for all equine businesses.

Lifetime gifting and relievable chargeable transfers

2.41

One potential consideration around the FA 2013 provisions combined with the 2021 Budget is gifting the APR/BPR achieving asset but retaining the liability within your estate. If the relievable asset is no longer part of the estate at death, the liability could not be deducted from it and, therefore, could be deducted against the rest of the estate.

However, IHTA 1984, s162B(7) states that "...to the extent that a liability is...taken to reduce value in determining the value transferred by a chargeable transfer, that liability is not then to be taken into account in determining the value transferred by any subsequent transfer of value by the same transferor". It is key to note it must reduce the value transferred by a chargeable transfer. If the lifetime gift was a potentially exempt transfer (PET) in which the donor survives 7 years, it will be exempt and so the liability may still be deducted from the estate on death as it will not have reduced the value of a previous chargeable transfer.

HMRC provides the following useful example of how s162B(7) takes effect in its *Inheritance Tax Manual* at IHTM28024:

"John, who has an estate of £3m, borrows £1m and uses this to purchase farmland which he then farms for 3 years. He then gives the farmland, now worth £1.2m to his daughter who farms the land herself, but he retains the liability. The individual has made a transfer of value when he gives the farmland to his daughter. The value transferred is the loss to John's estate of £1.2m. IHTA84/s162B(4) has the effect of reducing the £1.2m agricultural value by the amount of the liability to £200,000. This

£200,000 value then qualifies for agricultural relief, reducing the value transferred to nil.

With no changes to APR/BPR and CGT in the 2021 Budget and "Tax Day" much consideration needs to be given to equine lifetime gifts.

When John dies 2 years later, the £1m liability cannot be taken into account again due to IHTA84/s162B(7). Instead of the chargeable transfer on death being £2m (£3m less the £1m liability), it is £3m with no deduction for the liability."

Simply, if a debt is set against a relievable chargeable transfer, it cannot then be set against a subsequent chargeable transfer. This affects the position for lifetime gifts that farmers make.

Does the debt pass to the next generation or does it have to be repaid? That is a very topical subject at the time of writing. Consideration will be given to the forensic analysis and also the tax position. A key consideration will be whether it is possible for the liability to pass to the next generation secured on an asset without creating any IHT problems.

IHTA 1984, section 175A specifies that for the liability to be deductible for IHT purposes in the death estate, it must actually be repaid from the death estate. In many cases, this stipulation is satisfied because the asset upon which the debt is secured will be sold by the executors, the debt is cleared and the net proceeds are distributed to the residuary beneficiary. The only exception to the debt having to be repaid to remain deductible in the death estate is if:

- There is a real commercial reason for the liability not being discharged;
- Securing a tax advantage is not (one of) the main purpose(s) of leaving the debt outstanding; and
- The liability is not otherwise prevented, under any provision of IHTA 1984, from being taken into account.

There are a number of commercial scenarios in which this exception could be claimed. The beneficiaries could be taking over the business of the deceased, the borrowed money being used for working capital purposes, and the bank agrees to continue the lending facility.

Another example might be if there is a family or emotional attachment to the equine property and the beneficiary of the estate wants to receive the asset rather than the net sale proceeds and is happy to take on the debt. Throughout this book we consider the "emotional attachment" and passion of horses. If the lender is happy to move the mortgage with the property to the beneficiary, the debt should remain available for IHT purposes in the death estate.

Third-party debts from banks or building societies are more likely to attract relief under IHTA 1984, s175A, with HMRC taking more interest in less formal debts. Supporting paperwork and the terms of the loan will be vitally important. If only part of a liability is discharged from the estate, the debt is treated as having been discharged in a specific order. Liability that is attributable to financing excluded property is treated as having been discharged first, followed by the liability attributable to property that is eligible for BPR, APR or woodlands relief. The final tranche of borrowing to be treated as discharged is that not attributable to relievable property.

The sale of the asset by the executor could result in CGT, but the probate value should be correct. Historically, a large number of equine beneficiaries have wanted to continue owning the asset, but in recent years with high values and with Wills, which leave the asset (and liability) to a number of siblings/beneficiaries, the problem can become more complicated. There has been and possibly will be increased sales of equine assets not just to repay the borrowings but also to pay out the beneficiaries.

When equine business proprietors are instructing the writing of their Wills, it is essential for them to work out the repayment of both debt and other sibling entitlement in practical terms with realistic values prior to death. Where there is just one beneficiary, the settlement of debt to both comply with s175A and taking on the debt can be relatively straightforward but with multiple beneficiaries and serious levels of debt the problem can be more complicated.

What is the position of the debt in the hands of the next generation? Does it retain its nature from the death estate or can it change again? The position will almost certainly depend on the facts and the personal circumstances of the beneficiary. The IHT treatment and deductibility of the debt in their future death estate will be dictated by how the debt is acquired, how it is discharged, the use of the borrowing, lifetime gifts and whether they have their own IHT relievable assets.

A clear point for equine businesses and their tax advisers is to look at the estate with borrowings, lifetime transfers, and possible assets created by money owing to the deceased. All terms of security provided and monies borrowed should be understood by the lawyers, accountants and tax advisers when producing all documents relating to the equine operation, e.g. Wills, partnership agreement, accounts, tax returns etc. The impact on the practicalities of the loans must be considered at every stage. What will happen on probate? How are the IHT reliefs affected? etc. There can be very complex equine trading estates.

Conclusion

As mentioned in **Chapter 1** and throughout this chapter, advisers have a duty to try to maximise tax planning for a passion. Stud farming is farming and comes with a raft of beneficial agricultural tax reliefs. Inheritance tax reliefs can be a significant saving and will feature throughout the book as will capital gains tax reliefs. The thoroughbred (TB) and the non-TB, e.g. sports horse etc, are considered.

CHAPTER THREE

HMRC ATTACK ON THE NON-COMMERCIAL EQUINE BUSINESS

Following on from the topic of **Chapter 2**, this chapter looks into the recent scrutiny undertaken by HMRC against relief claims of 'hobby' equestrian businesses. This Chapter summarises the often overlooked but essential badges of trade, sponsorship pitfalls and commerciality of the equestrian business. Specifically, we look at:

- Hobby v commercial (**3.1**)
- Defining the taxable moment (**3.2**)
- Commerciality – badges of trade (**3.3**)
- Assets of the trade or personal enjoyment (**3.4**)
- Length of the period of ownership – an investment or a business (**3.5**)
- Frequency of transactions (**3.6**)
- Supplementary work (**3.7**)
- Circumstances of ownership (**3.8**)
- Motive of the equine business (**3.9**)
- HMRC attempt to tax profits on occasional sales (**3.10**)
- Late registration of an equine activity (**3.11**)

- When to register the equine business with the tax authorities (**3.12**)
- Racehorse sponsorship (**3.13**)
- Guidance given by HMRC BIMs (**3.14**)
- Equine sponsorship of competitors post GDPR (**3.15**)
- The facts of the *Crown and Cushion* case (**3.16**)
- Evidence of equestrian sponsorship (**3.17**)
- Benefit to the family member was an "incidental effect" of the sponsorship (**3.18**)
- The commerciality of sporting and equestrian business (**3.19**)
- The pursuit of equine profit (**3.20**)
- Use of private horses in the equine business (**3.21**)

3.1

This subject of the commercial equine business as opposed to the hobby was first considered in **Chapters 1** and 2.

This chapter aims to lead the reader through all kinds of equine tax planning from the tax position of the owner to the stud farm, training, breeding etc. The utilisation of losses will be considered, as will the business advantages of owning business assets for capital gains tax and inheritance tax purposes. All these subjects are then considered later in the book. The VAT registration is considered specifically at **5.4**.

Many equine businesses have become businesses from a simple leisure pursuit by a process of evolution rather than being planned as such from the outset. Hence the emphasis of the business plan (see **1.15**) to show HMRC that there has been a transformation and it can be profitable.

Because many proprietors' perceptions are one of racing being non-taxable one frequently encounters 'businesses' which have not been registered with the tax authorities as such at the proper time or, more pertinently, at the best time. The carrying on of a business with a view to profit is not recreation; it is a taxable activity. There will, of course, frequently be cases in which some elements of the business, e.g. the stud (see **CHAPTER** 7) are a proper taxable activity whilst others are not.

The case of *Sharkey (HM Inspector of Taxes) v Wernher (1955) 36 TC 275* (see **1.11**, **4.12** and **7.13**) demonstrates quite clearly that Lady Wernher's equine activities were similar to those seen in many other establishments and were indeed, in the eyes of HMRC, a mixture of business and pleasure. The case considers what elements of the mixed racing and breeding operation were 'within the scope of tax' and 'outside the scope of tax'. Although this case was about racehorses being transferred to stud at market value, the case also provides guidance for many equine activities that exist today. The court had to consider what were business activities and what were recreational activities or 'outside the scope'. The key question for the tax adviser to address can be when should a taxable business be registered with the tax authorities? Very often the answer here lies in encouraging the provision of better information transfer between taxpayer and tax adviser along with evidence of activities together with taking professional advice at a very early stage. Once the business is established as commercial the planning around the offset of losses can commence and this is looked at in **Chapter 8**.

Defining the taxable moment

3.2

Many people enter the equine world without realising that certain events are taxable or at least require disclosure to their accountant/HMRC.

The new move to Making Tax Digital (MTD) (see **5.5**) and the £10,000 limit could help some equine operations define the taxable moment in compliance terms.

Examples here could be where:

- a valuable racehorse becomes a stallion and stands at stud producing a very valuable income stream. Although there may be large pre-existing racing losses which absorb this profit in reality, from HMRC's viewpoint, one is a taxable profit and the other is not a tax deductible amount. The receipt of stallion fees therefore needs careful planning (see **CHAPTER 6**);

- a property is purchased to house some of the racing activities possibly including breeding (see **7.1**). There is already a principal private residence (PPR) and thus a second home is involved. If the property is sold at a gain the taxpayer could assume that it is all part of the 'racing is tax free' mentality. However, it needs full disclosure.

- a show jumping horse is sold at a very large profit. This involves extensive training expertise. No previous disclosure was made to HMRC as costs had been exceeding the income.

Identifying the change from commercial to non-commercial and vice versa often comes down to the accountant and tax adviser. At a practical level we would flag up non-commercial equine operations, e.g.

- Reduced or no sales

- Results well below business plan expectation

- Continued losses (see **2.3**)

and these would be monitored year by year.

To spot the hobby that has become a business is less easy. Examples can be:

- Direct approach by an equine client who has read an article (or their accountant has done so) on equine trading disclosure

- Generic questions around the tax return that identify sundry income

- High profile awareness to the equine world

- Sale/purchase of equine land and property with unclear status as to business hobby

I set out the tax advantages in broad terms of an equine business. Suddenly having a profitable hobby can have tax disadvantages:

- Undeclared output VAT on sales (see Chapter 5)

- Unclaimed input VAT on purchases

- Undeclared profits from the equine business

- Missed opportunities with CGT and IHT

Some of these could result in penalties if not dealt with in a timely maner.

Commerciality – badges of trade

3.3

Throughout this book considerable emphasis has been placed on the need to demonstrate that activities carried on within the equine industry are commercial business activities and that the so-called 'badges of trade' exist. This is crucial to obtaining tax benefits and trading tax status.

If an equine activity is proved to be commercial this will establish business status for assets used in that business. The benefits of entrepreneurs' relief (BADR) (see **2.4**) and rollover relief for CGT and BPR/APR for IHT can only be enjoyed by the taxpayer if the equine business is commercial and accepted as such by HMRC.

The similar subject of the 'reluctant farmer' is reviewed in detail in the author's *Tax Planning for Farm and Land Diversification* Sixth Edition (2020) Bloomsbury Professional, in **Chapter 12**. Some equine enthusiasts will inevitably become reluctant registrants for their businesses in order to protect CGT and IHT reliefs.

If HMRC is not satisfied with the commerciality of a business then it will not tax it as a trade but will treat it as a hobby (see **2.29**). This will lead to a denial of tax relief, particularly if losses arise, although HMRC may still pursue tax on profits eventually. Income tax losses are restricted to being carried forward

if commercial inspiration cannot be proven. Thus, if a large profit appears in one year there may be a problem. A bloodstock breeder who does not occupy a stud farm may find it more difficult to convince HMRC that he is operating a bona fide trade. However, each case must be judged on its own merits and if, in fact, the relevant criteria have been satisfied then the breeder should meet with success.

Although bloodstock breeding (see **6.1**), racing (see **2.7**) and other equine activities are a somewhat specialised industry, the well-known 'badges of trade' are equally applicable here and should be referred to in any case where it is necessary to convince HMRC that an activity is a taxable trade.

Asset of the trade or personal enjoyment?

3.4

While any form of tangible property can be traded, most commercial 'commodities' are rarely held as an investment – they offer the holder no 'pride of possession'. Property, which does not produce income simply by being held or which offers the owner any personal enjoyment, is more likely to be held for the purposes of trade. As the stallion or share in a syndicated stallion can be a positive income-producing asset, it is conceivable that HMRC could argue that it is being held as an investment and not trading stock (see **4.8**). Similarly, as an owner of a racehorse is likely to derive personal enjoyment from the activity, but is unlikely to realise profits, HMRC tend to argue that racing is a hobby and not a taxable trade.

However, in such cases it can be important to stress to HMRC that commerciality does not preclude personal enjoyment (see **3.21**). In the case of any equine business, are the horses held as an investment, for recreation or realisation at a profit? Likewise, with the ownership of equine property, is it held for investment, recreation or to house a business as part of a genuine trading activity?

HMRC have difficulty in accepting that expenses related to areas of the equine world are incurred wholly and exclusively for the benefit of a trade. In tax law this goes back to the concept of 'duality of purpose', where HMRC effectively try to argue that if someone enjoys what they are doing, any expenses associated with the activity are disallowable. They generally believe that such a trade is an attempt to achieve tax relief on the costs of a hobby (see **2.1**, **2.29**, **3.1**) and try to deny expenditure on the grounds that the taxpayer obtains private enjoyment from the expenditure.

HMRC are always concerned about duality of purpose (see **3.21**) and personal benefit. The concept of duality is best explained by *Mallalieu v Drummond* (1983) 57 TC 330 where black clothing needed for an appearance in court was held to be needed for the more conventional use of clothing the body as well. The legislation is contained in what is now ITTOIA 2005 s35 which states:

> '(1) In calculating the profits of a trade, no deduction is allowed for –
>
> (a) Expenses not incurred wholly and exclusively for the purposes of the trade; or
>
> (b) Losses not connected with or arising out of the trade.
>
> (2) If an expense is incurred for more than one purpose, this section does not prohibit a deduction for any identifiable part

> or identifiable proportion of the expense which is incurred wholly and exclusively for the purposes of the trade.'

Problems arise where HMRC believe that personal pleasure is being derived from elements of the stud farm or equestrian activity. Examples of this are escalating costs of vermin control, the horse or even the quad bike to inspect the farmland and farm/equine activity, equine clothing and farmhouse expenses.

A thorough review of possible areas of 'duality' is recommended for all equine operations.

Length of the period of ownership – an investment or a business?

3.5

Property, which is to be traded, will commonly be held for a relatively short term whereas an investment is normally acquired for long-term income and capital growth. HMRC accept that bloodstock breeding is a high risk, long-term trade and cannot be assessed on the results of the first few years.

The disposal of some horses at a profit after being held for a relatively short time will obviously enhance arguments of commerciality. This does not mean the business has to involve instant dealing or 'pinhooking' (the purchase of young stock to bring on to the next stage of racing).

In the VAT case *Commissioners of Customs and Excise v Lord Fisher (1981) STC 238* at page 245 Gibson identified six indicators, some or all of which should be satisfied to identify an activity or activities as a business. These indicators are equally applicable as a test for IHT purposes. Gibson said a business will exist where the activity:

- Is a 'serious undertaking earnestly pursued' or 'a serious occupation, not necessarily confined to commercial or profit making undertakings';

- Is 'an occupation or function actively pursued with reasonable or recognisable continuity';
- Has a 'certain measure of substance as measured by the quarterly or annual value of...supplies made';
- Was 'conducted in a regular manner and on sound and recognised business principles';
- Is 'predominantly concerned with the making of...supplies to consumers with consideration'; and
- Whether those supplies 'are of a kind which subject to differences in detail, are commonly made by those who seek to profit by them'.

Frequency of transactions

3.6

A key consideration to determine commerciality will be the frequency or number of similar transactions by the equine activity and this is indeed one of the 'badges of trade'. The larger the amount of bloodstock held, the more likely it is that the tax adviser can convince HMRC that a trade is being carried on. If only one broodmare is owned, then HMRC is likely to argue that a hobby is being enjoyed. On the other hand, if the investment encompasses a number of mares and stallion shares, then the tax inspector is more likely to be convinced that there is a bona fide trade.

We are often asked when does an equine business become a hobby. Generally the criteria are lack of sales, profit and inability to prove commercial intent with convincing business plans. Ironically the conditions in reverse are good indicators that a hobby has become a business, i.e. there are sales and profit and this has led to a commercial intent and, as a result, convincing business plans can be produced.

In the same way the quantum of losses can take equine businesses by surprise so can turning a hobby into a business.

The complex practical tax point is deciding when on the analysis of facts and timeline the business has ceased to be commercial and vice versa when has a hobby become accountable for tax. VAT can be a key issue and in that regard ironically it is the *Fisher* case that is often used.

However, it is important to note here that the average number of horses held by members of the TBA is currently only a few. Thus, it will be important to stress that commerciality is linked to motive and is not dependent upon volume.

Supplementary work

3.7

Another badge is supplementary work, i.e. has any work been undertaken in connection with the assets. For a genuine bloodstock breeder, the broodmare will need constant attention and the breeder will normally (but not always) own his own stud farm so that he is carrying out work on the mare, i.e. improving it, if possible, from its acquisition until it produces progeny. The ownership of a share of a stallion, for example, which is not kept at the breeder's premises, may not involve him in any supplementary work during its period of ownership, although he may be liable for his share of its upkeep. This could result in the stallion being classed as an investment as opposed to treatment as a trading asset. If a stallion is only being held for its income from nomination fees rather than to enable the owner to send his own broodmares to the stallion, then HMRC may regard the stallion as an investment rather than trading stock. If other equestrian activities are carried out in addition to breeding, this may provide evidence of an overall commercial entity being in existence, e.g. breaking and schooling. On the other hand, it has to be recognised that such activities might be classed as merely feeding and improving the animals' 'condition', and thus not be considered a trade.

Circumstances of ownership

3.8

Certain assets can either be held as an investment or as trading stock of businesses. Syndicate shares in a stallion or a freehold building are two such examples. The length of ownership is often an important factor in the view of the courts and HMRC.

For example, the owner of a freehold building who sells at a large gain after, say, two years is more likely to be held to be dealing in property than a similar property held for, say, ten years. However, the owner may have originally intended to hold the asset as a long-term investment but be faced with an urgent need for emergency finance which leads to the sale of the building after only two years. If the changed circumstances can be evidenced to HMRC, then he is likely to accept that the asset was acquired as an investment and not stock. If a stallion or a share in a syndicated stallion was, in reality, acquired as an investment, then its sale in the short term to raise finance for an emergency should not affect the nature of the asset when it was acquired. It is the circumstances surrounding ownership of the equine operation and trading activity, which is the key issue together with the original motives behind the acquisition of the asset. It could be a livery yard started as a hobby but soon developed into a thriving activity.

Motive of the equine business

3.9

There are many who consider motive of the equine operation to be the most important badge of trade. In some cases, it will be clear that the motive of the owner was to trade or alternatively hold the horse as an investment. However, there will be many cases in which the distinction is not so clear cut. Here, evidence of the motive of the owner when he acquired the horse will be extremely important. For example, if it can be shown that a share in a syndicated stallion was acquired with a view to covering a broodmare at the stud farm and that arrangements were made for the broodmare to visit the stallion, then HMRC may well have to accept that it is stock, i.e. part of a trade, even though, for some reason, the broodmare was unable to visit the stallion. It is intention and motive, together with the supporting evidence at the time of the original transaction, which are important in deciding tax status.

What is absolutely crucial here is the primary purpose behind the activity. If this can be shown to have been commercially inspired, the fact that a proprietor derives some incidental personal benefits or pleasure from the ownership aspects of the activity should not detract from the acceptance of the activity as a genuine trade.

One motive of the equine business can be the generous tax reliefs BUT there must be a commercial motive to make money. There are numerous tax reliefs that the equine business can take advantage of:

- The ability to rollover gains from business assets into another business asset, and the potential for BADR for CGT;
- BPR and APR for IHT;
- The ability to claim 'sideways' income tax loss relief where losses are sustained and include some 'lifestyle' expenses; and
- The ability to repair and improve the property whilst claiming maximum allowable input VAT and, where possible, maximum income tax relief.

All tax reliefs must be carefully scrutinised by the farm tax planner and it is essential that all the relevant conditions are met so as to take full advantage of each and every one of them. As with any business all expense claims must be wholly, and exclusively for the purpose of the farming trade or estate enterprise and the operation must be commercial and must be shown to be commercial.

However, if the pleasures of ownership were the original inspiration for the activity (often, in HMRC's view, evidenced by the proprietor's long-standing prior involvement in this sort of activity in general), then HMRC will seek to refuse the owner the bonus of qualifying tax relief status which would, in effect, be to subsidise the owner's personal hobby from the public purse.

The tax case of *McKnight v Sheppard (1999) STC 699* is useful in that it was held that the object of a taxpayer in making expenditure had to be distinguished from the effect of the expenditure.

HMRC attempt to tax profits of occasional sales

3.10

In most circumstances, HMRC generally regard the prospect of profit from racing and general sports horse ownership to be too remote and so do not accept that it is a taxable trade (see **5.4**). Rather, they regard it as a hobby or recreational activity or, in the case of a company, a non-taxable activity. This means that the costs of training are not tax deductible and any prize money is non-taxable. This book looks at this in depth.

Although the hobby equine business is not trading, HMRC may, in certain circumstances, still raise an enquiry into the treatment by the individual of the occasional profit which they may make under the Self-Assessment regime. HMRC are however expected to take a consistent view when considering profit and loss-making years. The offsets of losses against general income and capital gains as detailed in s64 and s71 of ITA 2007 (see **8.3**) are restricted where breeding activities are not considered to be both carried out on a commercial basis and with the view to making a profit. The usual carry forward of trade losses (s83) (see **8.8**) should however still be available, subject to the cap on claimable tax reliefs (see **8.12**) not restricting the claim (see **8.8**). The cap on sideways loss relief (see **8.12**) will not be applied to brought forward losses. It is advisable therefore that full records are maintained to provide concrete evidence of a trade being carried out commercially with a view to making a profit in such a situation. A business plan, continually updated, is very helpful in this regard (see **1.15**).

If there is any doubt as to the correct tax treatment, advice should be obtained.

Late registration of an equine activity

3.11

The lack of clarity between business and hobby status, together with lack of clarity over trading stock and investment stock, can cause a genuine business to be registered late for tax purposes. It could be that accounts have not been submitted when they should have been.

Genuine pre-commencement expenditure is expenditure incurred before the first day on which the business is carried on. Where the expenditure qualifies for annual investment allowances (AIA) there is a timing problem as these vary so much. Normally, such expenditure is treated for capital allowances purposes as if it had been incurred on the first day on which the business is carried on (CAA 2001, s 12). However, in determining whether expenditure is AIA qualifying expenditure, any effect of s 12 on the time at which it is to be treated as having been incurred is disregarded (CAA 2001, s 38A(4)). A similar rule applied when deciding whether expenditure qualified for FYA (CAA 2001, s 50).

A stud or general equine business might develop slowly from owning a few shares in a racehorse to breeding from a favourite mare to a significant activity. The taxpayer might consider this a 'leisure activity'. It may well cost a lot to run with outgoings exceeding incomings and every now and then there might be a valuable sale, albeit generating no profits as the costs already incurred exceed the sale price. The owner might want to proceed commercially. All these matters must be given consideration and clients must be encouraged to disclose the information to their tax adviser fully. This will be essential, not just to facilitate planning, but also to ensure that all compliance issues are also considered.

In relation to the late registration of an equine trading activity or stud, some questions that could be raised between tax adviser and taxpayer are as follows.

- Are there more VAT implications than the Weatherbys Racehorse Owners Scheme? Should normal trading registration be considered? (see **5.6**)

- Could the activities be considered trading and if so what are the compliance and planning considerations?

- Could the activity seek protection of IHT and CGT relief from the business status that would be accorded to business assets?

- Can losses be claimed and, if so, what are the time limits?

- Are there any other problems with late registration?

The importance of communication between client and tax adviser at an early stage must be very clear.

When to register the equine business with the tax authorities

3.12

Once it has been decided that there is indeed a business in existence and it is established that some or all of the 'badges of trade' can be seen to be in place, the inspector of taxes should be presented with a positive business plan showing commercial inspiration and the carrying on of the activity with a view to a profit. The important decisions at this stage will be to choose a start date which will be accepted by HMRC. Clearly, if losses have arisen, the earlier the better from an income and CGT viewpoint, as this will limit future exposure to tax liabilities because the losses brought forward can be used to offset current and future taxable profits.

Racehorse sponsorship

3.13

In 1994 owner-sponsorship was introduced in racing. This allowed owners to obtain sponsorship and the sponsor to advertise on the jockey silks, breeches, the horses' rugs etc. Before entering into any sponsorship agreement, businesses should consider how such an agreement can be best structured for tax so that the maximum relief is obtained. The subject of equine sponsorship is dealt with in Chapter 4 in the context of owning a racehorse (see **4.5 to 4.7**).

Claiming a deduction for a sponsorship payment should in theory be no different to claiming a deduction for advertising expenditure. In structuring sponsorship there are a number of basic principles which should be followed.

1. The sponsorship agreement should be entered into by the trading business whose trade is to benefit from the sponsorship and not, for example, by a non-trading holding enterprise. Equally, where a horse or race is to be named after the company it should be named after the said business in the sponsorship agreement and the sponsorship should have a clear benefit to that particular business.

2. The expenditure has to be revenue in nature, i.e. deductible against income, in the hands of the payer since no deduction will be given where the business is incurring expenditure on fixed assets, for example on the acquisition of a racehorse, or a share in a racehorse. Provided that it is for the recipient to decide how the money should be spent, then even if the recipient chooses to acquire a racehorse the cost to the payer's business should still be deductible as a revenue expense.

3. As mentioned above, the main benefit of the expenditure must be to the trading business which then needs to show that the sponsorship payment falls into the same category as its normal marketing and promotional activities. A deduction will be available if the business can show that the sole purpose of the payment is to

help market its products and services and that any benefit to an employee or director is purely incidental.

Guidance given by HMRC BIMs

3.14

HMRC produce supplementary guidance to help understand the relevant tax treatment in different scenarios. The Business Income Manuals, otherwise known as BIMs, advise on trading income and the following are particularly relevant when it comes to sponsorship:

- BIM42555 Specific Deductions: advertising expenses: sponsorship
- BIM42560 Specific Deductions: advertising expenses: sponsorship: entertaining and benefits in kind
- BIM42565 Specific Deductions: advertising expenses: sponsorship: purpose

Further details on race sponsorship are contained in the British Horseracing Board's publication: Racehorse Owners' Sponsorship Code of Conduct (see **5.6** and **5.7**).

Equine sponsorship of competitors post-General Data Protection Regulation (GDPR)

3.15

There is no doubt that GDPR will cause commercial operations to work to alternative advertising methods with concerns over electronic mailshots and newsletters. It is timely therefore to look at sponsorship as a renewed focus.

The case of *The Crown & Cushion (Chipping Norton) ltd v HMRC (2016) UKFTT 765 (TC)*, see more below, is a positive result for the potential sponsorship of high profile equine competitors when the details are applied correctly. The decision is of course provided that there is evidence that the sole object is to promote the business of the sponsor, i.e. that it is wholly and exclusively for the purpose of the trade. Currently trades are looking for new ways to market and achieve client awareness. It is thought by some that even where the marketing mailshot continues with authority to approach and a clear unsubscribe button, it will be useful to have areas of attraction to keep customers subscribed and this could be sponsorship. It is likely that many tax advisers and commercial operations needing to keep in touch with existing customers and potential customers post GDPR will be seriously looking at sports sponsorship as an alternative solution.

The facts of the Crown and Cushion case

3.16

The limited company in this case operates a family owned hotel business comprising six hotels. Originally established in the 1980s, the driving force of the business during the relevant period was the company secretary Mr Jim Fraser, who ran the company day-to-day. His two daughters own the company shares, and one (Mrs Eileen Powell) is the sole director.

In 2008 Mr Fraser put in place a sponsorship agreement between the company and his granddaughter, Miss Alice Powell, a promising young racing driver who began to attract substantial media attention. She went on to become the youngest female to race in Formula Renault in 2009, and subsequently was the first female to win the championship in 2010 in UK motorsport history. The agreement stated that in return for £160,000 + VAT annually over four years, totalling £640,000 + VAT, Miss Powell would undertake various promotional and advertising activities in relation to the hotel company business, including carrying branding on her car and driving overalls, as well as providing 15% of her racing earnings for the next 12 years. If other sponsors could be found, certain repayments would be due to Crown and Cushion Hotel Limited.

HMRC claimed that the motor racing sponsorship payments made had a duality of purpose and were not wholly and exclusively for the purpose of its trade. They were of the view that the payments were both advertising for the hotel chain and the advancement of Miss Powell's personal racing driver career, again breaching the guidance in BIM 42565. The company appealed the decision of HMRC and the case went to First Tier Tribunal (FTT).

The FTT disagreed with HMRC on the basis that the evidence presented pointed to Mr Fraser's sole object when making payments was to benefit the company by attracting customers to the hotels, the closest of which were situated close to the Silverstone race track. The duality of purpose argument once again could not be proved in this regard. The expense also matched, on a room by room basis, previous advertising budgets indicating the payments were not over and above what may have been considered appropriate for a business of this size. The FTT found that Mr Fraser was not motivated by a desire to further Miss Powell's racing career and any benefit she received was merely an incidental effect of the payments made.

In 2014, however, HMRC came back with corporation tax amendments for the appellant company, showing an additional £155,355 in corporation tax, due to payments in the years to 31st March 2011 and 31st March 2012 that it ruled were not made wholly and exclusively for the purposes of the appellant's trade under s54 CTA 2009.

The First Tier Tribunal allowed the appeal, finding that:

- The word 'exclusively' means that if the taxpayer's object when incurring the expenditure has any purpose other than or additional to the promotion of the business then it is not deductible.

- The 'object' of the expenditure must be distinguished from its effect.

- It could not be presumed that the existence of the close family relationship between the parties meant that the benefit to Miss Powell in furthering her career was inescapably one of the objects for incurring the expenditure.

- Evidence demonstrated that Mr Fraser's sole object in the company making the payments was to benefit the company by attracting customers to the hotels.

- Mr Fraser was not motivated by a desire to further Miss Powell's racing career and the benefit to Miss Powell was an incidental effect of making the payments.

The case can provide guidance for successful equine sponsorship.

Evidence for equestrian sponsorship

3.17

The *Crown and Cushion* case above has given hope to various commercial operations who have a strategy to use this type of sponsorship within the equine world. There is no doubt that the equestrian industries of show jumping, eventing and dressage attract a wealthy audience whether the event is seen live, watched via television or online, or is simply read about in magazines. Obviously Covid lockdown has put a lot "on hold". Both the *Crown and Cushion* case and the *McQueen* case clearly showed the emphasis of evidence.

The type of evidence to look for includes, but is not limited to:

- Details of negotiations, including correspondence and contracts;

- How did they become aware of that particular event or person?

- Why was it decided to sponsor that particular event or person?

- What alternatives were considered and why were they rejected?
- A copy of the business plan that is usually prepared in commercial sponsorship cases (see **1.15**);
- Copies of any material provided by the person or entity seeking sponsorship;
- Details of how the sponsorship was intended to bring the name of the business or its products before the intended target audience (including how prominent are any adverts);
- How is the sponsorship exploited in terms of point of sale publicity, the local media, or other available avenues?
- The arrangements to assess and refine the effect of the sponsorship.

The internet is a useful additional source of information:

- What is said about the sponsorship on the website of the business?
- Is there any information on general sites about that sort of activity?
- Is there evidence of previous involvement in the sport of activity?
- What does the person or entity sponsored have to say about their sponsors?

Benefit to the family member was an "incidental effect" of the sponsorship

3.18

Whether an expense has been incurred 'wholly and exclusively' for the purpose of the taxpayer's trade will of course depend on the individual facts of the case under consideration, but the decision of the *Crown and Cushion* demonstrates that it is possible for equine businesses to make sponsorship payments to family members and for such payments to be tax deductible provided that any benefit to the family was an "incidental effect" of the sponsorship payment and a full commercial strategy is in place.

As the case demonstrated, it helps if the rider is high profile. There must be a documental trail from the original plans to sponsor, board minutes, comparisons of cost effective marketing and business plans (see **1.15**).

In *McQueen v HMRC [2007] SpC 601* it could be shown that the marketing was more cost effective than, say, newspapers and proof of resultant customers was documented.

The commerciality of sporting and equestrian businesses

3.19

A key approach in the determination of business or hobby is to draw guidance from tax tribunals.

The recent First Tier Tribunal case of *Sir Keith Mills, Team Origin LLP v HMRC [2017] TC05844* considers whether sporting businesses can be deemed as trading, and if so, whether their losses could be off-set. Whilst this case is based on sailing, it very much resonates with issues that arise in the equine world, especially with HMRC's current enthusiasm to examine equine activities and losses.

The facts of the case are that Sir Keith Mills set up a limited liability partnership, Team Origin, as an entity for assembling a sailing team to win the America's Cup international sailing competition. In 2007 offices were opened in London, Valencia and Portsmouth; 67 people were employed; negotiations with Royal Thames Yacht Club began to act as the designated club for competition; and a boat was bought for the racing team.

Mills and his team drew up a business plan showing profit could be achieved in the long term if Team Origin won two successive cups and therefore gained the hosting income from defending the Cup twice. As with many equine activities, further income would also be earned through sponsorship, merchandising and other hosting-related sources.

However, by 2010 Team Origin ceased trading on the grounds it would not be commercially viable having claimed trading losses of £32m over the four-year period. HMRC thus opened an enquiry into its returns and issued closure notices on the basis that its activities did not constitute a trade (ITA 2007, s 989).

The FTT therefore had to consider whether there was indeed a trade and if so, was it operated on a commercial basis? First, they looked at whether racing was in fact a separate activity. The judge said: '*There was an interconnection, interlacing and interdependence between the two activities – the racing activity was conducted not only with a view to increasing the prospect of success in the America's Cup but also as a vehicle to make sponsorship attractive.*' Put simply, without the racing there could be no sponsorship income, nor merchandising or hosting income.

Encouragingly, the FTT also concluded that obtaining sponsorship constituted a trading activity. They cited the decision in *British Olympic Association* (SpC 28) which supports '*the idea that seeking and obtaining commercial sponsors against the backdrop of a sporting endeavour is something which is prima facie capable of amounting to a trade even though the facts of that case in relation to the set-up of the association were significantly different from the facts of the present appeal*'.

However, this was not enough. In the equine world, be it competing and training or breeding (see **6.1**) and selling, a juncture is often reached where a decision has to be made as to whether such activities represent a trade or private undertaking. The process of obtaining and receiving sponsorship, for example, is often a key indicator. At this stage, the aforementioned 'badges of trade' are used as reference. The case *of Eugene Blaney v Revenue & Customs [2014] UKFTT 1001 (TC)* illustrates the use of the 'badges of trade' approach in determining whether or not horse breeding activities amounted to a trade for the purpose of claiming relief for Capital Gains Tax. In this case, the FTT deemed that the operation was too small to constitute a trade and the judge considered that the 'principal motivation was his love of horses and horse racing'. Furthermore, the activity of horse breeding was not related to Mr Blaney's trade as a house builder, again proving the activity of horse breeding was related to his general enjoyment of horses. Similarly, in the case of *Thorne v Revenue & Customs [2014] UKFTT 730 (TC)* (see **8.21**), it was decided that Ms Thorne, a self-proclaimed 'equestrian breeder and farmer', lacked the badges of trade as she was not seriously interested in profit but was "*just an amateur*" (in the unkind eyes of HMRC) participating in what could be considered a hobby.

The pursuit of profit

3.20

To be more than "*just an amateur*" the pursuit of profit is thus a key factor in providing evidence to HMRC of commerciality (see **3.1 to 3.9**). However, whilst there was no suggestion in this case that Sir Keith would not have liked to have made a profit with Team Origin, the prospect of this was small. As such, the tribunal turned to ITA 2007 s66(1) and (2) (see **8.4**), which denies loss relief where a trade had not been performed on a commercial basis or with a view to realising profits. In *Seven Individuals v CRC [2017] STC 874*, the Upper Tribunal found that the likelihood and level of profit are central to commerciality and therefore the FTT determined that in this case Team Origin had not acted commercially – "*someone seriously interested in profit would not engage in a trade with such a likelihood of profit or level of return*".

Both sailing and racehorse breeding involve high infrastructure costs and this case very much echoes that of *R Murray (TC3474)*, a racehorse breeder and trainer. In both these cases although there may have been a reasonable expectation of profit at the start of the taxpayers' businesses, high running costs and consistent losses over time quickly diminish that hope. What is key in the case of Mills, and indeed any business venture intrinsically linked to a non-business activity, was the conspicuous absence of reference to profits in plans and documents and a failure to rework the business plan as changes and uncertainties arose. Given that many equine businesses record large trading losses it is therefore essential that, to protect the accrued losses, the adviser and client put the following steps in place:

- business plans to show that, from the outset, a profit can be achieved in future years under the proposed structure;
- revised rolling business plans responding to the actual trading results; and
- ideally, accounts showing an eventual profit for the operation.

All advisers submitting loss claims on behalf of clients must ask objective questions about potential profit and not just accept in good faith the information provided.

Use of private horses in the equine business

3.21

In addition to the working animals, there may be one or more that are only used privately (see **3.4**), perhaps for dressage, show jumping, eventing or other competition work such as show horses. Sometimes these special animals are not used at all in the business in case of injury.

The question of transfer of a horse for private use at market value as set out in *Sharkey (HM Inspector of Taxes) v Wernher (1955)36 TC 275* (see

1.11, **4.12**, **6.11** and **7.13**) has to be taken into consideration. If a horse is transferred from business to private use it must be made at market value.

Private usage of feed, tack, farrier, medicines, veterinary care etc, must also be ascertained and properly accounted for. Clearly, by extracting the private element of an equine business, this will make it a more commercial and viable venture that satisfies HMRC's close review (see **8.1** and **8.2**) but the treatment must be consistent.

Many equine businesses own private horses and it is often a matter of debate as to how the private use (see **3.4**) is treated in the accounts and tax computation. As always there are tax planning issues as well as compliance and the fair assessment of drawings for partners.

On the assumption the trade is a partnership there should be a verbal or written partnership agreement that establishes the basis for the taxable market value of premises or services supplied to partners for any private use. Where the private horses use the same stabling and consume grass from the fields along with "livery horses", it can be assumed that the grass and stable usage would be capable of being sold to livery customers.

There are arguments to support that what such a customer pays is the market value and is what the partner in the business should pay since the private use adjustment must reflect the market value. Of course, there may be different livery rates for different types of livery and/or different durations of livery but that can be factored into the calculation of the private use adjustment and this can be set out in the partnership agreement or minutes. ITTOIA 2005, s172 enacts the *Sharkey v Wernher* ((1955) 36 TC 275) market value rule to 'trading stock', ie private items should be taken at market value. HMRC in its *Business Income Manual* at BIM 33630 makes it clear that services rendered to the trader personally, or to their household, should have only the costs disallowed. The practical and fair way of dealing with the private element is through the accounts as a debit to drawings and a credit to income. The provision of livery 'services' on its own would not be taxed, although if staff or other costs are incurred, they should be posted to drawings and thus disallowed in the body of the accounts.

Where there is a farm with no liveries but private horses the value of grass being eaten by private horses in the fields will have a grazing market value per acre. Again, the basis of calculating the market value of the grass should be sufficient to pass HMRC scrutiny and the allocation between partners be agreed in the partnership minutes.

There is a protection for IHT relief if full market rent is charged so that they are "used in the business" under s110 IHTA 1984 and the income is recorded per *Balfour*. The probate valuation of assets with private use together with the description of use will be significant for the claim for BPR. Honesty and transparency of information supplied to the valuer is key. The RICS qualification required for the probate valuation should ensure that the correct analysis of private assets will be ascertained on a fair and reasonable basis. Where the assets are used for private purposes but full market rate is paid this should be shown on the valuation for transparency.

HMRC's approach to the question of allowing expenses against income from equine activities is generally favourable for the business of buying and selling horses where there is pure 'trade'. This is sometimes known as 'dealing' and sometimes 'pinhooking'. However, where the costs of producing horses for sale include competing HMRC can consider that it must give rise to considerable personal benefit. The tax adviser must try to protect this position.

Pony paddock income and gains

3.22

The income sources could be horse liveries, a grazing licence or the paddock could be let for events such as parties, weddings, local festivities and the like. All such income should be declared on the self-assessment tax return. The importance of the declaration of this income to the tax authorities can be seen above as support for claims to beneficial capital gains tax rates. But the importance of correct disclosure was also illustrated by the self-employed income support scheme (SEISS), enabling claims to be made when income was lost due to Covid-19 disruption.

The negative cost of production potentially exceeding sales and evidence to show a profit can be produced is key. There is a difference between breeders who board out their mares and stud farms that have their own land. The latter is farming for tax purposes and the former is not. The stud farm can take advantage of the 'hobby farming' rules, but there must still be evidence that the stud operation is trading commercially with a view to a profit. At the top end of all equine sports (such as racing, show jumping, dressage and the like) there are strong profits, but problems can arise at the lower end due to margins and, sometimes, inexperience. Equine profits can be achieved – there must be full allowance for private usage and a full understanding of the weak areas with rectification action.

The current rate of capital gains tax on any possible gain on paddocks and buildings will be 20% unless the land and the newly purchased asset were used for a business. In that case rollover relief can be claimed on both the purchase and disposal under TCGA 1992, s162. From a tax perspective, the disposal of bare land can be linked with a grand farmhouse and let cottages. The eligibility of the farmhouse as an asset against which a claim can be made for rollover relief is the subject of much debate. It has been known for tax advisers to claim full rollover relief on the purchase of the farmhouse, however there should be restrictions to defer only the business elements of the working farmhouse. Alternatively, business asset disposal relief (BADR) can be claimed if the conditions are met and 10% capital gains tax paid. Many UK residents have a misapprehension with regard to their homes and capital gains tax and assume 'it is where I live so no tax to pay', not realising that gains on 'pony paddocks' are potentially taxable.

Conclusion

In the light of the potentially 'fine line' between 'hobby' and commercial business (see **1.19**) it is essential for the equine business to take tax advice from an early stage of the planning. Such work should include preparation of business plans and a forensic analysis of what is happening and what can happen to maximise tax relief. The badges of trade must be reviewed in the context of the proposed business and consideration must be given to tax legislation and BIMs. Some equine businesses are dependent on sponsorship and the commerciality of such agreements must be reviewed in the context of HMRC's close review of such arrangements. Any private usage must be identified and reported for in a structured, honest and fully researched way working within favourable tax rules, particularly for agriculture and genuine business. With the large variety of 'motives' to run an equine operation that exist within the industry, the 'fact find' of the operation is key. Detailed analysis and understanding of the operation is essential for tax advisers to be able to provide 'full and complete' advice.

CHAPTER FOUR

OWNING A HORSE – TAX PLANNING

As the title suggests, the following chapter investigates the relationship between horses and their ownership by businesses and private individuals. The chapter aims to help the reader to understand the possible tax implications of owning, buying and selling competition horses within various business structures that can be used for the equine operation. The following topics will specifically be considered:

- 'Tax free' ownership v tax efficient ownership
- Business motives
- Interaction with the stud farm
- Interaction with the stallion
- Buying and selling horses

The detail is as follows:

- Achieving tax efficiency of competition horse ownership (4.1)
- Business motive of racehorse ownership (4.2)
- Ownership of racehorse – *McMorris* (4.3)
- Can a company pursue a hobby? (4.4)
- Sponsorship, entertaining, marketing, advertising and PR (4.5)
- Owning a racehorse in the corporate entity (4.6)

- Unincorporated business owning a racehorse (**4.7**)
- Ownership of the stallion – the income stream (**4.8**)
- Leasing racehorses (**4.9**)
- Share of winnings (**4.10**)
- CGT and horse ownership (**4.11**)
- Interaction with the stud farm (**4.12**)
- Buying and selling or loaning a horse (**4.13**)
- Planning the sale of the "tax free" racehorse (**4.14**)

Achieving tax efficiency of competition horse ownership

4.1

As mentioned in **CHAPTER 1** (SEE **1.11**), **CHAPTER 2** and throughout the book, horse-racing and the ownership of horses is generally regarded by HMRC as 'tax free'. Owning a horse is essentially not a taxable activity. The arguments put forward by the BIMs (HMRC Business Income Manuals) (see also **1.11** and **4.3**) for racing being non-taxable are strong and based on the desire to refuse loss relief for the high costs of involvement in this pastime.

However, the Government's decision to keep the Racehorse Owner's VAT Scheme (see **5.6**) is a significant opportunity for tax advisers, racehorse owners and racing authorities to work together and look at the maximisation of the commercial structure and tax efficiency of the industry of owning racehorses (see **CHAPTER 5: PLANNING FOR VAT**).

In order to establish that an activity is actually a properly taxable trade, it must be shown to be managed on a commercial basis with a view to the realisation of profit. As has been said, there is a case for racing to be regarded as taxable because a racehorse needs to be tested on the racecourse in order to determine whether it should be retained for a career in breeding. These tests are for speed, stamina and courage. If there is to be any prospect of agreement on this matter from HMRC it is perhaps more likely with fillies (the female of the species) since, statistically, a higher percentage return to the breeding function.

Racecourses are ideal locations for the entertainment of business contacts and although entertainment expenditures themselves are disallowable for tax purposes, other costs of racing ought to be tax deductible if a commercial venture is structured correctly.

Business motive of racehorse ownership

4.2

The 'motive' of the ownership of the equine business is considered throughout the book (see **3.9**).

Most directors whose companies own racehorses (see **4.6**) would claim that they do so for advertising, marketing or public relations (PR) purposes. Tax Inspectors will obviously look very closely at such claims, as they have to satisfy themselves that they are granting tax relief for legitimate business expenses and not merely subsidising a hobby of one of the directors. The key issue here is motive. The following points will be taken into consideration:

- Is there an entertaining motive behind the acquisition of the racehorse? If so, the claim is likely to fail or at least fail in part.

- Is this form of advertising in keeping with the company's size, structure and image? A company who has not previously had a substantial advertising budget is unlikely to succeed in a claim.

The same applies to a company which would not otherwise advertise to the public.

- Is there any evidence that the horse is being used for advertising purposes? If a horse is named after the company which owns it, there is a stronger argument in favour of treating it as a business expense.

- It might be wise to try and carry out an analysis of sales and to prove that there is a direct benefit. Alternatively, an independent marketing or PR bureau could prepare a report. This might keep fellow directors and the tax inspector happy at the same time.

- Is this form of advertising likely to generate more business? Has the decision to advertise in this way been based on sound commercial principles? If not, the claim is likely to fail.

For the VAT position of racehorse ownership see **5.6**.

Ownership of racehorse – McMorris

4.3

In this case the taxpayer had bought a half-share in a racehorse in February 2010 and agreed to meet half the livery training and racing costs. Initially, the racing results for the horse were positive and the owners refused an offer of £50,000 to buy it.

The success did not last and, in summer 2011, the owners sold the horse for £1,000, of which the taxpayer received half. In his 2010/11 tax return, he claimed loss relief in respect of a trade, which he described as "racehorse". HMRC refused the claim on the ground that owning a racehorse was a hobby, not a trade. The First-tier Tribunal referred to the badges of trade as explained in *Marson v Morton [1986] STC 463.*

The First-tier Tribunal decided that the deal was a one-off transaction. Further, because the taxpayer had not borrowed any money for the venture, there was no long-term plan for the operation and he "clearly derived pleasure" from the project, all of which pointed away from the badges of trade.

Overall, the tribunal decided that the activities did not amount to a trade. The judge added that, given the informality of the arrangements between the co-owners, ITA 2007 s 66 was not satisfied because the activities were not carried out on a commercial basis. The taxpayer's claim for loss relief failed as the operation undertaken was not considered a trade – the horse was in fact deemed to be 'tax free' (see **1.11**).

Can a company pursue a hobby?

4.4

The above case raises the question of whether company ownership would have had more success in arguing a trade existed. In principle, it makes no difference whether an individual or a company owns a racehorse since corporation tax is largely based on income tax rules with some specific extensions and revisions. Inevitably there are minor differences due to the legal distinction between a company and an individual.

For example, whereas HMRC regard racing as a hobby when carried on by an individual, it cannot be said that a company owning a racehorse is carrying on a hobby. It is either carrying on a taxable or a non-taxable activity – but what of benefits in kind for directors?

In *Chepstow Plant International Ltd v HMRC (TC01035)* the company financed the training expenses for several racehorses but given they were being run in the director's personal name and not in the name of the company, HMRC questioned the allowability of the costs of training for corporation tax and also the potential benefit in kind for the director. In this instance the director could successfully demonstrate that he had no real interest in the horses as had never even visited the trainer and as such, this is a positive case to support tax efficient racehorse ownership.

However, to ensure the case is more robust, the practical planning point to take away is to ensure the racehorse is run in the name of the business. This way racehorses can be a very effective means of advertising and entertaining for a company.

Sponsorship, entertaining, marketing, advertising and PR

4.5

Equine sponsorship is looked at in **Chapter 3** (see **3.13 to 3.18**).

Horseracing is one of the most televised leisure activities and is thus an extremely high profile sport which can in turn be used to promote products through advertising and sponsorship.

In general, an individual or a company cannot obtain tax relief for racing expenses and, conversely, will not have to pay tax on race winnings. The exception to this rule is where the HMRC accept that a racehorse is maintained for the purpose of advertising or marketing, in which case the owner can claim the cost of keeping and racing the horse as a business expense. The disadvantage is that prize money becomes taxable, but relatively few racehorses generate enough money to cover the cost of keeping them. The vast majority of owners who keep racehorses for marketing purposes will be companies, although the rules also apply for individuals.

The advertising world of the 1960s and 1970s has moved into the whole new industry of marketing and PR. The travelling salesman is almost a rare beast replaced by a marketing and PR team. How does the ownership of a racehorse fit into the twenty-first century business life?

1994 saw a turning point for sponsorship. Owner-sponsorship was introduced in racing which allowed sponsorship through the medium of horse rugs, jockeys' breeches and silks. The key is to ensure that the sponsorship agreement is tax efficient. It is essential that maximum tax relief is obtained.

In today's world, one of the ultimate aims of the taxpayer and tax adviser alike is to try to obtain tax relief for expenses that the taxpayer 'enjoys'. This does not mean trying hopelessly to claim relief for a hobby, but to ensure that the business relationship between racehorse ownership and the taxpayer's business is commercially sound, well structured and tax efficient.

The case of *Executive Network (Consultants) Ltd v O'Connor (HM Inspector of Taxes) [1996] STC (SCD) 29* can be a useful reference for the purpose of considering expenditure incurred by a company in sponsoring a horse riding business.

Tax efficiency of the sponsorship is a key issue. As set out at **4.2** above, the main benefit of the sponsorship expenditure must be to promote the trade of the company. The business should be able to show that the sole purpose of the sponsorship agreement is to help promote and market the company's products and services and that any personal benefits accruing from horseracing are merely incidental. The reason for the sponsorship should be documented. The BHB have guidance publications such as 'The Racehorse Owners' Guide to Sponsorship' and the 'Guide to Valuation of Ownership Sponsorship Sites'. The sponsorship should have a clear and defined benefit for the trade.

Another consideration is a structured corporate entertaining package for both staff and clients. Whilst staff entertaining is allowable there is a thin line between client entertaining and staff entertaining. When employees help entertain clients then this is client entertaining. However, where the business is entertaining employees only, e.g. paying for a day at the races, it can be tax allowable for the company although there is a risk that the staff will be taxable on the benefit received.

Owning a racehorse in the corporate entity

4.6

Ultimately, a company's ability to succeed in obtaining tax relief on a racehorse may well depend largely on the facts of the specific case and on the relative powers of negotiation possessed by the company's directors and advisers and by the company's local tax inspector. In practice, it should be relatively easy for a large company to claim relief if it has a substantial advertising budget and if the racehorse is named after the company's product. Conversely, a small company, which is unlikely to generate much business from this form of advertising, is unlikely to succeed in its claim for tax relief for the expenses, especially if its advertising budget would otherwise be a modest one.

HMRC will look at all cases closely. For a business to be able to obtain tax relief it will be necessary to satisfy HMRC that the expenditure is deductible as it is wholly and exclusively incurred for the benefit of the trade of the business. If a business can obtain tax relief for racing expenses, it will, of course, be taxed on any race winnings. HMRC will have to see that the expenditure is incurred to promote the trade, increasing awareness of its products and brands. As alluded to above however, successfully claiming a deduction for racing expenditure will generally be more troublesome when the owners or directors of the business have a known personal interest in racing.

The practical point for the tax adviser and the owner is to compile a plan in advance, a detailed folio of evidence about the reasons for the purchase of the racehorse looking at budgets, opportunities and possibly identifying by reference to marketing reports the expected benefits flowing from the purchase. Full consideration must be given to the previous section on sponsorship, entertaining, marketing, advertising and PR.

For all directors who pay UK income tax, and whose companies own racehorses, there is always a danger that HMRC will regard the company's financing of the horse as the provision of a benefit in kind for the director, especially in cases where the director has a keen interest in horse racing and has enough influence to bring a racehorse into the company. The benefit in kind will have to be declared on the form P11D if appropriate.

Unincorporated businesses owning racehorses

4.7

The same basic taxation principles apply whether a bloodstock activity is operated personally or through a company. In general, an individual is likely to be carrying on a taxable bloodstock activity but HMRC may regard his racing activities as a hobby and non-taxable. Here we must again turn to the fundamental principles set out previously. However, these principles may be modified somewhat when dealing with a company owning a horse rather than an individual. The ability to obtain tax relief for the unincorporated business may again depend on sponsorship, entertaining, marketing and PR.

The entertaining element of ownership will be disallowed in the tax computation and likewise the element of the expenses that is not wholly and exclusively for the business will be disallowed.

Again, great emphasis should be placed on sponsorship agreements which should ideally contain clear, well-structured and documented evidence that the expenditure is expected to produce distinct and identifiable benefits to the business.

Detailed work by marketing/PR consultants would demonstrate how the ownership could help the business and evidence of success will be imperative.

VAT registration for the unincorporated business can be conducted under the racehorse owner's scheme.

Ownership of the stallion – the income stream

4.8

Stallions are looked at in more depth in CHAPTER 6, however, it is worth looking at the summary position. It has been said that owning a racehorse is a dream, owning a stallion is an income stream and this is a taxable income stream.

As mentioned earlier, bloodstock breeding is a high-risk, long-term business. Mares do not generate income until they produce progeny and it will be a number of years before a judgement can be made as to the quality of the foals. The owner must pay for their upkeep, together with the nomination fees to enable the mare to visit a stallion, so losses are likely to be made for several years. Stallions, on the other hand, are income producers once they return to the stud farm. The likely value of the stallion will depend upon its success during its racing career, but a stallion can be an extremely profitable asset from the outset.

The owner of a successful colt has a number of choices at the end of its racing career. He could sell it and, as the racing activity is generally not taxable, the proceeds will be received tax free. However, the tax-free element will depend on what the horse costs – either purchased or bred. If he brings the stallion back into a stud farm it will enter the accounts at its then market value so that if it is sold by the stud farm at a later date, the increase in the value of the stallion during its racing career will be tax free. The stallion could be used to cover the mares of the stud farm or other owners could send their mares to the stallion for the payment of a nomination fee.

A successful stallion valued at, say, £1m could be expected to generate nomination fees of approximately £6,000 per nomination, so that the owner or shareholders could sell 40 nominations and produce income of £240,000 for that year. However, this income would be taxable and so the individual taxpayer would be liable to pay income tax at the highest rate of 45% under current legislation. Whether such income will be taxable as trade if part of a stud or under miscellaneous income is dealt with in CHAPTERS 6 AND 7.

Leasing racehorses

General

4.9

Due to the difficulties which may arise in funding the cost and expenses of keeping and running a racehorse, some owners of a breeding business acquire their racehorses personally and then lease them on to their business so that all the expenses are met by that business. It may be possible to show that the expenditure thus incurred is advertising expenditure so that the company receives tax relief, although, obviously, the commercial viability would have to be justified to HMRC. In addition, the company may pay the owner a rent for the use of the horse, although this would be taxable on the owner.

If the business leases and then races the horse, any winnings should accrue to the business. However, if the racehorse becomes extremely valuable, the terms of the lease could include a clause to terminate the agreement with the business and enable the breeder to sell it with the resultant profit being tax free on the assumption that the breeder's trading activity is not taxable.

There are various forms of leases, which can be arranged between the owner of the horse and the company. All leases need to be registered with the Jockey Club under the Rules for Racing. A form of lease can either be obtained from the Jockey Club or a legal document can be drawn up which will clearly define the relationship between the parties so that there can be no confusion at a later date. Again, the leasing arrangement, which may be required, will depend upon the tax position of the parties and the likely profitability of the activity.

Leasing arrangements may also be entered into where the breeder does not wish to sell a yearling filly, but to retain her for breeding purposes, and cannot afford training expenses. In these cases, similar leasing arrangements to those outlined above may be entered into. Imagine the situation where a breeder or stud farm wants to retain ownership but cannot afford training fees. The owner could lease the horse (at a relatively low cost subject to the quality of the horse) to the business who could then name it in their business name and organise marketing and PR around the activity. If successful, the breeder/stud has increased the value of its stock (and possibly associated stock) and the business has undertaken valuable PR/Marketing.

Obviously, if the business was a company and the company and owner were connected, there would be disclosure requirements under the related party transactions provisions. If the business was unincorporated, disclosure to HMRC would also be required.

Share of winnings

4.10

In *Norman (Inspector of Taxes) v Evans [1965] Al ER 372, 42 TC 88,* the taxpayer, a breeder of racehorses, appealed against assessments made on him under Schedule D Case Vl (now replaced by ITTOIA 2005 Part 5 – miscellaneous income) in respect of sums received by him under agreements whereby he received one half of the winnings of horses which he had leased to other persons for the purposes of racing. It was contended on behalf of the Crown that the sums received were taxable profits under a contract of 'bailment'. On behalf of the taxpayer, it was contended that he received one half of the winnings in his own right and not under the terms of a contract, and that racing horses was a non-taxable recreational activity. It was held that he was properly taxable since the sums received by him arose not from a recreational activity, but from a business transaction between him and the lessees.

Whilst tax and the equine operation, especially sports horses, have developed significantly since 1965, the mere existence of competition winning and success does not automatically provide justification of a commercial business operation. The pursuit of profit (see **3.3** to **3.9**), profit motive (see **4.2**) and the business plan (see **1.15**) are far more persuasive to HMRC.

Capital gains tax and horse ownership

4.11

Horses which form part of the bloodstock of the stud farm and racehorses in training should not be subject to capital gains tax (CGT). The bloodstock which forms part of the commercial activity of the stud farm will normally be treated as stock-in-trade and will not be a capital asset for the purposes of this tax.

The valuation of stock of a stud is dealt with in CHAPTER 7.

Racehorses were within the scope of capital gains tax from the introduction of the tax in 1965 until 1968. The Chancellor of the Exchequer at that time realised that as racehorses were more likely to produce capital losses than capital gains, a number of racehorse owners were accumulating substantial capital losses and these capital losses could be carried forward indefinitely and set against future capital gains. In the circumstances, it was decided to take racehorses outside the capital gains tax net.

What a pity this ruling was made. How useful the capital gains tax relief would be. But if losses are achieved through a trade such as a stud then income tax relief can be obtained under the correct legislation and this income tax relief is more advantageous.

CHAPTER 6 looks in detail at the principle of the sale of the stallion and the wasting asset.

Interaction with the stud farm

4.12

The stud farm is considered in depth in **Chapter** 7.

When the racehorse owner also owns a stud farm, when is the tax-efficient time to transfer to the racing activities? How can tax planning and stud ownership be reconciled?

As set out in **CHAPTER 3 AND CHAPTER 4** if, in general, breeding horses is a taxable activity (see **2.2**) and owning racehorses is a separate and non-taxable activity, then the transfer of horses from the stud to and from racing back to the stud will be awarded special tax treatment.

This matter was considered in the 1955 case *Sharkey v Wernher (1955) 36 TC 275* (see **1.11**), which held that the animal must be valued at 'market value' when it leaves the stud to go into racing. Reference to this case is used to determine that assets taken from a proprietor's business for private use must be at market value. The market value of the horse at that time will be reflected in the bloodstock accounts. Therefore, even though a horse has not been sold, any profit or loss from breeding is taxable or allowable when it leaves the stud and commences its racing career.

Such profit or loss will have been realised in this way even though the breeder will not yet have received any proceeds from the sale of the horse to meet the tax liability. However, if the cost of breeding the horse by the stud farm amounted to much more than its market value when the transfer to racing is effected, this would result in an immediate tax relief on the amount spent. The loss will be achieved in the stud accounts, and then in the tax computation.

When the horse returns to the stud, it is brought into the bloodstock accounts at its then market value. If a horse left the stud and became an extremely successful racehorse before returning to the stud at a much higher value during its racing career, the gain will have accrued tax free to the owner, but with no money received. Conversely, if the horse is worth less when it returns to the stud then a non-allowable loss will have accrued.

Thus, timing is an essential element in the tax planning here. Deciding precisely when horses go into training and when they should return to stud will generally be based on opinions as to their future development and potential. However, the stage at which this occurs can determine just how much tax they incur over their lifetime. The task of seeking to reconcile the opportunity to obtain all the tax-free gains of racing with the desire to obtain loss relief on commercial losses of the stud farm would seem an impossible task for the tax planner. The tax position of stud farms is dealt with in CHAPTER 7.

Buying and selling or loaning a horse

4.13

Horses are subject to the ordinary laws of contract and the sale of goods so far as the transfer of their ownership is concerned. The aim of this section is to emphasise the benefits of information provided by the BHS and other organisations on this subject and to provide examples of model agreements.

There is no implied condition as to the fitness of an animal for any particular purpose *except* where the seller carries on a business of selling such animals. Otherwise, there are no warranties whatever upon the sale of an animal, as to its quality or fitness for any particular purpose, in the absence of express agreement. The rule of *caveat emptor* (or 'buyer beware') applies, and there will be no comeback over unidentified defects or other problems. Therefore, when the purchase is from a private individual, it is vital that there is a written agreement, which expressly provides that the horse is of the particular quality or possessed of the particular virtue that the buyer desires. It is also prudent to have the horse examined by a veterinary surgeon prior to purchase.

The buyer will also want to ensure that he has an appropriate remedy in the event of breach of any express term of the contract as to the condition of the horse. If there is no express provision, the buyer cannot return the horse for a breach of warranty as to the condition of the horse, unless the term of the contract, which has been breached, is regarded as going to 'the root of the contract'. As such, the buyer will be restricted to a pecuniary claim in damages. It is therefore best to provide expressly when and how the buyer will be allowed to return the horse for breach of warranty. Notice of any defect should be given to the seller as soon as possible. Where the contract specifies a time limit within which a complaint must be made or the animal returned, no action could be brought if this time limit has passed.

If the seller *is* in the business of selling horses, the Sale of Goods Act 1979 imposes a statutory expectation that the horse should be 'fit for the purpose for which it is sold and is of satisfactory quality'. There is a right to return the horse upon discovery of a breach of either of these terms, following a reasonable time for examination. This can lead to uncertainty, and there can be dispute as to whether the seller was aware of the purpose for which the horse was to be purchased. Therefore, it is still highly advisable to have a written contract.

Two model agreements can be obtained from the BHS. Precedent VI is an agreement for a straight sale and purchase of a horse and Precedent VII is an agreement for a loan coupled with an option to purchase.

A solicitor should draft all legal agreements. The aim of these agreements is to give guidance (and guidance only) so that when the meeting with the solicitor is arranged, various complex matters have been given due consideration.

Planning the sale of the 'tax-free' racehorse

4.14

Consider the following.

1 *The successful racehorse is good enough to stand as a stud. When is the most efficient time to sell?*

Racing is tax-free. What happens when a racehorse becomes a stallion? Is this still tax-free?

The sale of a successful racehorse can be 'tax free' (see **1.11**). The sale of the syndicate is taxable. A racehorse owner might not want to own the whole of the stallion. As per HMRC's Business Income Manual at BIM 55730, this is set out as follows:

> *"Since the cost of buying a successful stallion outright is prohibitive for some bloodstock breeders, ownership may be shared in a syndicate. The usual form of syndication is into forty equal shares, representing the number of mares which, traditionally, was regarded as the standard for a stallion to cover in one season. Each syndicate member contributes towards the costs of keeping the stallion and is entitled to one 'nomination' each season per share owned. The member may use the nomination to cover one of his or her own mares, or it may be sold on the open market. The shareholders appoint a committee that deal with the day to day management of the stallion".*

The sale of part of the racehorse is, as stated, tax free, however, once the stallion is an established syndicate animal, the sale of the shares in the syndicate are taxable as a miscellaneous income (or as a trade if part of stud activities). Clients must be advised prior to establishment of the syndicate of the ability to take advantage of the tax planning opportunity.

The situation will be confused if the stallion is part of a stud operation.

Stud fees and sale of nominations will be taxed as miscellaneous income unless:

- the owner of the stallion share is not carrying on a trade of stud farming or horse breeding;

- the owner is carrying on such a trade but does not use the stallion share for the purpose of obtaining service for his own mare.

As mentioned above, these will be taxed as trading income. Each case *must* be looked at on its merits. Every alternative *must* be planned in advance. Clients with racehorses must be encouraged to discuss and disclose their activities in full as there could be tax savings to achieve or tax pitfalls to avoid.

2 The sale of a racehorse is tax free but is the sale of a foal from the racehorse (broodmare) tax free?

The activity of breeding can be taxable and each case must be looked at individually. If the disposal is deemed to be taxable then obviously the expenses surrounding it will be taken into account. Breeding is an activity based on luck. A foal of very high value could be bred and sold.

Conclusion

Owning a horse (racehorse and competition) is generally considered to be 'tax free' or 'owned privately'/ 'outside the scope' of tax. However, there are situations where horses are owned commercially and ownership can be part of the commercial operation. There is a lot of tax planning to be put in place to maximise tax reliefs whatever direction is taken and it should always be held in mind that HMRC have a negative approach to ownership they consider to be personal and to tax losses that are incurred without the profit motive (see **Chapter 8**). Where the 'ownership' is considered to be within the scope of tax, detailed evidence must be produced from an early stage to support that view.

CHAPTER FIVE

PLANNING FOR EQUINE VAT

VAT and the equestrian industry can be an extremely complicated topic to understand and needs strong professional guidance. **Chapter 5** aims to distinguish the differences between VAT rates, the relevant schemes available and to establish the potential VAT liability of the whole equine industry with specific emphasis on livery, tuition, selling horses and the livery business. In addition, this chapter summarises the differentiating VAT treatment of racehorses and their owners in comparison to other schemes open to the more commonplace equine scenario. We specifically consider:

- The VAT margin (Second Hand Goods Scheme)
- Farmers flat rate scheme
- Place of supply
- Temporary movements
- Supplementary returns
- Bloodstock
- Racehorse Owners Scheme
- Partial exemption

Planning for Equine VAT

5.1

Value Added Tax (VAT) always seems to be the forgotten tax – one that is ever present but is largely ignored as just a cost component of a transaction. This is highlighted by the pragmatic use of the 'margin' or second-hand scheme which even ensures that the cost of VAT is hidden in the sale or purchase price of horses so that few are even aware that the tax has been paid. In practical terms a large amount of equine businesses have incorrect VAT treatment.

The equine business should be seeking steps to ensure that VAT recoveries are maximised, whilst minimising the output liability due to be paid. This chapter seeks to explain some of the VAT basics that equine individuals or businesses can use to minimise this VAT burden. The topics covered are summarised below:

- Planning for equine VAT (**5.1**);
- Background to VAT (**5.2**);
- The basics of VAT (**5.3**);
- The business question (**5.4**);
- Making Tax Digital – VAT (**5.5**);
- Registration scheme for racehorse owners (**5.6 to 5.8**);
- The supply of land (**5.9**);
- Flat-rate farmers' scheme (**5.10**);
- Margin scheme for horses and ponies (**5.11**);

- Haymaking for horses (**5.12**);
- Place of supply – goods (**5.13**);
- Place of supply – services (**5.14**);
- Sale of part share of a horse (**5.15**);
- Supplementary returns (**5.16**);
- Boodstock – services (**5.17 and 5.18**);
- Syndicates (**5.19**);
- Supply of additional services (**5.20**);
- Livery services (**5.21**);
- Tuition (**5.22**);
- Partial exemption – the basics (**5.23**);
- Land and property – the basics (**5.24**);
- Land and property (**5.25**);
- Commercial property opting to tax (**5.26**);
- Bloodstock agents (**5.27**);
- Racehorse trainer (**5.28**)

Background to VAT

5.2

VAT was introduced almost 50 years ago on 1 April 1973. Since that time the principles of the tax have remained relatively constant, but the complexities have ensured that the VAT adviser is kept busy and that the 'simple tax' has become unintentionally complicated with much scope for misinterpretation and unintended error, especially with regard to the equine industry. Some of the VAT has been dealt with within the specific chapters. For example:

7.35 – VAT planning around the stud farmhouse

7.36 – Repairs to the stud farmhouse

The basics of VAT

5.3

In the UK we have three 'taxable' rates, being a 0% zero-rate, a 5% reduced rate and a 20% standard rate. By supplying goods or services at a taxable rate, the right of VAT recovery is secured on the cost of related purchases. There are also exempt supplies which do not carry VAT but the making of them means that there is no recovery of the input VAT incurred on related purchases, unless such input VAT is beneath a 'de-minimis' limit.

When a mixture of supplies is made at both the taxable and exempt rates by the equine business, then the business will be able to recover a proportion of the input VAT incurred. This proportion is calculated under a 'partial exemption' method and it is essential to consider which method will allow the fairest recoverable percentage.

A VAT registration can only be sought if the business makes some taxable supplies. If only exempt supplies are made a VAT registration will be invalid. The current VAT registration limit is £85,000 per annum. This is the value of gross income in a rolling 12-month period. If the taxable turnover is above this limit, then a compulsory VAT registration must be sought.

If the taxable turnover is below the VAT registration limit, then a voluntary or intending registration can be applied for. This gives the benefit of input VAT recovery on costs whilst the business is still in its infancy or prior to the actual making of any taxable sales. These voluntary registrations mean that VAT must still be accounted for on the taxable sales made; but do offer significant cash flow advantages and formed the basis of the Registration Scheme for Racehorse Owners.

The business question

5.4

The ability to register for VAT, and to recover input VAT on expenses, is wholly conditional upon there being a taxable business purpose. For the equine industry in particular, this has often been the root of its VAT problems. When does a hobby become business or a business become a hobby? (see **1.19**, **3.1**, **3.2**, **3.11**). Only if HMRC are satisfied that there is a genuine commercial business activity will they allow a VAT registration to be considered. If the activity is being carried out under the umbrella of an existing VAT registration, then HMRC will need to be satisfied that the activity is still one of business – if not, then any associated input VAT cannot be recovered.

Whether an activity is one of business or hobby has been the subject of many VAT Tribunals and there are a considerable number covering the equine activities carried out by sole proprietors, partnerships and companies alike. Some of the more important cases include *Ian Flockton Developments Ltd v Custom & Excise Commissioners [1987] STC 394*, *Triangle Thoroughbreds Ltd (VTD 5404) AQ 1990* and *Brian Gubby Ltd (VTD 1961) AQ 1985*, which concerned whether the racing of horses was carried out for private pleasure or for the furtherance of continued economic activity.

Goodman Equine Ltd (TC 2243) is another important VAT case. The business claimed input tax of £73,167 for a horse called 'For Fun'. HMRC disallowed the claim on the basis the company was not a business for the purposes of VAT. The company appealed. The key question was whether the taxpayer had met the business tests as laid out in *CCE v Lord Fisher [1981] STC 238.* The company traded at a loss and seemingly relied on the financial support of its sole director to continue. It was decided the sole aim was "pleasure and social enjoyment of equestrian activities" for the director. There were no horses sold despite offers – this was the key point of the loss of the appeal. This case highlights that existing personal interest can make reclaiming input tax difficult where the business case is marginal.

For the proposed activity to be considered 'business' for VAT purposes, there must be a clear and realistic intent to make taxable supplies on a regular and continuing basis.

It could be argued that there is much similarity between the passion for horses and music. Against this background, it is important to note that HMRC is vigilant for cases where input VAT is claimed on private activities. However, a recent case *Gravel Road Records (TC05598)* shows there is a difference between a "hobby" and a "failure" with regard to business activities.

Many businesses involving horses have a high commercial potential but do sometimes fail to make a profit. The *Gravel Road* case explains the need to show evidence of "intended business" to avoid unrecoverable tax charges. The facts are that Gravel Road spent considerable sums creating a recording studio; but delays in completion of the work caused their planned customers to go elsewhere at a time when the recording industry suddenly went into decline and alternative clients could not be found. Gravel Road Records had to cease trading before making any supplies and disposed of the facility. HMRC assumed that the business had spent the money on a 'hobby' activity, i.e. for private pleasure.

HMRC could neither show, nor provide, evidence of any use of the recording facility for private recording purposes and it did not appear to try to do so. Instead, HMRC went through the Lord Fisher tests (*CEC v*

Lord Fisher [1981] STC 238) for what constitutes a business activity, ignoring the fact that the Court of Appeal had recently cast doubt on these in *Longridge* (*Longridge on the Thames v HMRC [2016] EWCA Civ 930 (2016)*).

The tribunal upon review of the facts could see no evidence of hobby use, but plenty of evidence of an intended business use. Examples of business intent were the high level of cost and the involvement of equity investors. The taxpayer won, having endured the problems of having to go through the business failure in depth at tribunal level.

The tax lesson for anyone in the equine industry starting a true commercial business is that HMRC might try to say the operation is not commercial. It is imperative to have a business plan in place and third-party evidence where appropriate. In the *Gravel Road* case the investor had no interest in music and only wanted to make a profit on its investment. It was considered by the tribunal that it was the original intention and evidence that was important, rather than the end result. This case is a useful reference for tax advisers to quote in situations where HMRC challenge input VAT claims on the cost of either abortive or loss-making projects. The 'original intention' question is one that equine businesses have to consider with regard to both VAT and income tax. Often the equine business is started with an 'original intention' of a hobby not a business, however when there is a genuine business the evidence of intention must be retained and tied into the business plan. It is vital to retain evidence of all areas of commerciality.

Making tax digital – VAT

5.5

Making Tax Digital (MTD) is HMRC's attempt to digitalise UK tax, in an effort to improve services, calculations and accuracy. In this section we look to address the following common questions for equine operations:

- What is MTD?
- Who is affected?
- Why is it happing?
- How will it affect you?
- What are the benefits?

Making Tax Digital is legislation that requires the majority of businesses and individuals to send quarterly updates to HMRC on their income and expenditure via MTD compliant software.

The primary aim is to make tax administration more effective and efficient for businesses and individual tax payers to submit, maintain and manage their tax affairs though the mandatory use of technology and digital systems. Speaking in broad terms, the digitalisation of tax services will eventually affect most businesses and individuals, deeming this law one of the biggest shake ups in HMRC's history.

One of the main incentives and reasons behind making tax digital is the amount of incorrect information and errors submitted to HMRC, leading to a loss in tax revenues. It is deemed that a modernisation of the tax system will reduce the amount of avoidable errors and help guide businesses and individuals to establish their correct tax position without costly corrections and unforeseen demands for additional payments.

The aim was further to reducing errors, MTD will lead to the reduction in administration time for businesses, individuals and HMRC. A single digitalised system will also mean there will be no need to re-submit information that is already held by HMRC, as is currently required under the existing system.

The first phase of Making Tax Digital launched on 1 April 2019 for VAT reporting.

By April 2022, all VAT registered businesses must then switch to MTD for VAT, regardless of their turnover level. The next stage of the initiative is to extend MTD to all self-employed and those with property income from April 2023 for the purpose of income tax. This applies to both England and Wales.

Equine businesses and landowners have so far not been required to join the MTD regime if they are not VAT registered. However, from 6 April 2023, the MTD for income tax could apply to all such operations. It is expected that there will be an exemption for those with an annual turnover (across all sources of self-employment and property income) below a threshold of £10,000.

The Registration Scheme for Racehorse Owners

Background

5.6

General VAT registration can be in the name of a sole proprietor, a partnership, a corporate entity or an unincorporated body, i.e. a Club or Association. It is important to remember that if a sole proprietor is VAT registered then all of his business activities will be covered by that VAT registration – he does not need to register for each activity and it is crucial that VAT is declared correctly on all business supplies made by him, no matter how diverse his supplies are.

The Racehorse Owners VAT Scheme is designed to recoup some of the costs involved in having a horse in training, making the activity more affordable and allowing owners into the game that may have otherwise not been able to afford to take part.

On 16 March 1993, HMRC introduced the Registration Scheme for Racehorse Owners ('the Scheme'). This acknowledged that those owners who were actively seeking sponsorship and appearance money for their horses would be treated as being in business and therefore could apply to be VAT registered. Once registered, owners must account for VAT on their 'business' racing income, including prize money, sponsorship income and sales of horses, and can recover, subject to the normal rules, VAT incurred on the purchase and upkeep of racehorses and other general overhead expenses associated with the ownership.

In 1997 the scheme was reviewed and, with effect from 1 January 1998, all owners with racehorses wishing to register can only apply for VAT registration if:

- the racehorses are covered by a sponsorship agreement registered at Weatherbys; or

- the racehorses are covered by a trainer's sponsorship agreement registered at Weatherbys; or

- the owner can demonstrate that they have received, and will continue to receive, business income, i.e. from appearance money or sponsored number cloths.

Note that a sponsorship agreement must obtain a minimum level of fees to be seen as a business activity, even if these are, in fact, very modest. Full details on the sponsorship requirements can be found in 'A Code of Conduct for Owners' Sponsorship' which is available free of charge from the British Horseracing Board (BHB).

The agreement reached by HMRC and the British Horseracing Board came about following a long period of negotiation between the parties and all those involved in the bloodstock industry. HMRC's refusal to accept that the business test was being met had the effect that VAT at the standard rate was being suffered as an additional cost to all those struggling to keep the British racing industry alive. The extremely generous tax and VAT treatments in place in other EU Member States (particularly France and Ireland) meant that the UK authorities were being forced to reconsider the impact that its decisions were having on the nation's equine industry.

The Scheme

5.7

Full and comprehensive information on the Scheme can be found in HMRC's VAT Notice700/67 (last updated 24 July 2018) and can be found at their website. The BHB also provides 'A Guide to the VAT 'Scheme'' which can be obtained free of charge from their website at www.bhb.co.uk or by calling 020 7152 0000.

The Scheme registration requires completion of a VAT 1 registration form, just like any other VAT application. However, it is also necessary to complete a D1 form (for sole ownership of horses) or a D2 form (for shares in horse ownership) and to send this completed form to Weatherbys. The 'D' forms are obtainable from Weatherbys and they have a useful VAT team on the helpdesk number which is 01933 440077. The 'D' forms confirm that there is a sponsorship agreement or that business income has been received from the horses owned. Weatherbys will confirm the details that they have been given and then return the stamped 'D' forms to the owner. Once received, the certified 'D' forms and the completed VAT registration forms should be sent to the address on the VAT 1 form.

Once approved by HMRC, a VAT registration number will be sent out, along with the effective date of registration (normally the date the completed D form was received by Weatherbys). The normal VAT rules should then be applied to all sales and purchases (bar the exceptions listed below). It is important to notify Weatherbys of the VAT registration number as soon as it is allocated as this will ensure that any prize or appearance money is paid with the addition of VAT (rather than as VAT inclusive).

Registered person

5.8

The legal entity to be registered for VAT should be the owner of the racehorse who is registered at Weatherbys, i.e. sole proprietor, partnership or limited company. If only a part share in a racehorse is owned, then registration as a sole proprietor will only be allowed if this share is at least 50% of the horse. If less than 50% is owned, then registration will only be accepted in the name of a partnership with the other part share owners.

Where a business is already registered for VAT and it purchases a racehorse for advertising and promotion purposes, they should treat the activities under normal business rules. This means that if the racehorse is used partly for advertising purposes and partly for providing entertainment or private purposes, then the input VAT should be apportioned to reflect this use.

Note that prize money is only standard rated if the horse is covered by the Scheme and thus no output VAT will be due if the horse is unregistered – such prize money remains outside the scope of VAT.

The normal VAT rules for output VAT and input VAT vary slightly under the Scheme and, in particular, the following VAT liabilities apply:

- sponsorship income – standard rated supply;

- prize money/appearance money – standard rated supplies. Note that the value of prize money for VAT purposes is the amount calculated under the Rules of Racing as receivable by the owner, less entry fees etc. collected by the racecourse;

- sale of racehorses – standard rated supply if the horse is in the UK;

- racehorses given away or put to a non-business use – output tax is due on the market value at the date at which non-business use takes precedence;

- sale of a share or shares in a racehorse – this is a standard rated supply unless the sale of the share creates a new partnership, in which case the supply is disregarded for VAT purposes. Note that the sale of a share is a supply of services and thus will be standard rated if the owner is established within the UK.

With regards to the recovery of input VAT, HMRC allow the following:

- The purchase, training and maintenance of a racehorse put to training is a business expense. VAT may be recovered on such costs, including any costs incurred when the racehorse is unable to run due to injury, provided there is an expectation it will run in the future.

- Owner subsistence – where the horse is racing some distance from the principal place of business, and it is unreasonable to expect the owner to travel to and from the principal place of business, VAT may be recovered on hotel accommodation and breakfast/evening meals in line with the normal VAT rules. Note that HMRC will not normally allow the VAT recovery on meals or drinks taken at the racecourse.

- Telephone usage has been agreed at 10% VAT recovery unless there is evidence to support a higher percentage.

- Lease of executive boxes – where an owner leases a box at the racecourse, the VAT recovery will depend upon the extent of business use. If used for meetings with potential customers and suppliers during racing, as well as for their own personal use or for corporate entertaining, then HMRC will allow 50% of the VAT incurred on the lease of the box to be recovered as input VAT. If the owner feels a higher percentage recovery is warranted, evidence should be retained to justify the amount of VAT reclaimed.

The supply of land

5.9

Everyone is aware of how important it is to understand the tax treatment of the supply of land and indeed how complex the VAT treatment is thereof. The "Tax Day" 2021 included consultations on the tax treatment of the supply of the land. Guidance is provided in VAT Notice 742: VAT on land and property. Paragraph 2.2 defines the supply of land as:

> "*You make a supply of land by making a grant of an interest in, right over or licence to occupy land in return for a payment or consideration*".

What sounds so simple in such an explanation is extremely complex in terms of all tax consideration, not just in income tax terms regarding trading or not trading for income tax (see **1.11**) but also in the context of inheritance tax (IHT) and VAT. For all tax advisers and landowners, decisions are challenging.

Much has been discussed within the domain of the tax tribunal concerning the supply of land for VAT purposes. While some might see contradictions, others might see a very clear need for clarification.

The help of income tax advisers, VAT consultants and inheritance tax advisers are needed every time an equine business or stud owner decides to diversify or plan alternative land use in an entrepreneurial manner.

Further review of the grey area or fine line between the supply of land or the supply of a serviced business is a necessity supported by research and evidence. For example, *Vigne v HM Revenue & Customs (HMRC)* [2017] *UK FTT 0632* (see **1.7**) showed how having sufficient document evidence of the service provided allowed business property relief for enhanced livery to be obtained.

Perhaps greater clarification is needed by HMRC on this grey area at a VAT and IHT level. Stud farmers (see **Chapter 7**) need to understand what their legal, professional and tax position is with regard to any diversification they undertake. If a farmer/landowner moves from pure farming by way of diversification into livery services, holiday accommodation or the supply of land/buildings, there needs to be clear definition of how the tax and VAT rules apply (see 1.6).

It is the role of the professional adviser to provide the correct VAT warnings against the background of possible improved income streams. The whole strategy must be looked at with a holistic approach to all tax areas.

Flat-rate farmer's scheme

5.10

The flat-rate scheme for farmers was introduced as an optional scheme for businesses. This might apply to a stud farm or farm integrated with an equine activity. The scheme refers to supplies made by farmers, but the nature of activities included within the scheme means that any business supplying farming and agricultural goods and services could be eligible. By registering under the scheme, the 'farmer' receives certification and is no longer VAT registered. The scheme can only be used for designated supplies but means that VAT no longer becomes due on sales made and that there is no VAT recovery on costs. Instead, the farmer is able to add a 'flat-rate' charge of 4% on sales of designated produce to VAT registered customers. The farmer can retain this 4% addition and the VAT registered customer can recover it on his normal VAT return. As the farmer is able to sell to the public without the addition of either VAT or the flat-rate 4%, he can increase his sales price in order to make a little more profit whilst these prices still remain below his VAT registered competitors.

The designated supplies covered by the scheme are varied but include stock farming, crop production, forestry, fisheries, certain processing of farm products and supplies of agricultural services. However, activities that involve animals which are not eaten by humans or produce food which is eaten by humans are largely excluded. In particular, the training of horses bred for racing, specialist training of horses and activities involving animals such as pony trekking, riding and hunting are excluded. This means that these supplies must be treated outside of the scheme and, if the value of these taxable supplies exceeds the VAT threshold, the farmer must leave the scheme and a VAT registration is required to cover all supplies.

The main benefit of the scheme is to those stud farmers that have a majority of sales included within the designated services but who also have some stabling or livery that produces a small amount of additional income each year.

The following is an example where VAT planning in the use of the scheme may bring benefits.

Example

A business currently lets 20 acres of land to a tenant farmer (an exempt supply) and has 150 acres of managed woodland. In addition to this, he also has a couple of stables where his horses are kept and where he charges ten other horse owners for the care, exercising and stabling of their horses. Currently, the farmer is VAT registered and has to account for VAT on the charges that he makes for his livery services. Note that these livery services do not qualify for exemption as they are primarily care related, not DIY livery services. In order to be competitive, the farmer has to meet some of the VAT cost himself as he does not want his customers to feel that they are being charged VAT. By using the flat-rate scheme, the farmer could de-register from VAT until such time as the livery income exceeded the current VAT threshold. He would need to charge VAT registered customers 4% flat rate on the woodland timber sales (which he retains), however he can avoid accounting for 20% VAT on the livery services and on any timber sales to the public. He needs to consider the loss of recoverable VAT on assets and overheads but, if these costs are low, then the benefits could be very welcome.

Encouragingly, a recent European Court case, *Shields & Sons Partnership v HMRC [2017] C262-16*, decided that HMRC cannot withdraw a farmer from the VAT flat rate scheme merely because that farming business would be substantially better off than if they registered for VAT. In 2012, HMRC had removed the farming partnership from the agricultural flat rate scheme on the grounds that the partners had benefited from the scheme by approximately £375,000 over seven years. Shields challenged HMRC's decision, and eventually won their case when it reached the Court of Justice of the European Union (CJEU). The scheme was devised to reduce the administrative burden of VAT registration and the CJEU explained that a farming business must be able to objectively assess in advance if the business can legitimately expect to meet the criteria to access and to remain in it. However, whilst the European VAT Directive does allow the exclusion of "categories" of farmers, this does not extend to those who are simply good at working the system as HMRC contended. Such farming or stud farming businesses are allowed to stay in provided they meet all the other requirements.

Margin scheme for horses and ponies

5.11

A margin scheme operates for second-hand horses and ponies and is available to a VAT-registered person, although not in conjunction with either the flat-rate farmers' scheme (see **5.10**) or the flat-rate scheme for small businesses. The margin scheme can, however, be used by persons registered under the Registration Scheme for Racehorse Owners (see **5.6** to **5.8**). These rules should also be considered in the context of bloodstock agents (see **5.27**) where most of the customers are VAT registered.

The use of the margin scheme is optional and can be applied to all or just some of the horses or ponies owned. The basis of the scheme is that the VAT to be declared on the sale of an eligible animal is calculated on the margin made between the purchase and selling price. This margin is treated as being VAT inclusive and therefore one-sixth (16.67%) of the margin must be declared to HMRC as output VAT.

There are a number of conditions that must be met in order for the scheme to apply so care needs to be taken as inappropriate use could result in hefty VAT liabilities.

The scheme cannot be used for:

- horses or ponies which have been bred within the business as these are not 'second-hand' animals;
- horses or ponies that have been purchased from outside the EC and have therefore been subject to import VAT;
- horses or ponies whose purchase price was subject to a VAT charge.

Providing the purchase has not been subject to VAT, the scheme can be used either for purchases of equine animals for resale or for retention within the business.

It is a legal requirement that a stock book, or similar record, is retained and that details of the purchase (stock number, name of vendor, purchase price and date of purchase), sale details (invoice number, buyer, sale price and date, margin made and VAT due) and description of the animal are clearly shown. The description of the horse must include the following:

- unique identifying passport number;
- colour;
- sex;
- type or breed (e.g. cob, or thoroughbred);
- age;
- height;

- stable name; and
- any distinctive markings.

The purchase and sales invoice should normally have a declaration that 'input tax deduction has not and will not be claimed in respect of the goods sold on this invoice'. This is the evidence that shows that the animal is eligible for use within the margin scheme. If buying from a private individual it is important to ensure that an invoice or purchase document is still obtained.

As an alternative to the above accounting rules, HMRC also allow the use of a special three-part invoice set which is available through the British Equestrian Trade Association (BETA). These forms comprise:

- Part A for the stock records;
- Part B acts as the seller's sales invoice; and
- Part C as the buyer's purchase invoice.

The use of this three-part form obviates the need to retain the stock book and declarations mentioned previously.

The purchase or sale of animals through an auction will still be eligible for the margin scheme providing all the accounting conditions are met and that the auctioneer is aware that the margin scheme is to be used.

There are also restrictions on the amount of VAT that can be recovered in relation to the costs of caring for a horse that has been purchased for sale under the scheme, and it is recommended that these rules are checked carefully before deciding the scheme's benefits. Full details of the margin scheme can be found in VAT Notice 718.

Given that the sports horse industry has such a large mix of business and non-business 'players', i.e. VAT registered and non-VAT registered interactions, this scheme can be very useful to minimise the VAT disadvantage.

The recent tax tribunal cases of disputing the commerciality of equine businesses, *Thorne* (see **8.21**) and *Murray* (see **3.26**), have highlighted the need for equine operations to consider evidence of commerciality. This scheme can be used to improve the structure of the operation including VAT registration and optimising VAT opportunities. This in turn can help with commerciality and profitability.

Haymaking for horses

5.12

The question of haymaking for horses is considered at **1.5** and **1.6**.

Food and livestock sold for human consumption is generally zero-rated. VAT Notice 701/15: Animals and animal food at paragraph **2.2** gives examples of zero-rated animals as:

- Meat animals;
- Dairy animals;
- Poultry (except ornamental breeds), including those for egg production;
- Honey bees
- Fish (except ornamental breeds and coarse fish), including those for production of edible roes.

At paragraph **2.3**, the guidance states that an example of standard-rated supplies includes horses. But what of the sale of hay and food for horses? The sale of hay for consumption by livestock is zero-rated, but some animals that may normally be considered livestock could be kept as pets.

At paragraph **6.3**, the list of animals that are not pet species but may be kept as pets include horses, ponies and sheep. For these animals, their food can be zero-rated unless it is packaged or held out for sale in a way that shows it is intended for a pet. Thus, if hay is sold and marketed for consumption by livestock it can be purchased for consumption by horses and still be zero-rated. There are similarities with the inheritance tax interpretation of 'haymaking for horses' as an agricultural activity.

VAT Notice 701/15 demonstrates that, if the hay sold was grown for generic consumption and could be purchased by livestock farmers *or* horse owners, it is fundamentally an agricultural product. Again, this shows that all diversifying farmers *must* check and evidence the impact of various moves away from traditional farming by their business. For the elderly farmer, such provision of evidence needs the help of family and advisers alike.

Place of supply – goods

5.13

It is always important to determine where a supply is deemed to take place under the VAT legislation, as that will determine who has to account for any VAT due on that sale. Generally speaking, if a supply of goods does not involve their removal from or to the United Kingdom it will be treated as supplied in the UK if the goods are in the UK and otherwise will be treated as supplied outside the UK.

Place of supply – services

5.14

The rule for determining the place of supply of services varies according to whether the supply is business to business (B2B) or business to consumer (B2C).

It should be noted that it is the supplier's responsibility to determine whether or not his customer is in business, and evidence should be retained to demonstrate to HMRC the basis for this decision. A VAT number is a clear indication, but a customer could be in business even if he is not VAT registered, e.g. he is trading below the VAT threshold or he is a flat-rate farmer.

The basic rule for determining the place of supply of B2B services is that it takes place where the customer belongs. A supplier shall be treated as belonging in a country if he has a business establishment or some other fixed establishment in that country. Therefore, if the recipient of the service belongs in the UK then that service is deemed to be supplied in the UK. There are some exceptions to this rule, e.g. services relating to land, but they are unlikely to be regularly encountered in the bloodstock industry.

Sale of part share of a horse

5.15

There is an important quirk for horse owners to watch out for. VATA 1994, Sch 4 para 1(1) confirms that although 'any transfer of the whole property in goods is a supply of goods', the transfer of any undivided share of 'the property in goods' is a supply of services. Thus, because a horse is deemed to be undivided property, the sale of, say, a 50% share is deemed to be a potential supply of services as long as the business:

- Holds a valid VAT registration;
- Has passed the various badges of trade tests; and
- Is trading in the sale of horses.

As mentioned, the only variance to this rule is when all shareholders dispose of their shares simultaneously. In such cases, the entire horse is being disposed of and this counts as supply of goods.

Treating a horse share sale as a service opens further complications involving the place of supply, which again can determine whether a VAT charge should be levied. The result is that, in such a scenario, advisers must follow the place of supply rules and *VAT Notice 741A* as follows.

If the transaction undertaken is business-to-business (B2B), with a company or business dealing in horses in the normal course of their trade, the service is deemed to have originated in the place where the customer belongs. If this is outside the UK, no UK VAT should be charged, although the transaction may be subject to local taxes in that other country.

If the transaction undertaken is business-to-consumer (B2C) – a private individual or a company that does not deal in horses in the normal course of trade – the service is deemed to have originated where the supplier is based; in other words, the UK, and therefore full UK VAT should be charged.

For example, if a half-share of a horse is being sold and the other half is being retained, the supply being made is deemed by HMRC to be a service. If the sale is made to an Irish VAT-registered company that deals in horses in the normal course of its trade, the transaction will be deemed to have originated in Ireland, and no UK VAT should be charged because this transaction is 'outside the scope' of UK VAT. However, if the other party was an individual resident in Ireland, but who had no business interests in horses, the transaction would be deemed to be B2C and will originate in the UK with VAT chargeable on the transaction.

If a horse is being sold by a partnership, when one joint owner is selling a share to a third party, the VAT treatment will again need to be considered. Such action is akin to an individual partner selling a share in a business partnership. It is considered, particularly given HMRC's stated policy on shares of less than 50% in the notice, that this should be treated as an investment transaction (outside the scope of VAT) rather than an economic activity. VAT should therefore not be charged on such transactions.

The sale of private horses and horses used in a business can be easily confused and the different VAT approaches can complicate the determination of the correct treatment by advisers. As well as identifying when VAT should be applied to an equine transaction, advisers should have an understanding of both the racehorse owners' scheme and the margin scheme, while remaining aware of the complications involved with the sales of part shares in a horse. An eye should also be kept on the final post Brexit position. The *McMorris* case gave guidance on the complexity of the commerciality question.

The key is to consider all horse sale transactions on their merits and plan ahead. Nothing is straightforward in such transactions and where appropriate specialist advice should be sought.

Supplementary returns

5.16

Post Brexit it is essential to ensure that all cross-border movements are correctly recorded and specialist advice is taken.

Bloodstock services

Breeding

5.17

HMRC will allow a Breeder to register for VAT prior to the making of any taxable supplies (sales or leasing of the foals or yearlings). This is known as an intending trader registration. However, HMRC must be satisfied that the breeding is a genuine commercial activity and they will require evidence to demonstrate this. As a mare will not produce a foal each year, HMRC normally expect the breeder to have more than one mare in order to meet the 'commerciality' test. If the intention is to breed with only one mare then a good business case is needed to support the application for VAT. The sponsorship rules that apply to the registration scheme for racehorse owners do not apply to owner breeders.

Syndications – supplies of shares

5.18

Colts which are to become stallions are often syndicated into shares. These shares will be sold to owners giving them an interest in the stallion and/or the right to a nomination during the breeding season. It is important to identify whether the share is for a nomination or for an interest in the stallion (or for both) as the VAT treatment will vary.

The sale of both types of share is treated as a supply of services, rather than a supply of goods.

For *shares of interest*, a UK VAT registered breeder will have to account for VAT whether the purchaser is an UK or non-UK resident.

The purchaser of the share will be entitled to VAT recovery only if he is VAT registered and will be using the 'share' for business purposes. If input VAT is recovered, then the onward supply by the owner of his share will also need to be standard rated for VAT purposes. This assumes, of course, that the owner is established within the UK.

Should the owners come together to sell all the shares in the stallion then this will be a supply of goods and HMRC will accept that the normal VAT rules should be applied to determine the VAT liability of the sale. In these circumstances, the individual sale of the shares is normally ignored for VAT purposes when the stallion is sold to a purchaser outside the UK.

The *supply of a nomination* is normally deemed to take place in the country where the covering takes place. This means that if the stallion is within the UK then the nomination will be subject to 20% UK VAT. When sending mares abroad it is key to take specialist VAT advice.

Syndicates

5.19

Normally a syndicate will be formed to control and manage the transfer of the shares of interest and nominations. As this syndicate is also responsible for the upkeep of the stallion, the owners will contribute to the syndicate who disburses this income to the stable. The syndicate may also sell nominations over and above that of the 'share' entitlement of the owners. This income is used to offset the stabling and veterinary costs incurred. With effect from November 2000, HMRC accept that a syndicate making supplies of these surplus nominations is making a business supply. It must therefore register for VAT if this income exceeds the VAT-registration limit. The registration can either be in the name of the syndicate, as a partnership of its members, or the syndicate secretary can register as an agent for the entire membership.

The syndicate can consider a voluntary registration if the value of its taxable supplies is below the VAT-registration limit. This should, however, be considered carefully as the level of administration will increase and the value of syndicate input VAT may not justify the VAT obligations.

HMRC have an agreement with the British Horseracing Board and Thoroughbred Breeders Association with regards to keeping of stallions at stud'. This agreement can be found on HMRC's website, Notice 700/57 section 20, and includes fairly comprehensive information on the valuation and VAT treatment of stallion nominations including those provided free of charge.

Supplies of additional services

5.20

When nomination services are supplied there will often be additional services supplied as ancillary to the nomination. These may include veterinary services, blacksmiths services and consultancy and breeding advice. Providing that these services are ancillary to the nomination, and are not separately invoiced or supplied, the VAT liability of the nomination service will also apply to the additional services.

In cases where separate supplies are made the following rules apply:

- stable rental and services relating to land are supplied where the land is situated. Generally, bare stabling is exempt from VAT (see **5.21**) unless the stable owner has 'opted to tax'. Where there is a high level of care (which there usually is with the nominations and mares in foal) then the services are not treated as land related and will remain taxable;

- the vast majority of other services, such as veterinary and blacksmiths services, are supplied where the supplier belongs and will therefore be taxable at 20% if these are invoiced by UK suppliers.

Equestrian activities

Livery services

5.21

HMRC always held the view that the livery services provided by stables to horse owners were taxable at the standard rate. The only exception to this was the single supply of grazing rights (being zero-rated) or the letting of a bare stable or field which was accepted as exempt unless they have elected to opt to tax (see **5.26**).

However, this view was slowly being eroded by the way in which stables continue to diversify in order to raise further sources of income. In particular, they are now far more flexible about the level of services offered and there is a continued growing trend for all land owners to be more aware of 'tax planning' incentives and to take advantage of ways in which their services can be provided at a better value than a competitor's.

The ruling in the VAT tribunal case of *John Window [2001] VTD 17186* confirmed that the stabling of horses should remain exempt from VAT unless the option to tax has been made. However, it then ruled that where livery services are provided as an incidental part of that stabling then the whole supply should also be exempt. It does not become a wholly standard rated supply, and nor should an apportionment of the supply be made between the taxable and exempt elements.

The *John Window* case was the lead case of several others and although the principles of the 'single supply' rule were established well before this hearing; the decision opened the door for many liveries to save VAT and for the horse owner to pay less for the services received.

However, care should be taken in determining the VAT liability as the nature of the supplies made will vary from customer to customer – some owners may only require DIY livery services (clearly exempt, subject to the option to tax) whereas others will request full livery such that the level of care becomes the most predominant part of the supply and therefore makes the whole charge standard rated.

The higher the level of care required by the customer then the more likelihood there is that the entire supply will remain standard rated. Indeed, the level of care given by racehorse trainers, stud farms and breaking-in schools are such that HMRC will not accept that the exemption can be applied, instead classifying these services as 'specialist' and insisting such supplies are standard rated.

For those liveries that might have opted to tax, the availability of exemption is removed entirely although it is hoped that the majority of stable and land owners have not taken this route.

The ability to exempt livery is, as mentioned, very dependent upon the level of care offered. For the DIY livery or one where the owner is offered simple turning out, mucking out and feeding services then probably the exemption would apply. When exercising and grooming is added to the package then the predominant supply is becoming one of care. There can be a very fine line between the VAT liabilities and it is essential that any contracts, written or verbal agreements and what actually happens in practice is structured to ensure that there can be no future arguments with HMRC concerning the VAT liability.

For those liveries that feel they have been incorrectly charging VAT on their supplies then they have the opportunity to revisit their VAT treatment and to make a 'voluntary disclosure' to HMRC for VAT overpaid. However, it should be remembered that whilst the exemption gives rise to opportunity for keeping the charges at a competitive level, the businesses will lose the ability to recover VAT on costs relating to the exempt supply. Any refund of VAT by HMRC will need to take into account the repayment of input VAT that might have been made on livery expenses. HMRC have also stated that they will not repay output VAT unless this was previously suffered out of profits, i.e. not separately charged to horse owners.

It is also notable that some horse owners have demanded a refund of VAT from their liveries and it is suggested that if such demands are met, then any refunds should take into account the cost of irrecoverable VAT and reasonable expenses in seeking the refund from Customs (including any professional fees incurred!).

Tuition

5.22

The riding school operation is reviewed at **1.8**.

Commercial supplies of horse riding lessons and tuition are considered to be educational and are normally standard rated. However, when provided by a partner, sole proprietor or non-profit making organisation, the VAT liability becomes exempt. Corporate entities should treat the supplies as standard rated unless they are also non-profit making and plough any 'profit' from this educational activity back into the furtherance of those activities.

A sole proprietor or partnership offering tuition should be aware that the exemption does not extend to services offered by employees of the business. Thus, if a partnership employs other tutors, only the partners' teaching services will be exempt – the services of the staff remain taxable. This might be enough to ensure that the level of taxable income remains beneath the VAT threshold but care still needs to be taken to ensure that the turnover levels are monitored. There is a way round such a problem by trading through an LLP and making salaried staff members. This supply is then exempt which has distinct advantages for the survival of the riding school.

Unless hacking and trekking services can be linked to an educational supply, these will remain standard rated whoever they are supplied by.

With the complex exemptions available for both stabling and educational tuition the business will need to consider the benefits of structuring such activities to maximise its VAT position. Whilst exemption will bring savings to the end consumer, the business should consider the loss of VAT on related costs and overheads very carefully.

Riding lessons have a complicated history when it comes to establishing whether VAT is chargeable when providing them to private clients. Because riding lessons have previously been defined by HMRC as 'being taught in a number of schools on a regular basis', they can be subject to an exemption from VAT as confirmed by HMRC's VAT Education Manual at VATEDU 40200. There is a proviso that they are taught to a level similar to those being conducted by educational establishments across the country.

However, issues can arise over what counts as a basic riding lesson conducted to an educational level and thus qualifying for the exemption, and whether the instruction given is classified as specialist training beyond this level. The second example is universally accepted, following guidance from HMRC, as a standard-rated supply as detailed on VAT Notice 701/30: Education and vocational training.

Unfortunately, there is no clear distinction from the tax authorities as to what qualifies on either side and the defining characteristics that need to be identified to differentiate between the two. This can be problematic for equestrian businesses when trying to determine whether to charge

VAT. It therefore becomes necessary to investigate further and look at the individual facts of each case.

Probable defining factors when reaching a decision on whether to charge VAT for riding tuition at a specialist level may include the following.

- *The reputation and skill of the person conducting the lesson.*

  If the instructor has a world-class reputation and is an internationally recognised sportsperson – to use an extreme example – it is highly unlikely that that individual would be giving basic educational lessons to a standard usually taught in schools. It would, in this example, be expected that people learning to ride would start elsewhere and only come to that person to hone their skills for competing at a regional, national or international level. This would indicate that the standard would be well above that ordinarily taught in schools and would thus qualify as professional coaching and be standard rated for VAT purposes. On the other hand, an instructor with little reputation beyond the local area is far more likely to be giving educational lessons. There would be little point in a professional rider coming to this individual for further guidance, so the tuition would be deemed to be at a level more readily taught in schools. In this second situation, the VAT exemption is more likely to apply.

- *The amount charged for the service.*

  Riding lessons are readily available for £35 to £50 an hour across parts of the UK. If the proprietor is charging this level of fee, the argument would be that the riding lesson would be of an educational level, priced to match local competition and therefore qualifying for the VAT exemption. If, however, the proprietor was to charge significantly more, this would indicate that specialist coaching was being undertaken. The extra charge must represent more than simple educational advancement; otherwise why would the client pay a premium? In this situation, it is more likely that the exemption would not apply, and the standard rate of VAT should be charged on the transaction.

- *The level, skill and experience of the individual receiving the instruction.*

  If the client being taught is a beginner, with no reputation, national or international standing – again, using an extreme example – the argument follows that a basic educational service, qualifying for the VAT exemption, is being provided. If the client had international experience, the benefit of being coached by someone would not be to a standard 'ordinarily taught in schools' and would thus qualify as specialist training, subject to the standard VAT rating.

- *The invoice raised and details on it.*

  What the invoice specifically states as to the service has a direct bearing on whether a riding service can qualify for the VAT exemption. If the invoice states 'for specialist training and coaching services', the service would have to be standard rated. If the invoice raised reads 'for basic riding lessons and general equine instruction' it is more likely that the VAT exemption will apply.

- *Similar transactions and prior treatment.*

  Precedent is important. If the proprietor has given similar specialist training and charged VAT on the transaction, that is the service primarily provided by the business and HMRC will expect VAT to be charged on all similar transactions. If, however, the proprietor has taught basic lessons and the precedent for claiming the VAT exemption has already been set, the continuation of this stance would be more readily accepted by HMRC.

Several variables must be considered when judging whether the VAT exemption applies. In summary:

- If the proprietor gives regular basic riding lessons to a standard ordinarily taught in schools, for a value charged at a rate not in excess of local riding schools for the same service, to a person who has a similar background knowledge to a school or college-based student before going for the lesson; this would qualify for the VAT exemption. This is as long as the invoice explicitly states the basic nature of the service offered.

- However, if the proprietor gives instruction only to top level riders who have previously competed at national and international competitions and charges significantly above the market rate for riding lessons and states on the invoice that services given are for 'specialist training', the VAT exemption would not apply. In the eyes of HMRC, the service would be deemed to go beyond what is ordinarily taught in schools.

It is fair to say that many small equine businesses that provide tuition as part of their business model need the VAT exemption to survive commercially. Understanding the rules around the exemption and the provision of tuition is thus key. The fact that there are so many tribunal cases on the subject in recent years, including tuition given in, for example, pilates, belly dancing and bridge, all show that the rules can be subject to misinterpretation and can have an impact on many areas of small business life.

Partial exemption – the basics

5.23

Guidance regarding the application of partial exemption can be found in HMRC's VAT Notice 706. We have already noted the "Tax Day" consultation in this regard.

When a business makes a mixture of exempt supplies it does not have to charge its customer any VAT on the sale value. This can mean that the pricing structure becomes more competitive or that the business can make a little more profit as it can still undercut the price of suppliers who may have to charge VAT. However, the business needs to be aware that the cost of exempt supplies is the inability to recover input VAT incurred in making those supplies. This restriction is known as partial exemption. VAT relating to these supplies can only be recovered if it falls beneath a de-minimis limit.

Any business making a mixture of exempt and taxable supplies should carefully consider the impact of partial exemption so that it can first determine how much VAT is likely to be lost as a result of making these supplies and then what planning can be put in place to ensure that any loss is mitigated.

The first step for a business making exempt supplies is to attribute all input VAT incurred either directly to a taxable supply, directly to an exempt supply or to an overhead cost (such as professional and running costs). Having identified the amount of overhead VAT, this must be apportioned so that only the proportion relating to taxable supplies is recovered. Any costs directly relating to an exempt supply and the exempt proportion of the overhead cost are added together and are known as exempt input VAT. If the total amount of this exempt VAT is less than the de-minimis limit (£625 per month and less than 50% of all input VAT in the relevant period) then all VAT is recoverable. If this limit is exceeded, then none of the exempt VAT can be claimed in the VAT period.

The method used to apportion the overhead VAT needs to be determined very carefully. The 'standard method' is the most common method and does not need the prior permission of HMRC. It is the method that must be used if no other method is requested or granted. The amount of overhead VAT that can be recovered is determined by the percentage that taxable supplies bear to total (taxable plus exempt) supplies. This percentage is rounded up to the next whole number.

Alternative Methods

5.24

If the standard method does not produce a fair and reasonable result, a business can apply in writing to HMRC for approval to use a special method. Once accepted, the special method can be applied to the start of the current partial exemption year or from the start of the next year.

A special method can take any form – the business needs to consider which is the most fair and reasonable and whether the business has all the information to be able to calculate the figures each period.

Land and property

5.25

The VAT treatment of land and property transactions can be extremely complex, and it is recommended that the sale or purchase of property is always checked for VAT purposes to ensure that the business can plan or at least be aware of the VAT impact.

In summary, the sale of a brand new residential building is zero-rated whilst the sale of an existing residential property will be exempt. Repairs, maintenance work, annexes and extensions to existing properties will be standard rated but there are reliefs for works of approved alterations to listed dwellings. This relief enables structural work to be zero-rated providing that the work required and received listed planning consent.

It is also possible to benefit from a reduced rate of 5% when works are carried out to convert a non-residential building to residential use and to modernise a dwelling that has not been occupied for three years. In these cases, the builder carrying out the work should only charge VAT at 5% and not at 20% (see **7.34** and **7.35**). If the property is listed, the zero-rating will take precedence.

The rental of residential property is always exempt, and the owner cannot choose to 'opt to tax'. The only exception to this is the rental of holiday accommodation that might be included in the equine operation – this is automatically standard rated.

Commercial property – opting to tax

5.26

The VAT position on the supply of land is considered at **5.9** and VAT planning around the stud farmhouse is considered at **7.35**.

The sale of a new commercial property is standard rated but, unlike a residential property, 'new' for commercial properties means within three years from the date of construction completion. All other commercial property sales will be exempt from VAT unless the owner has 'opted to tax'.

The option to tax is a mechanism that allows a VAT-registered person to choose to charge standard rated VAT on the supplies of commercial property. The option is made on a property by property basis so that a business can choose to opt to tax one building and leave another 'united'. Once the option has been made it is largely irrevocable until a period of 20 years has elapsed. Great care must therefore be given before the option is made. The option can be made on any commercial property or on land, so it is possible that an owner could opt to tax stables, pasture land and/or commercial buildings. It is unusual for equestrian land and buildings to be opted as most owners choose to keep their buildings VAT free in order to keep fees low for their clients, but this point should always be checked.

Once the option has been made, all disposals, leases and lets must be taxed at the standard rate unless the lessee or purchaser is to use the site for charitable purposes or for residential use. Under these circumstances the option is disapplied for those transactions and will become exempt.

Works to commercial properties will be standard rated and it is irrelevant whether the work is to a listed building or whether it is an extension, repair or refurbishment.

If an equestrian business incurs VAT on a commercial property construction, repair or lease then it will be entitled to recover this VAT providing that the cost has been incurred for wholly taxable business purposes. There will be no need to opt to tax to recover this VAT unless the business intends to sell or let the property for what would otherwise be an exempt supply.

Bloodstock agents

5.27

Bloodstock agents often operate in a number of different countries and therefore have to be particularly careful to ensure that they do not fall foul of VAT regulations in any country in which they arrange transactions.

Where agents act in their own name in a supply of goods (e.g. where they issue an invoice for the purchase or sale of a horse even though they have only acted as agent) then for VAT purposes the supply is treated as having been made to them as principal and by them as principal. The agent will therefore have to account for VAT on the sale of the horse in accordance with the rules set out above. This in theory can mean that a horse sold on behalf of a non-VAT registered owner can become subject to VAT when the agent invoices the sale in his own name.

Where an agent acts as an intermediary, the place of supply of his intermediary services will depend upon whether his principal receives the supply in a business or private capacity.

As such, when acting for a business, the normal B2B rules apply, albeit sometimes in a somewhat counter-intuitive way.

Racehorse Trainers

5.28

The general understanding of the role of the racehorse trainer is looked at in **1.9** and **1.10**.

In broad terms all supplies made by racehorse trainers will be subject to VAT although supplies of training services to owners who are in business outside the UK will not be subject to UK VAT as it is a B2B supply. There are, however, a few areas where confusion can arise, and these are dealt with below.

A trainer will often own or have shares in horses in his yard. This may be because a horse has been bought as a speculative purchase, or a trainer has retained a small interest in a horse in his yard at the request of the other owner(s).

If these interests are retained for genuine business purposes then they can be treated as being part of the VAT registered business and the normal rules will apply (for example, a trainer who owns and retains horses might do so to attract owners or buyers and to provide rides for apprentices, provided the number of horses is not disproportionate to the main activity of training).

If a racing partnership under which the trainer owns a share in the horse, registers for VAT, then the trainer can recover any related input tax on his share through his own registration if the interest has been taken for business reasons, although he is not required to do so. In most circumstances it will be best for all concerned if the trainer's share is included in a partnership VAT registration under the Racehorse Owner's Scheme (see **5.6**).

It is quite common for trainers to incur expenses going to the racecourse etc. in the UK or elsewhere. These expenses will then be re-charged to the owner on the normal monthly training bill. These expenses are part of the cost of training the horse and as such the VAT treatment follows that of the training supply itself. The only time this does not apply is when the trainer has incurred the cost on behalf of someone else, e.g. he has paid the owner's air fare. In this case the expenses can be treated as disbursements. Generally, this will not be the case, so if disbursement treatment is claimed the trainer should be prepared to demonstrate that the supply of the underlying goods/services was made to the owner and not to him. Disbursement treatment could never apply to the trainer's own travel costs.

Conclusion

VAT registration and associated concerns are possibly one of the most complex and misunderstood elements of equine tax. All areas of equine tax must be researched in advance and none more so than the VAT position. The technicalities around the dealer (the margin scheme), the racehorse owner scheme and all angles around breeding, stud ownership and property together with livery must be given full consideration. The import and export of horses is also a matter needing careful understanding of the legislation.

In light of this, every area of VAT and tax planning must be tailor-made for the variety of different elements and the complex (though interesting) individuals contained therein.

CHAPTER SIX

TAX PLANNING FOR THE BREEDER AND THE STALLION OWNER

Taxation surrounding stallions, mares and foals is complex. The chapter below looks into the ownership of stallions, the associated allocation of stud fees and tax pitfalls, the ownership of stallions as a syndicate, and the valuation of stallions as assets/stock within business to include specifically:

- Leasing mares for breeding (see **6.2**)
- Foal sharing (see **6.3**)
- Sale of stallion to a syndicate (see **6.12**)
- Fiscally transparent stallion syndicates (see **6.17**)

What Type of Breeder?

6.1

There is normally a complete variety of bloodstock breeders. However, we will divide the breeder into two basic categories at this stage. First, the one who owns horses but not the stud farm itself, and so keeps his horse at a public stud (without land). Secondly, the one who owns horses and owns or leases a stud farm (with land).

The breeder who occupies a stud farm will be taxed in the same way as a farmer, as if he were breeding cattle or sheep.

The profits of a business of horse breeding, with a view to the sale of the progeny, will be taxable as this is classed as a form of farming.

In principle, there should be no distinction between the tax treatment of income and expenses of keeping mares and stallions to be used for breeding purposes. This point was well illustrated by the case of *Lord Glanely v Wightman (HM Inspector of Taxes (1933) 17 TC 63*. Lord Glanely received stallion nomination fees from the owners of visiting mares. He contended that relief should be given for the cost of maintaining both his stallions and his broodmares at the stud. Lord Wright, in judgment, said:

> *"The fee which is received for the covering of the visiting mares corresponds to the gain which the appellant has, or at least hopes to have, in respect of the foals of his own mares. But I think the similarity is deeper than that. The profit or income is, in truth, from the reproductive capacity of the animal and it is that which has the money value however realised, whether in cash or in kind. There is a natural tendency to think only of the procreative activity of the female animal, the mare, and ignore that of the male, the stallion."*

Clearly the activities of stallions and mares are an integral part of the stud farm's breeding activities and should be taxed accordingly. However, in some circumstances the receipts from a stallion are taxed separately under miscellaneous income under the heading of non-trading (previously Schedule D Case VI) (see **6.4** below).

Once it is established that a breeder is carrying on a trade, it is necessary to calculate the profits on which he or she should be taxed. Accounts will be prepared as for any trader, taking credits to income for horses sold or transferred to racing. Deductions are then made for costs of sales and other overhead expenses.

Leasing mares for breeding

6.2

The situation may arise where the breeder either cannot afford the purchase price of an expensive mare or would prefer to use a particular mare for a limited period of time without the need for a large initial outlay. This problem can be overcome by the breeder 'leasing in' rather than actually buying the mare. Normally, the leasing payments will be at an agreed figure which is to be included in the lease agreement signed at the time of commencement. The breeder will bear all costs of the mare during the lease period and such costs, including the leasing payments, should be allowable for tax purposes in the normal way. The leasing income will accordingly be taxable on the recipient, normally under miscellaneous income (non-trading), unless they are themselves a breeder, in which case the receipts are likely to be taxable as normal trading income.

Foal sharing

6.3

Due to the fluctuating nature of the demand for the services of certain stallions, in some years it is difficult to provide a stallion standing at stud with a full complement of mares. The price of the nominations is obviously a determining factor and can be reduced in order to increase the supply. However, in recent years the practice of 'foal sharing' has evolved. This is where the owner of a share in a stallion will agree with the owner of a broodmare to split, in varying proportions, the resulting proceeds from the sale of the foal or yearling which is the outcome from the mare visiting the stallion concerned. This can have the advantage to the mare owner that no nomination fee is paid up front in cash but is set at a figure dependent upon eventual foal sales. Again, this can introduce some complications with regard to stock valuations. The stallion owner is taxed on the stallion fees as well as the percentage of the foal proceeds for that year. If the stallion fees are part of the trade, the potential value of the foal should arguably be included as an asset in the balance sheet. Where barter is involved there must be the correct disclosure (see **7.12**).

Stallion fees not as a trade

6.4

Stallion income is historically taxable, although not as a trade, with nomination fees taxed as miscellaneous (non-trading) income. However, a stallion standing at an owner's stud covering the stud's own mare integrated into that business will be allocated differently. The stud is a trade and thus income generated in this way is deemed to be trading income.

As the future value of the stallion and its income producing life is uncertain, the owner may prefer to realise 'cash' and still receive an element of future taxable income through nomination fees, as well as retaining the right to send his/her mares to the stallion – this is where a stallion may be sold to a syndicate, where the original owner is a member. If the racehorse was held "outside the scope of tax", *(Sharkey v Wernher)* then any disposal by an owner to a stallion syndicate will be tax free. Income from an investment in a stallion is a taxable miscellaneous income. Many small studs look after stallions themselves directly, this however comes under the definition of trading income and no miscellaneous income on these animals is declared.

Stallions – relevant tax cases

6.5

Malcolm v Lockhart (Surveyor of Taxes) (1919) 7 TC 99 provides an example of stallion fees not treated as trade receipts.

A farmer, who was assessed to income tax under the now obsolete Schedule B provisions, owned a stallion that was used for breeding purposes. In addition to serving the farmer's own stock, the stallion served mares belonging to other farmers for which 'service fees' were received. The farmer claimed that the fees, which he received in respect of the stallion's services, should be deemed to be part of the profits of his farm, the income tax liability in respect of which was covered by the then relatively nominal Schedule B assessment.

The court held that the farmer was chargeable to Income Tax under what would later be Schedule D Case VI (now miscellaneous income) in respect of the service fees.

There is clearly some debate on whether the keeping of a stallion to serve mares for the public in return for service fees has any direct relationship to the occupation of a farm. It is, however, clearly not the occupation of land. A stallion kept for this purpose would seem to have no direct or 'necessary' relationship to the farming activities of a farmer. Such an animal may be kept in a separate stable and may even be owned and looked after by a person who is not a farmer. There may well be obvious advantages of keeping the stallion at farm premises, but these are arguably indirect considerations. The stallion may not bring the farmer any profits or gains other than those derived from his keep and thus has nothing to do with the other activities of the farm. As this simply involves the consumption of farm produce it is arguably just one way of marketing or realising the fruits of the occupation of the farm.

In this context it is worth quoting direct from *Malcolm v Lockhart*:

> *"It is quite possible that an entire horse may be used by a farmer in connection with his farm in such a manner that its use outside will, in relation to its use for his own purposes, be so trivial and unimportant that there would be no tax eligible in respect of profits received for its services; or on the other hand it may be that the real use and purpose of the animal and its real advantage to its possessor lie in the moneys which can be obtained by the use of its services outside.*
>
> *My lord, this question is essentially a question of fact; the commissioners in this case have decided that the use by the Appellant of this stallion is a use that provides a profit, which does not arise in respect of the occupation of his lands. This seems to me no reason whatever why that finding of fact should be investigated more closely. Had it been found*

in terms it would have been outside the competence of a court to discuss it further. It is not found in exact language, but it is found inferentially, and the facts to which I have referred – namely, the number of mares on the Appellant's farm, the number of entire horses that he possesses, and the extent of the profits which this horse has earned – are, in my opinion, abundant to justify the conclusion which has been reached.

For these reasons in my opinion this Appeal fails and should be dismissed with costs. The fees were not therefore an integral part of the stud".

This case produced an adverse view to the case of *Lord Glanely v Wightman (HM Inspector of Taxes) (1933) 17 TC 634* (see **6.1** and **6.8**) and therefore considers the degree of integration with the activities of a stud farm to be more important, but each case must be assessed on fact.

There have been a number of cases where taxpayers have been assessed under the old Schedule D Case VI classification, in respect of payments for the provision of facilities or the hiring of property. In some of these cases, it was held that the payments could be alternatively assessed under Case I as trading receipts.

It has also been held that a subsidy or contribution received by a statutory body not carrying on a trade can be assessed under Case VI. In *Severn Fishery Board v O'May (Surveyor of Taxes) [1919] 2 KB 484, 7 TC 103* licence fees, which the Fishery Board was empowered to charge, were assessed under Schedule D Case VI. It was held in that case, however, that the Fishery Board did not carry on a trade, and that there was no liability to tax in respect of the receipts. The basis of the decision was that the source from which the fees flowed was not analogous to a trade (see **6.4**).

This decision was questioned later by the House of Lords in *Forth Conservancy Board v IRC [1931] AC 540, 16 TC 103* where the Conservancy Board was empowered to levy dues on vessels, goods, and passengers coming within its jurisdiction. It was held that the Conservancy Board's surplus revenues from these dues were profits or gains within Schedule D Case VI (now recorded as miscellaneous non-trading income).

Local authorities and local authority associations are wholly exempt from income tax. Where a statutory body which is not so exempt carries on a trading activity, it is assessable as trading income (and not as non-trading income) on the amount by which any subsidy or contribution received by it exceeds its relevant expenses.

In *Carlisle and Silloth Golf Club v Smith (Surveyor of Taxes) [1913] 3 KB 75, 6 TC 198,* the court decided that profits derived by the club from visitors' fees were assessable under either Schedule D Case l or Case ll (again, trading income).

The cost of replacing stallions has been allowed as a deduction from the service fees they produce, but not an allowance for depreciation in their value.

Gifts of free shares or nominations

6.6

The demand for excellence in the training and racing of potential stallions is such that top trainers and jockeys command very high fees. In certain cases, inducements are offered and are eventually paid on successful results. In this connection, trainers and jockeys may receive free shares or nominations on the syndication of a stallion when it retires to stud. The income which arises from this source is clearly taxable in the recipient's hands. Indeed, the value of a share in a stallion given to a trainer or a jockey would itself be taxable on the recipient as income arising from the particular profession of trainer or jockey. The precise tax position will depend upon whether the recipient is an employee of the provider or a freelance self-employed individual.

In order to reduce the costs of the syndicate committee in respect of a stallion's keep, it is sometimes agreed that a stud farm will receive free nominations in lieu of these expenses. Any income which arises to the stud farm from the sale of the nominations will be taxed in the normal way as part of its trading income. If a stud uses the nominations for its own mares this will, of course, be reflected in the valuation of the stock for the stud farm (see CHAPTER 7).

Strictly, the owner should show the offset of free nomination as income and the cost of boarding which has been set off as an expense. The accounts and tax treatment of this will be important, especially as regards timing issues and the correct treatment of 'barter' (see 7.12).

The complexity of the taxation of stallions

6.7

In *Earl of Derby v Aylmer [1915] 3 KB 374, 6 TC 665* it was held that stallions are *not* plant, i.e. not fixed assets.

The Appellant owned two stallions at stud and was assessed in respect of the profits derived from stallion fees. He contended that in the computation of these profits for income tax purposes he was entitled under the legislation of the time to a deduction for depreciation "by reason of the diminished value of the stallions year by year".

It was held, that the claim did not fall within the scope of the legislation and could not be allowed. The judge said:

> *"I am clearly of opinion that the diminished value of the breeding animal, merely due to the fact that having lived a year it is a year nearer its end and therefore is from that point of view less valuable, is not within this section."*

The judge took the view that any diminution in value was not "by reason of wear and tear"; it was simply a loss arising from reduction in value of an asset which was a source of production which was a wasting source of production.

Business Income Manual 55710 states that HMRC accept that stallions can be depreciated in certain circumstances, but that this treatment is not generally accepted for mares. Stallions can be depreciated on a straight-line basis until they are 10. However, if their market value is higher, depreciation is not appropriate. Mares are always valued at the lower of cost and net realisable value.

Stallion fees part of the stud farm

6.8

The favourable case of *Lord Glanely v Wightman (1933) 17 TC 634* (see **6.1** and **6.5**) ruled that breeding, where the serving has been limited to animals on the farm, can be viewed as stud farming, i.e. part of a farming trade. The likely practical tax advantage will be that more expenses can then be claimed in respect of the keeping of the stallion.

In *Glanely*, the appellant was the owner of both a racing establishment and of a stud farm, comprising arable land, stud paddocks and pasture land; at which he maintained a stock of selected horses and carried on a breeding operation. Horses bred from the appellant's stock were sent to his training stables and raced, and those, which were considered satisfactory, were subsequently sent to the stud. Additions to the stock of horses at the stud farm were made, by purchase, from time to time and unsatisfactory horses were sold.

Mares belonging to other owners were served by the appellant's stallions at his stud farm in return for fees, and, on occasions, the services of the appellant's stallions to others' mares were exchanged for the service of other stallions to the appellant's mares.

The appellant was assessed to Income Tax under 'Schedule D' (now trading income) in respect of profits from stallion fees. He appealed to the special Commissioners contending:

- that any profit derived from stallion fees was covered by the tax assessment on the stud farm; alternatively

- that the stallion fees should not be the subject of a separate tax assessment, but were receipts of the trading undertaking of breeding and racing horses, in which, as a whole, no profit had been made;

- that if the stallion fees were assessable as a separate item, a deduction should be allowed of the cost to the appellant of the service of his mares by the stallions of other owners, and therefore should not be exchanged for the service of outside stallions.

The Special Commissioners rejected the appellant's contentions and upheld the assessments in principle. The degree of integration in the stud is important in arriving at this decision.

It was held that the occupation of the land being for the purpose of a stud farm, the use of the stallions upon the farm was not separable from the purpose of the occupation and the fees for their services were not taxable as trading income.

It is interesting to look at other points raised in the case. Success in breeding thoroughbred horses could only be attained by submitting them to the test of the racecourse in order to find out whether they possessed the necessary speed and stamina. The test was essential to ascertain the value of both stallions and mares for producing high class progeny. It was only by the successful racing of the progeny of a stallion that the fee for his service could be assessed accurately. The potential and actual capabilities of the horses bred from him were only capable of being tested on the racecourse by the purchasers. The method followed by the appellant is the one usually adopted.

It is not generally believed to be conducive to successful breeding to send a mare every year to the same stallion. Better results will arguably be obtained by sending a mare to different stallions in different years. Furthermore, over time fillies bred will finish their racing career and then return to the breeding stud. However, it is not uncommon to find that as a result of their close blood relationship to the stud stallions, they cannot be mated with any of them for fear of the ill-effects of inbreeding. Consequently, in *Glanely*, it was sometimes necessary to procure for the appellant's mares the service of a stallion or stallions belonging to other owners, for which fees were paid, or for which the services of stallions to the appellant were given in exchange. In these instances, the appellant, in addition to the stallion's fees, paid for the keep of his mares at the stud visited and the necessary travelling expenses.

Thoroughbred stallions must stand at a properly equipped stud farm and it is often not practicable to send them around the country to serve other owners' mares. The owner of stallions must therefore either occupy sufficient land to accommodate the stallions and the visiting mares, or else the stallions must stand at some other similarly equipped breeding establishment.

In the case of a stud with 40 visiting mares such as in *Glanely*, a large number of paddocks are required for the accommodation of the visiting mares and the owner's own mares, in addition, a number of spare paddocks and loose boxes are also needed.

After foaling, mares must not be crowded and only two or three mares at a time can be put into a six or eight-acre paddock. It is usual to find a high-class stud farm with the paddocks divided by fences, lined by trees, with water laid on, and equipped with loose boxes lit with electric lights.

The appellant in *Glanely* did not have sufficient mares to keep his stallions fully employed. He was therefore obliged to let their services to the owners of other broodmares. Apart from keeping the stallion in health, the obtaining of nominations from first class mares is the best way of proving the value of the stallion as the sire of good progeny.

The appellant in *Glanely* did not expect to make a profit out of racing alone but hoped he might make a profit out of the breeding and racing establishment as a whole. This might be possible if he obtained at least one more really first-class stallion commanding a fee of 400 guineas. He contended that he had always run the whole establishment on what he considered to be commercial lines.

This case ruled that stallion stud fees could be regarded as an integral part of the profits of the farm, provided these were fully integrated into the stud in the ways mentioned above.

Syndicate share in a stallion not a trade

6.9

The case of *Benson v Counsel (Inspector of Taxes) [1942] 1 All ER 435, 24 TC 178* gives a clear example of the tax position of the syndicate and the sale of stallion rights to nominations (stallion fees) as non-trading income.

The appellants were two members of a syndicate formed in 1932 to purchase a thoroughbred stallion. By an agreement entered into after the sale, defining the rights and interests of the members of the syndicate, members became entitled each season to one free nomination to the stallion in respect of each share they held in the syndicate. There were no restrictions on a member selling his right to a nomination, provided the mare of the purchaser was approved by the syndicate.

During the seasons 1934 to 1940 inclusive, the appellants sold some of their nominations. On appeal, it was held by the Special Commissioners that the payments so received, while not receipts of a trade within the then relevant Case 1 of Schedule D, were actually receipts of annual income chargeable under Case VI – now miscellaneous income.

It was held that the Commissioner's decision was correct.

If the tax planner's objective is to have stallion fees treated as trading income, it is essential to look at reasons behind the appellants' failure in this case. The key issue is the identification of the existence of an 'integrated stud farm'. This is of paramount importance. If a syndicate share is used on a farmer's own mares then the income from the share should be taxed as farm income, i.e. trading income.

Stallions as a wasting asset

6.10

For the purposes of UK capital gains tax, no chargeable gain or allowable loss accrues on the disposal of (or of an interest in) an asset which is tangible movable property, and which is a wasting asset. On the assumption that a stallion qualifies as a wasting asset then it is worth looking at the detailed CGT position associated with a wasting asset.

The exemption does not apply to a disposal of, or of an interest in, an asset if:

1 throughout the period of ownership of the asset by the person making the disposal, the asset has been used solely for the purposes of a trade, profession or vocation and that person has claimed or could have claimed any capital allowance for expenditure on the acquisition or enhancement of the asset; or

2 if the person making the disposal has incurred any expenditure on the asset or interest which has otherwise qualified in full for any capital allowance.

Expenditure on an asset is not deemed to have qualified for capital allowances for the purposes of (2) above unless the expenditure continued to be eligible for capital allowances at the time of the disposal of the asset. If capital allowances were originally given but were subsequently withdrawn because the expenditure ceased to satisfy the requisite conditions, the taxpayer is treated as if the allowances had never been made, in accordance with the decision in *Burman (Inspector of Taxes) v Westminster Press Ltd [1987] STC 669, 60 TC 418*. In that case, first year allowances made to the company in respect of expenditure on a printing press were withdrawn retrospectively because the press was never brought into use in the trade. It was held that the expenditure on the press had not satisfied the conditions of eligibility for capital allowances, and therefore the gain accruing to the company on the disposal of the press was exempt.

The most common example of assets to which exemption does not apply is plant and machinery used for the purposes of a trade.

Where an asset or interest has been used partly for the purposes of a trade, profession or vocation and partly for other purposes, or has been used for the purposes of a trade, profession or vocation for only a part of the period of ownership, or has otherwise qualified in part only for capital allowances:

- the consideration for the disposal, and any expenditure on acquisition or enhancement, are apportioned by reference to the extent to which that expenditure qualified for capital allowances; and

- the computation of gains or losses is made separately in relation to the apportioned parts of the expenditure and consideration.

Consequently, the exemption does not apply to any gain accruing in respect of the part of the consideration apportioned to use for the purposes of the trade, profession or vocation, or to the expenditure qualifying for capital allowances. The restricted exemption would apply, for example, where plant and machinery were used for non-business purposes.

Where a chattel is not exempt as a wasting asset, because expenditure in respect of it has qualified for capital allowances, the £6,000 exemption limit and associated marginal relief may apply instead.

Where a wasting asset is only partly exempt because of partial eligibility for capital allowances, it would appear that the limit applies to the part of the disposal consideration apportioned to the expenditure qualifying for capital allowances.

As it is extremely unlikely that a stallion will have been eligible for capital allowances, it is therefore clear that no chargeable gain or allowable loss accrues on the disposal of a racehorse or stallion, because a racehorse or stallion is tangible movable property which is a wasting asset. This is so even if the racehorse is immature. There should therefore be no capital gains tax concerns on the disposal of the racehorse.

Valuation of stock and transfers to racing

6.11

It might be that an individual carries on breeding activities which are regarded as merely a hobby and which do not have a commercial motivation. If so, this section should be regarded as reference material in the event that the motivations behind the activity change and become commercial at some stage.

On the assumption that the breeder is trading, the complex area of the valuation of stock is covered in detail in CHAPTER 7. Assuming that the breeder is paying fees at a public stud the calculation of costs should be relatively easy to calculate as opposed to operating a stud himself where the costs are internal.

As decided in *Sharkey v Wernher (1955) 30 TC 275* (see **1.11**, **4.12** and **7.13**), for tax purposes the transfer of breeding stock from a commercial concern to a racing stable has to take place for tax purposes at full market value. This would apply to a small breeder as well as a stud farm.

However, as can be seen in CHAPTER 7, for the valuation of stallions (see **7.8** below), a 'rule of thumb' method of valuation can be used to write off the stallion by equal instalments. This method is, however, only acceptable when a more accurate figure cannot be obtained. Similarly, with stallion syndicates the cost of the share in a stallion syndicate could be depreciated by equal instalments.

Potential 'Tax free' sale of racehorse (stallion) to a syndicate

6.12

As the future value of a stallion and the likely length of its income producing life is uncertain, the owner may prefer to realise capital and still receive future income through nomination fees whilst also retaining the right to send his mares to the stallion. This could be achieved by the owner selling the stallion to a syndicate of which he would be a member. If he retained, say, 20% interest in the horse, on the above assumptions, he could receive a large amount of cash tax free. The definition of 'tax free' is debatable here as it could be that the owner originally paid £2m for the horse and so has effectively made a loss with no tax relief. If he used, say, some of his nominations for his own mares, he could receive income from a sale of the other nomination fees and this income could meet the expenses of the stud farm.

The difference between the sale of nominations to the stallion (the right to have a mare served), the sale of shares in a syndicate and the sale of shares in a potential stallion must be looked at. They are three different and separate activities.

Establishment of syndicates

6.13

Because stallions can generate high income as soon as they have been retired to stud, they generally have a much higher value than broodmares.

The breeding season generally runs for over four months from mid-February to early July. On average, each mare will be covered once or twice by the stallion, thanks to the advances in veterinary technology in recent years. Because of the earning potential of high quality race stallions, in order to spread the cost and risk, syndicates are formed with nominations being provided to each shareholder i.e. the right to send one of the breeder's mares to the stallion each season.

From the outset, UK bloodstock breeders were very interested in the principle of the syndicate as it was a way of owning an interest in a successful stallion at a relatively small initial outlay when compared with the entire cost of the stallion, and also the owners would only be responsible for their share of its upkeep. If the stallion became more valuable by producing successful progeny, then the value of their asset, i.e. the syndicate share, would accordingly increase. If the member did not want to send one of his or her own mares to the stallion, he or she could sell the nomination for that breeding season to another breeder. The proceeds from the sale of the nomination would be subject to tax as miscellaneous income, depending on the investment of the stud (this was looked at in **6.8** and **6.9** above).

Taxation of nomination fees from shares in syndicated stallions

6.14

As we have seen, the ownership of a share in a syndicated stallion by a bloodstock breeder can be used to enable his broodmares to be covered or can enable them to produce income by selling the nomination. As the syndicate share could be used as an income producing asset, there is a danger that HMRC could treat the share as an investment and tax any net income from the sale of nominations as miscellaneous income and not trading income, as in the case of an investor who does not own broodmares. Any excess of the share of the upkeep of the horse over the nomination fees would be a miscellaneous income loss, which could only be set against other miscellaneous income, but not against any trading or other income. It follows that if the syndicate share is held to be an investment, its cost would not give rise to a trading deduction for tax purposes, nor will it be valued as stock at the balance sheet date.

This line of argument by HMRC could be supported if the number and value of syndicate shares exceeded the number of broodmares. For example, if eight syndicate shares were owned and the stud farm only had five broodmares, then, at that time, three of the shares could not be used in the trading activities of the stud farm. Clearly, each case will be judged on its own merits, but if the number of shares were restricted to the number of broodmares then it would be easier to contend the shares were acquired with the express intention of being used for the stud farm's activities. Even if the nominations are then sold, the proceeds may have been used to finance the costs of an alternative stallion nomination fee for a broodmare.

HMRC can apply a similar argument where stallion shares are to be included in a herd basis election, i.e. if the number of syndicate shares exceeds the number of mares owned by a breeder, the surplus nominations cannot be required for the breeder's mares and are not therefore part of the herd. For further information about the herd basis, SEE CHAPTER 7.

Taxation of syndicate committees

6.15

A syndicate committee is normally formed to protect the interest of the stallion concerned and to be responsible for expenditures such as advertising, keep costs and insurance of the animal. To cover this expenditure, the committee can be allocated a number of free nominations to the stallion to be used to raise revenue. Initially, the number is determined by the estimate of the quantum of the costs mentioned above. However, in certain cases where the stallion has become successful, profit can be generated for the syndicate committee. It is in these circumstances that HMRC may seek to tax the resulting profit.

Where stallions are less successful and it is difficult to sell nominations, a call may be made on syndicate shareholders to cover the syndicate committee's excess expenditure and, in these circumstances, the claimed apportionment from the shareholder may be a tax deductible item.

The taxation of the resultant profit can be looked at from two alternative approaches:

- Is the syndicate an unincorporated association?
- Is the syndicate a 'fiscally transparent entity' where the income is being taxed on the syndicate members in the appropriate proportions.

Unincorporated association

6.16

Where a syndicate is taxed as an unincorporated association it is taxed as if it were a company. The syndicate is under the control of a syndicate manager and committee. They have the power to distribute or accumulate any surplus income. In addition to the sale of nominations there will be the member's share of the income from the sale of surplus nominations.

Any breeding income will be treated as trade income where the member carries on an established breeding trade on a commercial basis with a view to profit. The income from the sale of surplus nominations will be taxed on the unincorporated association under corporation tax rules. Any surplus income generated by the syndicate will be regarded as distributions when it is paid out to members. The syndicate has to produce annual accounts for each stallion and profits shown in the accounts will be subject to corporation tax. The syndicate members will be taxed on the distributed income as if they are dividends received.

Fiscally transparent syndicates

6.17

A fiscally transparent syndicate (FTS) is one which is set up for the mutual benefit of the members directly and where the syndicate committee acts only as agent for the members. The difference between the unincorporated association and the FTS is that the income and expenses will be treated as accruing directly to the members in proportion to their shareholding, rather than to the syndicate. In effect, an FTS is somewhat akin to an investment club and treated in much the same way for tax purposes.

The applicable tax treatment turns on the wording of the syndicate agreement. If it is made clear that all rewards and risks of ownership are underwritten by the members, this will be an FTS. In this case, the income and expenses will be treated as accruing directly to the members of the syndicate and the division will be based on the proportion of their shareholdings. The syndicate manager will have no discretion as to distribution and the taxation of income will depend on whether the syndicate shareholder is a taxable breeder or a non-taxable breeder.

Tax planning around breeding income

6.18

The aim of this chapter is to try and highlight areas of activities of the small breeder or stallion owner which could be charged to tax or which may need to be disclosed on the individual's tax return. Owners should make their adviser aware of all their breeding activities to ensure the correct declarations are made.

The fact that income arising from owning racehorses can be regarded as 'tax free' does not prevent income receipts from the breeding elements of these activities being properly regarded as taxable – as soon as a horse retires from the racecourse to the breeding shed there is the potential for a taxable activity to commence. It is incorrect to assume that the racing losses and costs 'cancel' the taxable element of the breeding income.

The key points to be reviewed are as follows.

- Will a profitable small breeder incur tax liabilities on a 'one-off' high profit on sales?
- Will the profitable small breeder achieve full tax relief where a high profit is followed by large losses?

- Will income produced by an 'investment' stallion be taxable under miscellaneous income?
- What are the income tax implications of the allocation of future stallion nomination fees to jockeys and trainers (whether they are employed or self-employed)?
- What will be the tax status of shares of winnings paid to third parties as nomination fees – will these be taxed as miscellaneous income?
- Could stallion leasing produce more income – normally taxable as miscellaneous income but possibly trade receipts in some cases?
- Will there be tax liability on foal shares as miscellaneous income?
- Will free 'board and lodgings' for the stallion in return for stallion nominations be taxable?
- What is the true status of Irish 'tax-free' stallion nominations taxable in the UK unless a 'bridge' is in place?

Conclusion

The understanding of breeding with (the stud) and without the land ownership needs to be reviewed in tax planning terms. Likewise, so must the taxation of the 'stand-alone' stallion syndicate and the stallion integrated into the stud. The taxation, valuation and recording of the stallion is often complex and tax advisers must ensure that they are aware of all the details.

CHAPTER SEVEN

TAX PLANNING FOR STUD FARMS

Following on in greater depth from **Chapter 6**, here we investigate the entire view of taxation of Stud Farms. **Chapter** 7 aims to explain the common misunderstandings and 'tax pitfalls' surrounding the Stud business and explore the associated tax reliefs available. We discuss the trading structure and how it affects the reliefs available, the valuation of stock and future tax planning for 'the stud farmer', including:

- Studs trading as a limited company (7.4, 7.32 and 7.33)
- Achieving agricultural property relief and business property relief around stud ownership (7.7 to 7.31)
- Tax planning around stock values (7.8 to 7.11)
- The need for the correct recording of barter (7.12)
- Non-thoroughbred studs (7.15)
- Tax and VAT planning around the farmhouse
- VAT and general planning around the stud and stud farmhouse (7.34 to 7.37)

Stud farming is farming for tax purposes

7.1

As mentioned in **1.2** and **2.2**, stud farming is regarded as farming in the UK for the breeding of horses (see **1.19**). Ensuring full compliance with the definition will therefore mean access to valuable tax reliefs. Failure can mean extra costs both in the short and long term.

Whether or not an equine business qualifies as a farm depends on a number of factors. To qualify for agricultural property relief (APR – see **1.5** and **2.2**), property must be occupied for 'agricultural purposes'. Agriculture is not defined in IHTA 1984, but HMRC's Inheritance Tax Manual provides some useful guidance on land uses that would fall within this category (see IHTM 24068). HMRC accepts that stud farming can be regarded as husbandry and therefore as a form of farming (see **1.19**).

If a stud farm is run on commercial lines, then the trading results will almost certainly be taxable as a trade; whereas racing activities are not normally regarded as a taxable trade, as already considered at **1.18**. These principles apply whether the activities are run by an individual as a sole trader, through a partnership or a limited company. Before deciding on the operating or trading vehicle for the bloodstock and horseracing activities, it is necessary to consider the funding of the operation and the likely future trading results.

If the stud farm can be established with HMRC as a taxable trading business entity, it ought to obtain some of the benefits of the available reliefs for capital gains tax and inheritance tax, which may, in some cases, cover the stud house. These reliefs should not be put at risk as they can prove to be invaluable at later dates.

Equine property repairs v improvements

7.2

There have been strong cases for expenditure on repairs and renewals of properties being allowed as deductible expenses, as opposed to capital improvements that do not impact on the tax returns. These include:

- *G Pratt and Sons v HMRC [2011] (TC1269)* – "It was there before". Review of all expenses, repairs and replacement.

- *Cairnsmill Caravan Park v HMRC [2013] (TC02580)* – the replacement of the surface

- *Hopegear Properties Ltd v HMRC [2013] (TC02734)* – not just "patch repairs". Plan carefully to maximise repairs with tax efficiency.

- *Steadfast Manufacturing & Storage Ltd v HMRC [2020] – highlights the resurfacing of yard can qualify as a repair. Significant as a lot of equine businesses need repair.*

With the huge expenditure required on equine property, the question as to what counts as a repair or whether something is more capital in nature, is an important question with major ramifications. Expenses classified as repairs can be key to increase losses (see **8.1**) but these must not jeopardise commerciality. Repairs to the farmhouse and VAT planning are also important (see **7.3** to **7.6**).

Stud liveries in addition to husbandry

7.3

The activities of a stud farm may include a number of activities other than just the act of husbandry, i.e. the raising of livestock and the production of horses. The stud may also introduce mares as livery 'boarders'. This will be very common with the public stud that has stallions standing for use by the wider industry. Visiting mares will require board and lodging, and frequently stay for some weeks as part of the breeding process. A number of smaller breeders also do not want the responsibility of foaling the mare (being present at the birth) and will rely on the technology of a larger stud farm offering modern facilities such as CCTV, 24-hour staff etc. and thus leave their mares stabled at a stud for longer. These livery services are not generally regarded as farming activities and will not be eligible for the agricultural reliefs which follow. However, they should still be regarded as eligible for various business tax reliefs possibly, for example, qualifying for Enterprise Investment Scheme (EIS) status (see **2.2** and **7.16**).

As the income from livery activities is not regarded as farming income, the profits will have to be removed from the farming trading computations before any 'farmers' averaging' adjustments to taxable profits are undertaken. Similar adjustments will need to be carried out if claims under s397 for the eleven-year loss relief are to be made. The latter is of some concern as some studs approaching their eleventh year of loss have been known to take in 'boarders' to boost profits. This is, of course, another source of income not strictly regarded as farming income. The stud tax computation must be adjusted for non-stud farming income which must be disclosed separately on tax returns.

For IHT purposes, although these elements will not qualify for Agricultural Property Relief (APR) (see **7.17**), they will qualify for Business Property Relief (BPR) (see **7.21**).

Studs trading as a limited company

7.4

The choice of which trading structure is to be preferred must be looked at in detail (see **1.3 and 1.4**).

Many stud businesses might look to the protection of limited liability in view of the high risk nature of the stud industry. Particular tax problems which may arise here, however, are that trading losses might become 'trapped' in the company (see **CHAPTER 8**) and the stud land and buildings will not qualify for business asset disposal relief from capital gains tax. Obviously, the latter will only apply to stud businesses which own their own land and buildings. However, all equine businesses which own land inside a limited company, will suffer the same problem.

If the stud activities are carried out at a stud farm, it may be advisable to own the stud farm personally and to operate just the trading the activities through a company. The shareholder would then be the landlord and grant a lease over the stud farm to the stud company. The owner could receive a market rent from the stud company for the use of the farm and this may offset any interest charge payable on the mortgage used to originally acquire the land.

The subject of letting equine property is touched upon later in this chapter. However, a specific problem area here will be reconciling the structure chosen with the need to try to retain entitlement to valuable capital taxation reliefs currently available in respect of agricultural and 'business' property for both capital gains tax (CGT) and inheritance tax (IHT) purposes. Fundamental to this situation will be ensuring that there is in place a properly drafted lease agreement which retains the right to vacant possession within 12 (or in some cases, 24) months for the landlord.

Similarly, the fact that generally the activity of the stud farm is taxable whilst horse-racing activities are not can also pose some difficult questions for a limited company carrying on a stud activity.

It may even be more convenient to separate taxable and non-taxable activities into separate limited companies. If this is not practical it will be important to ensure that the respective income and expenses from each source are clearly distinguishable from the company's records.

Alternatively, the non-taxable income could be retained outside the company in the taxpayer's own name. Consideration should also be given to looking at areas such as sponsorship, entertaining, marketing, advertising and PR. For example, does the stud owner have a separate business that could incorporate a sponsorship agreement? This is considered in chapter 4 sponsorship of owning a horse (see chapter 4.5).

For inheritance tax purposes, it is only controlling interests in shares in a limited company that may qualify for APR (IHTA 1984 s122), however, a minority interest may attract BPR. If the company does not qualify as a trading company but as an investment company, then BPR will not apply. Furthermore, APR will only be relevant where one is dealing with a limited company trading as a stud farm. Other forms of equestrian businesses are not counted as agricultural but many still attract some BPR.

To attract the full APR on shares in a stud company the company must have occupied the relevant agricultural property for the purposes of agriculture (i.e. the stud farm) throughout the period of two years before the transfer of the shares. 100% APR is also available against the value of shares in such a company, if the company has owned the agricultural land and it, or another, has used it for agriculture, throughout a period of seven years before transfer, for example, where a company leases its land out to be farmed under a tenancy.

Where the shares have been acquired as consideration for agricultural land (normally on the incorporation of a pre-existing partnership or sole-trader's business), the shares issued as consideration are deemed to *stand in the shoes* of the original property in calculating the period of ownership, and in ascertaining whether the original property is still held on death (important for 'replacement property').

The inheritance tax relief of APR is restricted to the agricultural value. Agricultural value is set out in IHTA 1984 s115(3) and is defined as:

> *"The value which would be the value of the property if it were subjected to a perpetual covenant prohibiting its use otherwise than as agricultural property".*

Agricultural value applies to that part of the value of shares in (or debentures of) a company, which is attributable to the agricultural value of qualifying agricultural property, provided that the particular conditions set out in IHTA 1984, s122 are satisfied. This will be determined by the Shares Valuation Division (SVD) who will also notify the District Valuer (DV) of any agricultural property owned by the company which qualifies for relief (form VAL 63 or 63A) -see **7.20** and **7.29** below.

A stud house owned by a limited company will potentially cause income tax accommodation benefits to be assessable on the occupants where they are the directors or are otherwise employees of the company. There will also be potential capital gains tax issues as there will be no principal private residence relief available on the stud house if it is not owned by the individual in occupation. These difficulties can sometimes be surmounted via the use of trust arrangements under which a qualifying beneficiary occupies the property which is let to the company in which the trust is also a shareholder.

Capital allowances

7.5

The cost of the land used for stud purposes does not give rise to a trading deduction for bloodstock breeders. A breeder may however qualify for tax deductions on subsequent qualifying expenditure on assets used in the business. These deductions, known as capital allowances, are considered further.

There were changes in 2012 in the way capital allowances (see **2.18** and **8.15**) are claimed on the purchase of a property (land and buildings) and it is important that all advisers take capital allowances into account before finalising the purchase as failure to do so could result in allowances being lost (see **8.15**).

Averaging of stud farming profits

7.6

On 26 October 1977, the then Chancellor announced a range of measures designed to relieve the exceptionally high income tax liabilities within the farming industry at that time – these measures equally applying to stud enterprises.

The weather had produced substantial fluctuations in output, and therefore income, between one year and the next; which – under a graduated rate system – pushed liability into higher rate brackets in one year, without necessarily providing adequate compensation for that in next. This caused issues with cashflows and had the knock-on effect of actively discouraging capital investment – as farming is a highly capital-intensive industry, high taxes during one good season discouraged investment whilst a poor season would result in a lack of available funds to invest with.

The system enacted was based upon the simple concept of adding together the profits of two successive years and dividing by two. Baldly stated, that may sound initially attractive, but in practice a variety of limitations are imposed. The complete rules are now contained in ITTOIA 2005 Pt 2 Ch 16 and strong consideration by the tax adviser is needed before choosing to adopt this approach.

With effect from and including the 2016/17 tax year, farmers – including stud enterprises – now have the choice as to whether they average their profits over five years, two years or not at all. The changes to the averaging legislation made by FA 2016 s 25 have been incorporated into ITTOIA 2005 ss 221–225. For those who have been in business for fewer than five years, only the option of two-year averaging is available until they have established a five-year trading history, excluding the tax year of commencement.

An averaging claim cannot be made in the year of commencement or of cessation of a trade. It is key to note that this also includes individual partners joining or leaving an existing partnership. Tax losses in a year are treated as 'nil profits' for the averaging calculation, with the loss available to offset in the normal way. The 'nil profits' rule applies to five-year averaging and has always been the case for the two-year averaging calculation. Profits for the averaging calculation will still be calculated after any capital allowances claim.

Contract farming/stud arrangements

7.7

A contract farming/stud arrangement is essentially a landowner using the services of a contractor or another stud owner to farm the land. The landowner supplies fixed cost items, i.e. the property of the stud, and the contracting farmer supplies labour, machinery and management.

A contract farming arrangement can be used effectively at the time of intending retirement of a stud manager; or when a tenanted stud has fallen vacant due to the departure of the tenant and the landlord does not wish to manage the stud himself. He may lack the capital or the inclination to do so but, nonetheless, wishes to retain vacant possession, perhaps having in mind that one of his family might wish to have a stud career in the future.

Generally, the contractor receives a set fee for the services provided and a bonus as a percentage of the calculated surplus from the venture. The contracting income received by the contractor must be reviewed carefully.

Contract farming agreements generally centre around a memorandum of 'joint venture', which will contain an arithmetical calculation to establish how much the contractor should be paid for the services. It is often advisable in a contract farming agreement to set up a separate bank account in the landowner's name with all transactions relating to the agreement going through the account. This would automatically apportion the interest calculation on working capital as the account becomes overdrawn to fund variable costs. It is essential that a correctly drawn up agreement should aim to enable the landowner to carry on the stud trade and provide reasonable return for both parties, even within the current falling income position in the UK. This should then ensure that the landowner will preserve his business reliefs, not just for IHT, but also for CGT. Additionally, the IHT reliefs on the stud house are also preserved as this is normally one of the assets specifically dealt with in the arrangement.

Although contract farming arrangements might not be as universal to the equine industry as they have been to the farming industry, they should not be dismissed by the equine world. They can prove a cost-effective and tax-efficient way of dealing with stud land management.

Valuation of trading stock used in the stud farm

7.8

The principal guidance from HMRC for equine stock is in their factsheet, *HS232 Farm Stock Valuation 2017,* and at BIM 55710. For a stud farm to be treated as agriculture it must be carried out in conjunction with the occupation of the land, whether freehold or leasehold. This is not the case if mares are boarded at stud for a keep fee and, as such, the mare owner is not carrying out an agricultural activity.

The Business Income Manual says:

"The stud fee or 'nomination' fee paid by the owner of a mare for the services of a particular stallion can be a substantial sum. Unless:

- *The mare has already given birth to the foal, or is known not to have conceived, or has aborted, by the accounting date; or*

(1) *An "adjusting event" (see BIM33140) occurs – for example, the discovery between the balance sheet date and the date the accounts were finalised of a congenital defect rendering the foal valueless;*

(2) *The fee paid should be reflected in the balance sheet by one of the following methods:*

  (1) *Including the fee in a stock valuation of the embryo or foetus of the foal;*

  (2) *Increasing the value of the mare while she is carrying the foal by the amount of the fee;*

  (3) *Carrying forward the fee as a prepayment."*

Foals should normally be in the stock valuation at cost including the stud fee, the depreciation of the mare and the cost of keep to date at the year end. If the foal has any defects, the net realisable value at each year end must be considered.

Requests for specialist advice on open market valuations of thoroughbred horses can be made to the Bloodstock Section, Shares and Assets Valuation, Ferrers House, Castle Meadow Road, Nottingham, NG2 1BD, and should include: the name(s) of the horse(s) to be valued; the valuation dates; and any opinion of open market value together with reasoning.

The deemed cost method should not be used for the valuation of thoroughbred horses. This would, however, be used if the stud farm is integrated with farming and the farm animals need to be valued and costs of breeding and rearing to maturity home-bred animals are not available or readily extracted from the farmer's own records.

When the foal is born the stud fee becomes part of the cost of the live foal.

Foals are also included in stock at the lower of cost or market value. However, as the foals may have been bred and not bought, the cost of foals and yearlings is the aggregate of

- the stallion nomination fee;
- the cost of keeping the mare for the whole year of gestation; and
- the cost of keeping the foal from weaning until it is sold or transferred to training.

In cases where no nomination fee has been paid because the nomination has been acquired via a syndicate share, generally the annual depreciation allowance on the share is substituted for the nomination fee. If a foal is purchased then it is included in stock at cost.

The value of the foals should be increased each year by the cost of the keep. Industry standards have been agreed, with £75 a week being the guidance from *The Thoroughbred Breeders' Association Bloodstock Taxation Guide.* However, different methods can be used if the reasoning and basis can be evidenced. Again, it is important that net realisable value is considered so that, if the cost of production is greater than net realisable value, it must be included at the lower figure.

Valuation of stallions and mares for stock

7.9

The valuation of stock is complex and the wrong workings can result in the incorrect calculation of profit or loss (see **2.10**). Equine businesses should prepare an annual reconciliation of opening and closing stock and the movements between. First, there are foals, most often born in the spring. Then yearlings, who the next year become two year-olds and so on.

When considering each category of potential valuation, remember that the 'deemed cost' will be needed if accurate figures are not available. For example, the cost of keep of each category may need to be included. However, the 'lower of cost and net realisable value (NRV)' rule applies so, if an animal has problems that place the value *below* cost, this must be considered. All stock valuations must be consistent and accurate so that they are not manipulated for the benefit of the taxpayer.

The general rules, under BIM 55710, state:

> "*Except where the herd basis has been adopted, both stallions and mares should be dealt with as stock in trade and valued individually at the beginning and end of each year in accordance with relevant GAAP on the usual basis of (i) cost or net realisable value…, whichever is the lower, or (ii) at fair value less costs to sell where FRS 102 or IAS 41 are applied. Stock valuations should also include any foals and, where appropriate, stud fees paid...*
>
> *In the case of stallions (but not mares) a rule-of-thumb method of valuation, whereby the cost of the animal is written off by equal annual instalments until it reaches the age of 10, is acceptable. This method is an attempt to arrive at an acceptable figure for net realisable value*

where this is less than cost. It is not appropriate in either of the following circumstances:

- *Where a better figure is available because the animal is valued at the balance sheet date,*

- *Where it would give an unreasonable result. For example, in those exceptional cases where the value of an animal increases or drops at a rate significantly slower than that used in the rule of thumb, because, for example, of very successful progeny, the figure computed using the rule of thumb should be increased to an amount not exceeding cost."*

Importantly, market value cannot be used unless this is to identify the NRV.

Valuation of stud fees paid

7.10

The stud fee or 'nomination' fee paid by the owner of a mare for the services of a particular stallion can be a substantial sum – please see **7.8** for the Business Income Manual guidance on this.

The valuation of stallion held by a syndicate share is very similar to the valuation of the stallion held separately.

As far as stallion syndicate shares are concerned, and because there will frequently be considerable difficulty in obtaining agreement among the shareholders on a market value of a share at any particular moment, a concessionary treatment is available. The cost of a share can be depreciated by equal annual instalments. If, however, at any date the market value of such share is clearly above the written-down value, the share can be revalued upwards subject to a maximum value equal to original cost. If the value increases in any year above its written-down value, a breeder may need to temporarily refrain from any further depreciation of the share until such time as actual value falls back below the depreciated value.

Part of the stock of a stud business may well consist of shares in stallion syndicates. Strictly, the value of such shares should be determined by reference to the lower of cost or realisable value. However, since many shares might be held in one stallion, and each share owner might adopt a different approach to market value, HMRC accept a straight-line depreciation method which produces a £nil valuation for an animal by the time it reaches 15 years (this was reduced to 10 years from 2000), to reflect the likely or expected breeding life of a stallion.

If the owner of a syndicate share cannot convince his Inspector of Taxes that he is holding the share as trading stock, surplus income from it will be taxed under miscellaneous income. However, although the share will be a 'wasting asset' and will eventually become totally worthless, no trading deduction will be granted for the cost of the share by way of depreciation allowances.

Thus, the use of a stallion in the stud is a matter which merits close attention as this will impinge closely on tax planning issues as discussed above.

Practical tax planning around stock values

7.11

The equine industry is unique. It could be said that stud stock values are more volatile than teenage fashion. Outside factors such as the racing achievements of animals from associated bloodlines can have dramatic effects. Keeping stock fit and healthy and injury free is a real problem. Equine stock valuations may be viewed by some as an unimportant paper exercise but they can, in fact, produce tax refunds resulting from the tax losses that arise from an accurate valuation producing a loss. If potentially valuable equine stock is held at cost, the timing of the profit can be planned around the date of the sale. However, if a disaster awaits in the form of a valuation fall, it can be realised as soon as possible by means of being reflected appropriately in the stock valuation, therefore accelerating the tax loss (or reducing the taxable profit).

The stud farmer must, therefore, take full cognisance of the importance of year-end valuation of stock for his or her bottom line. The timing of the sale of good and bad stock is critical as is the timing of any transfer to racing; owners and tax advisers alike need to give appropriate weight to this subject. It will frequently determine exactly when a profit is achieved. As with all tax planning issues, however, commercial common-sense should take priority such that when a good sales price can be achieved the adviser may need to accept that the owner will very likely ignore the tax planning advice given previously.

Mares and stallions will have been either purchased or transferred from training, i.e. racing. Those purchased in the market will have been brought in at cost, while those transferred from training will be brought in at market value. The accounts will reflect these amounts unless the current market value of the animal is lower, in which case this will be substituted. A number of factors can influence the market value of a horse, including its past performance, racing career, market conditions and breeding prospects, etc.

As stock values considerably affect the taxation position, HMRC tend to examine them closely and so it may be worth seeking a written independent valuation in certain cases.

Barter and the stud farm

7.12

Barter is often used in the bloodstock industry and is looked at in the context of free shares and nominations (see **6.6**). Stud farms particularly can involve a large amount of barter. For example, free use of a stallion, work in return for free boarding, keep of mares, foal sharing etc (see **6.3**) have all been recorded at various enterprises across the country. It is essential for those who produce the accounts to ask stud owners about the existence of any barter transactions that might be incorporated into the accounts and also the stock valuation.

Various tribunal cases show that HMRC has been scrutinising claims to sideways income tax loss relief (see **8.2**). Such intense HMRC review has included rural businesses such as a tree surgery and woodmanship business – *Kevin Johnson [2016] (TC4805)*. The *Johnson* case involved no monetary income, but there was 'barter' income. The tribunal considered the impact of this on the taxpayer's ability to offset tax losses sideways against other income. The case reminds taxpayers and advisers of the need to show the correct 'barter' or 'non-monetary' transactions in business accounts and to disclose these correctly on the tax return. The First-tier Tribunal clarified the understanding that the activity of bartering is no less capable of being defined as a trade than one involving money. However, the barter transactions must be recorded correctly in accounts, tax returns and all submissions to HMRC for all equine businesses.

As an aside, this subject of trading income received in non-monetary form was included in the 2016 Finance Act which confirms the existing law and practice that the value of trading income received in 'non-monetary form' is taxable in full as trading income. All barter transactions in studs must be recorded in full.

It is a practical reality that stud farms operate with barter arrangements across a multitude of areas, e.g. with tree surgeons, farm contractors, livery services etc, especially as farmers become elderly and need more help from outside. As the equipment becomes more expensive and the tasks more onerous the swapping of skills versus land use becomes more attractive. However, such barter must be correctly recorded for tax and to provide a full understanding of the trading operation. The need to record barter as correct in income tax and VAT terms might result in some extra fiscal payments by the stud farming partnership. However, such amounts could be very small compared to the millions of pounds in future IHT that could be saved through the farm being able to show the act of agriculture, the supply of services, the commercial use of woodland etc. In farming estates there could be fundamental barter which the executor fails to uncover by *not* asking the right questions of those with the correct information when reviewing the farm accounts as part of probate and producing the IHT400.

With diversification there can be increased barter across all levels of the stud farm enterprise operation and the tax spectrum, not just income tax and IHT but also VAT.

Transfers to and from racing to the stud

7.13

Sharkey v Wernher [1955] 36 TC275 (see **1.11**, **3.2**, **4.12** and **6.11**) sets out the tax allowability of the stud and the tax-free status of ownership, alongside the need to split the stud and the racing activities and sort out transfers to and from the stud.

Transfers to racing from the stud are made at market value. Transfers from racing to the stud are also made at market value. In both cases, an independent third party may be required to support the numbers used in each transaction. If, in general, breeding horses is a taxable activity and racing is non-taxable, then the transfer of horses from the stud to racing and back will be accorded special tax treatment.

The *Sharkey v Wernher* case established that a horse must be valued when it leaves the stud to go into training. The market value of the horse at that time will determine the profit or loss realised by the stud from breeding, and this will be reflected in the bloodstock accounts. Even though the horse has not been sold – merely transferred – any profit or loss from breeding is taxable or allowable when it leaves the stud and commences its racing career. Such profit or loss will have been realised 'in kind' rather than in cash so that tax is payable on any profit even though the breeder will not yet have received any proceeds from the sale of the horse to meet the tax liability. Sometimes the transfer values are used as tax planning and thus are checked by HMRC.

In the case mentioned above, Lady Zia Wernher carried on a stud farm, the profits of which were agreed to be chargeable to income tax under

Case I of Schedule D, the regime in place at the time. She also carried on the activities of horse racing and training, which were agreed not to constitute trading. Five horses were transferred from the stud farm to the racing stables. The cost of breeding these horses had been debited in the stud farm accounts. On the question of the amount to be credited as a receipt, Lady Wernher contended before the Special Commissioners that the proper figure to be brought in respect of the transferred horses was the cost of breeding.

The Crown, in contrast, contended that the market value of the animals, which was considerably higher, was the proper figure. It was held that the figure that should be credited was the market value.

Many breeders who have not been able to sell their stock at a reasonable price have been forced to put their horses in training, in order to achieve stronger prices and advertise the animals to a wider pool of owners. This principle will be tested in the future. What stock sells varies from 'year' to 'year' and from 'sale' to 'sale'. At times, untried horses just do not sell. When the horse returns to the stud, it is brought into the bloodstock accounts at its market value. Conversely, if the horse is worth less when it returns then a non-allowable loss will have accrued. Many breeders argue that the racehorses that return to the stud should stay in the stud accounts throughout, however HMRC try and argue 'training is just a jolly' and reduces value.

Integrated studs and racing activities

7.14

There are strong arguments to say that racing activities cannot be split from a stud farm. In this context it is worth looking at one of the specific points raised in *Lord Glanely v Wightman (1933) 17 TC 634*. It was argued in that case that "success in breeding thoroughbred horses could only be attained by submitting them to the test of the racecourse." (see **6.8**).

This matter was again considered within the *Sharkey v Wernher* case already mentioned (see **1.11**, **4.12**, **6.11** and **7.13**) and the principles from the case were later enacted by Financial Act 2008 Schedule 15 Part 1 which inserted the rules in ITTOIA 2005 Part 2.

How can a profitable horse be brought into the 'tax free' arena? HMRC want horses 'tax free' as so many lose money (like gambling). The tax planning that should be considered is to have potentially profitable horses in private ownership, however, this needs to be genuine and well evidenced.

Non-thoroughbred studs

7.15

This subject was considered in chapter **1.14** and **2.29** above.

Artificial insemination (AI) or embryo transfer are prohibited by the rules of racing, although used routinely in other areas of equine sport. Through AI, stallions can compete at the same time as being used at stud, although even those used for natural covering on mares can be frequent competitors too. Good performance mares in show-jumping, eventing and polo can also continue to compete while their genetic offspring is developing in another mare by way of in vitro fertilisation.

If the stud has sports horses competing at the same time as their breeding activities, it can be argued that competing expenses should be treated as wholly and exclusively incurred for business purposes. This is on the basis that it is the current performance in competition of a sports horse stallion and the quality of its offspring, rather than its breeding, that determines the number of mares being sent to it. It is very important that the business plans can show the commercial benefit and correlation between competition expenses and improved trading results.

The adviser must understand into which category their equine client falls – bloodstock, sports, competition or stud – and ensure the ground rules for accounting and tax treatment are established. Matching of costs and forensic analysis is essential with all horse trading operations. Consistent treatment of private horses through the examination of expenses and valuation of stock is key.

EIS – Can it apply to a stud farm?

7.16

The Enterprise Investment Scheme (EIS) was first looked at in **CHAPTER 2** at **2.2** and **2.13**. Stud farming currently does not qualify for EIS as, by definition, it is within the exclusion currently contained in the legislation aimed at 'farming'. Where the breeding operation does not involve land, in principle EIS opportunities can be investigated.

Agricultural Property Relief

7.17

Agricultural Property Relief (APR) has been looked at throughout the book.

Where certain conditions are satisfied, relief from inheritance tax is available on the transfer of agricultural property in the UK, the Channel Islands and the Isle of Man. The relief known as APR is a percentage reduction in the value transferred by a transfer of value and is given automatically without claim.

Relief is also available on occasions on which tax is chargeable under the provisions relating to settlements without interests in possession. (IHTA 1984 s115(1)(5) and 116(1)), broadly discretionary trusts. This tax relief is of prime importance to the stud owner. The commercial stud farm (and commercial equine business) can be an enjoyable and efficient way to shelter wealth from inheritance tax.

It is imperative to look at the definition of 'agricultural property' or 'farmland'. Some guidance is given in IHTA s115(2) for the purposes of this relief. 'Agricultural property' means agricultural land or pasture and includes woodlands and any building used in connection with the intensive rearing of livestock or fish if the woodlands or building are occupied with agricultural land or pasture and the occupation is ancillary to that of the agricultural land or pasture.

It also includes such cottages, farm buildings and farmhouses (see **7.24**), together with the land occupied with them, as are a character appropriate to the property. The breeding and rearing of horses on a stud farm and the grazing of horses in connection with those activities is to be taken to be agriculture and any buildings used in connection with those activities to be farm buildings.

Agricultural land or pasture (IHTA s115(2)) means the bare land and does not have any wider meaning derived from the interpretation Act 1978 (*Starke v IRC [1995] STC 689*). It will, however, include any interest, servitude or right over land. In the past it was argued that farmhouses were by definition 'agricultural land' and immediately qualified as such. The bare land or pasture must be used for the purpose of agriculture to qualify as 'agricultural' land or pasture. 'Agricultural' is not defined in the legislation though it is likely to include that within the Agricultural Tenancies Act 1995 s38(1) wherein 'agricultural' includes horticulture, fruit growing, seed growing, dairy farming and livestock breeding and keeping, the use of land as grazing land, meadow land, osier land, market gardens and nursery grounds cottages, farm buildings and farmhouses (together with the land occupied with them) as are of a character appropriate to the property (IHTA 1984 s115(2)).

Death of the stud farm owner

7.18

The liability to inheritance tax (IHT) primarily arises on death or on chargeable lifetime transfers. The deceased's estate is valued at that time and if the chargeable assets exceed the nil rate band (see **7.37**) tax will be payable on the excess at the appropriate rate, currently 40%. If assets are left to a surviving spouse, IHT will normally be deferred until the death of the surviving spouse.

For stud farms there are various tax planning issues raised by the availability of APR, BPR, the nil rate band and the 'surviving spouse' exemption and these must be given due consideration. It is for this reason that will planning is of such importance.

It is hoped that the stud will escape inheritance tax liability under the provisions of APR (see **2.2** and 7.17). Careful attention to will planning should attempt to ensure that the business assets are covered by APR/BPR and that non-business assets are covered by the nil rate band and make optimum use of the surviving spouse exemption. Lifetime gifts of the equine property including the new residency nil rate bands are dealt with at **2.25**.

The risk of not using land capital accounts

7.19

As set out in **1.3**, many studs are run as a sole trade or as a partnership. The agricultural property relief (APR) (see **1.2** and 7.17) applies to the land whilst BPR applies to the business. It is essential to establish which partners own the stud land property, as reflected in both the land capital accounts and the capital accounts, to ensure the relevant rates of relief are applied.

APR takes precedence over BPR

7.20

Stud property will probably qualify for a mixture of APR (see 7.1) and BPR (see **1.2** and 7.21). APR takes precedence over a claim for BPR if both forms of relief are available on the same item.

To ensure that the stud qualifies for APR it is essential to conform to the basic conditions for APR. The relief is available where an individual or partnership transfers land and buildings used for agricultural purposes (i.e. at death or by lifetime gift). It is also available against shares or securities in agricultural companies to the extent that their value is attributable to agricultural property. This is provided that the transferor has control of the company immediately before the transfer. Land and buildings at a stud farm used for the breeding, rearing and grazing of horses should generally qualify for APR.

Relief will only be available if one of the following conditions is satisfied:

- the property has been occupied by the transferor and used for agricultural purposes for a period of two years prior to the date of the transfer; or

- the property has been owned by the transferor for a period of seven years prior to the date of transfer and has been used for agricultural purposes throughout that period either by himself or another;

- if a transfer of agricultural property falls to be included in the gross estate of an individual on death (i.e. before reliefs are deducted), normally because it was made within seven years of the death of the donor, it must be held by the donee throughout the period up to the donor's death and still remain agricultural property and be occupied for the purpose of agriculture during that period for relief to be retained.

APR is restricted to Agricultural value (see **2.33**). The expression 'agricultural value' of agricultural property is defined to mean the value which the property would have if it were subject to a perpetual convenient prohibiting of its use otherwise than as agricultural property (IHTA 1984 s115 (3)) (see chapter 7.4 above).

The effect of the definition is that APR only applies to the agricultural value of the property, not any enhanced value attributed to development or 'hope value'. Provided that the conditions are met, BPR should apply to any balance not attributable to agricultural value.

When a stud farm fails in its claim for APR it may well be possible that BPR can still be claimed.

Obtaining 100% BPR on stud property

7.21

Many areas of the overall stud property will require the protection of BPR as opposed to APR, e.g. potential development land, cottages, equine elements that are not a stud and other diversified activities.

In considering the eligibility for a BPR claim, it is key to note that BPR is a percentage of relevant business property. For unincorporated stud businesses (sole traders and partnerships, as is the case with most stud farming businesses), the most important categories of relevant business property are:

- A business or an interest in a business (e.g. a share in a partnership) (s105(1)(a) IHTA 1984) rate of relief for BPR 100%; and

- Land or buildings, or machinery or plant used wholly or mainly for the purposes of a company controlled by the transferor or a partnership of which he was a partner (s105(1)(d) IHTA 1984) rate of relief for BPR 50%

A stud business which consists wholly or mainly of making or holding investments is not relevant business property (s105(3) IHTA 1984). In recent years, HMRC has been trying to argue that many land-based businesses fall over the 'investment line' and do not qualify as relevant business property. As was noted in *Pawson*, there must be no presumption that a business which involves property is an investment business. HMRC will try and attack property used in a partnership that is not partnership property and therefore it will restrict BPR to 50%. However, denying BPR because the operation has 'crossed the investment line' is a 100% IHT relief prize for HMRC, not just 50%. As a result, all the BPR on the genuine trading element could be lost with the attack on the overall business status.

Acquiring stud land on death of another person

7.22

The owner of a stud farm will also want to ensure that the person who acquires the stud will themselves satisfy the relevant inheritance tax conditions for the future.

Where the deceased acquired the land on the death of another person, he is treated for the purposes of the conditions as having commenced to occupy the land on the death of that other person (IHTA 1984 s120(1)(a)).

If the land was acquired on the death of the deceased's spouse, then if the spouse satisfied the conditions at the date of death, the deceased is treated as having also satisfied the conditions at that date (IHTA 1984 s120(1)(b)).

When grazing of horses is not agriculture

7.23

Stud farms engaged in the breeding and rearing of horses, and for grazing associated with that activity (IHTA 1984 s 115(4)), qualify as occupying agricultural land for the purposes of APR.

However, in *Wheatley v IRC [1998] STC (SCD) 60* (see **1.2** and **2.33**) the Special Commissioners held that APR was not due in respect of a meadow which was the subject of a grazing agreement between the deceased and a grazier. It was accepted that the meadow constituted pasture within the meaning of IHTA 1984 s115 but the claim failed because the horses were used for leisure pursuits and were not connected with use for agriculture or with a stud farming business. This decision has been criticised on the grounds that the act of growing grass, which can properly be regarded as a 'crop', should be treated as an act of husbandry, irrespective of the way in which the crop is exploited or utilised, i.e. grazed by horses.

The stud house – APR

7.24

There have been a number of court cases over the years involving farmhouses and whether APR (see **1.5** and **2.2**) is available against the agricultural value of the farmhouse (see 7.17). On the basis that the stud farm is farming the tax planner should look to a claim for APR on the stud farmhouse.

The main tests are as follows.

- Is the property a farmhouse?
- Is the surrounding land farmland?
- Is the farmhouse of character appropriate (see 7.17) to the surrounding agricultural property?

The first two points are fairly straightforward. The latter is more difficult to satisfy. HMRC looks at all three tests and then reviews the whole picture. The current trend seems to be for HMRC to consider each of the above aspects in turn and then to apply the 'elephant test' – 'a farmhouse is difficult to describe but you will know one when you see one!' So how would the stud farmhouse be viewed by HMRC?

For the property to qualify it must be at the centre of stud farming operations and must be of a 'character appropriate' to the surrounding land over which the owner and occupier of the stud house must have beneficial interest.

For instance, if the owner and occupier of the stud house no longer own the surrounding stud land, even though it is being actively used by the stud itself, the stud house would not attract any relief. This is because the owner of the stud house does not have a beneficial interest over any stud land to give the stud house the necessary 'character appropriate'.

Conversely, if the owner of a stud house had given away the farm land, perhaps to his son, subject to the retention of a tenancy for him and his son as a partnership, he will retain a beneficial interest in the land, and the stud house will still attract relief.

Historical association

7.25

Has relief been given on the property previously under the current inheritance tax rules? Provided the transferor still has a beneficial interest in the acreage which satisfied a previous transfer, the 'character appropriate' test can probably be satisfied.

Geographical comparisons

7.26

Comparisons are made with similar holdings of land in the surrounding area. Although the size of the stud house does not form part of the character test, it is often a feature referred to in disputes over the availability of the relief. Other studs in the area would be compared.

Financial viability

7.27

This is a test being used more and more by HMRC. They attempt to question whether stud activities undertaken are sufficient to maintain the stud house. Many experts in this field believe this is an unfair test as it concentrates on activities conducted, not those that could be conducted. For instance, an elderly stud owner may reduce his farming operations concentrating more on letting land for grazing, which in turn may reduce his return from the land. This could then affect the availability of APR on the stud house.

The stud house – '*Antrobus*'

7.28

The inheritance tax advantages of stud farming have been that the farmhouse and farm cottages are potentially business assets and eligible for inheritance tax relief as well as the stud land and buildings. There have been several cases, including *Lloyds TSB (Personal Representatives of Antrobus deceased v IRC SpC 336,* which challenged the availability of IHT relief on farmhouses and introduced some new aspects to the debate.

The APR on a farmhouse is restricted to the agricultural value, although again it is generally to be hoped that BPR could be claimed on the balance of any value not relieved by APR.

This can be a complex issue for the tax adviser. Throughout the period of ownership of a stud house, care must be taken to ensure that for capital gains tax purposes, best use is made of the CGT Principal Private Residence relief whilst trying to ensure that the farmhouse does not 'fail' but win as in *Antrobus* for inheritance tax purposes.

It is worth noting that in the past it was argued that farmhouses were by definition agricultural land (IHTA 1984 s115) and immediately qualified as such.

Although these cases relate to farming and not stud farming, they are still relevant to the potential tax relief on the farmhouse. Perhaps a test case will give the equestrian world more guidance at some stage on the future.

The main points on IHT and farmhouses raised by *Lloyds TSB (Personal Representative of Antrobus Deceased) v IRC* were as follows.

- Is the house appropriate by reference to size, content and layout to the stud buildings and land being used in the stud?

- Is the house proportionate in size and nature to the requirements of the farming activities conducted on the land in question?

- Does the house meet the so-called 'elephant test'?

- Would the 'educated rural layman' describe the property as a 'house with land' or as a stud farm?

- The historical dimension – how long has the house been associated with the land in question and has there been a history of agricultural production or stud activity?

The limitation of relief to farmhouses described as 'of character appropriate to the property' has caused difficulties. HMRC's view has been that in interpreting this section, 'agricultural property' means agricultural land or pasture. Farm buildings and farmhouses qualify if (and only if) they satisfy the stated condition. If they are not 'of a character appropriate to the property' they do not qualify for relief. A large and expensive 'farmhouse' standing in a relatively small acreage would thus be disqualified as 'inappropriate'.

The farmhouse must be of a character appropriate to the land that surrounds it. One of the tests of 'character appropriate' is that the occupiers of the farmhouse must be treated as farming the land.

Agricultural value and the stud house

7.29

Agricultural value is considered in 7.4.

Agricultural value can have significant relevance to the farmhouse in view of current high property values.

Assuming the relief is available it is now important to ascertain the agricultural value of the stud house. This is the value of the property subject to a hypothetical restrictive covenant prohibiting the non-agricultural use of the property.

There are many who consider that the agricultural value is around two-thirds of the open market value of the property, but this is subject to debate. Tax practitioners have argued that this should not be the case, particularly where the farmhouse is transferred together with the rest of the farm property. In this instance, the agricultural value of the whole unit should not be much less than the open market value of the farm as a whole.

There is also an argument put forward that the agricultural restriction is a restriction on use not occupancy. A non-farmer may wish to purchase such a property because the agricultural restriction on surrounding land protects the amenities sought. In this case, the agricultural value should be equivalent to the open market value. The relevance of this argument will depend upon the area in which the farmhouse is situated and whether it is attractive to non-stud farmers.

At the time of writing, land prices appear steady after a sharp rise from 2005. Furthermore, the 'hope' value for possible development is high due to the shortage of houses.

The rented stud house

7.30

Reference should be made here to HMRC's BIM 55255 – Farming: Farmhouse Rent. This will be of particular use to the rented stud farm and how the farmhouse should be dealt with.

The stud owner or farmer can let grazing rights and still be a trader with all the associated business reliefs. This can be essential if a large gain is in prospect.

The criteria for a well-drafted grazing agreement have already been set out. There are also important inheritance tax advantages under IHTA 1984 s117(a). It is considered that the case for the claim for APR in the future is stronger when there is an established trade as opposed to a letting arrangement.

The *Farmer* and *Balfour* cases – the stud cottages

7.31

Most stud farms employ staff who require accommodation on the premises so that they can deal with problems on site. The case of *Farmer (Farmer's Executors) v IRC (1999) STC (SCD) 321* (see **2.6**) is likely to be of great importance with regard to the availability of IHT reliefs, particularly Business Property Relief (BPR), available for stud farm cottages and may even extend the availability of the relief to cases in stud cottages, which were previously part of the stud operation but have since been let out. However, the capital gains tax eligibility of each property has to be looked at on a property-by-property basis.

In the *Farmer* case, Mr Farmer gave evidence that the farm was run for a profit but that it is very difficult to make a farming profit without the subsidies from the European Union. The evidence of HMRC was that the farm could have been run at a profit if there had been no lettings: there would not be a large profit, but the farm could be self-supporting and there would be a healthy profit in some years. Over a ten-year period, the farm would be viable.

The judge said that it was necessary to consider the business in the round. Of the five relevant factors, the overall context of the business, capital employed, the time spent by the employees and consultants in the business, and the levels of turnover, all supported the conclusion that the business consisted mainly of farming. The profit figures, and more particularly the net profit figures, on the other hand, supported the opposite view. Taking the whole business in the round, and without giving predominance to any one factor, the conclusion was that the business consisted mainly of farming.

The resultant theme of *Farmer* and *Balfour* and the significance to the tax planner is that of 'unified management' with all aspects of the business being examined. Where this can be demonstrated, the case for the availability of the relief will be that much stronger. The letting of some *surplus* properties was indeed relevant but not fatal to the case. Until further cases emerge it will be essential for the tax planner advising studs to work very closely with land agents and the farmers alike. Key factors appear to be:

- ensuring that the letting of surplus stud buildings is incorporated into the stud as one unit;
- ensuring integrated accounts, i.e. treating all the financial activities as one integrated business unit;
- recording time spent on properties;
- using organisations such as the CLA and TBA to monitor APR/BPR claims and to report back on success and failures.

HMRC's statement that the business 'could have been run at a profit if there had been no lettings' is of interest. Could this statement still be made today? Also, the business 'consisted mainly of farming'. Is this still likely to be the case in an age where farm diversification is key to survival? Hopefully, direction from case law or the Government will give future clarity, but in the meantime, the taxpayer should take note of the main points stressed above as far as possible in order to achieve maximum IHT reliefs.

The question of cottages as 'surplus to requirement' has been looked at in detail in the case of *Farmer* mentioned above. However, it is also important to look at the main cottages used by a stud.

To ensure retention of favourable tax status, all stud cottages should be checked for the status of their tenancies, the amount of legal protection the tenants currently have and the tax efficiency of such arrangements then reviewed. The advice for all equestrian activities is to review the tax status of the assets held and that includes cottages. Stud farms traditionally require a lot of staff and this will probably result in property being provided for their accommodation with all the potential tax consequence highlighted above that this may entail.

BPR is also needed to protect “hope value” or development value that the stud might have (see **2.34**).

The equine limited company and APR

7.32

The limited company is first considered at **1.4**.

The IHT position and the availability of APR (see **7.17**) on the value of land used for stud farming but owned inside a limited company deserves specific attention.

Under IHTA1984, in order to obtain APR, agricultural property, which is the subject of the transfer, must form part of the company’s assets, and part of the value of the shares or securities of the company must be attributable to it. The transferor must also have control of the company immediately before the relevant transfer.

‘Control’ is defined as control of powers of voting on all questions affecting the company as a whole, which if exercised, would yield a majority of the votes capable of being exercised (IHTA 1984 s269(1)). The fact that a company has one or more classes of shares with voting rights limited to the question of winding up the company, or any questions primarily affecting shares of that class, does not prevent an individual from having control (IHTA 1984 s296(4)). No account is to be taken of the capacity of the shareholder or that of any other shareholders to exercise their votes.

In *Walding’s Executors v IRC (1999) STC 13* the deceased held 45% of the voting shares of the company, and her four-year-old grandson held 24%. Her executors contended that as her grandson lacked legal capacity to exercise his votes, she therefore had control, but this argument was rejected, i.e. APR was denied. She was found not to have overall control.

In the later case of *Walkers' Executors v IRC (2001) STC (STD) 86*, the deceased held 50% of the shares and was chairperson of the board of directors of the company, in which capacity she had a casting vote. The Inland Revenue contended that when exercising her casting vote, she owed a fiduciary duty as an officer of the company, and if there had been conflict between her personal interest as a shareholder and that of the company, her use of the casting vote would have been constrained by her position as a director. The Special Commissioner held that, having particular regard to IHTA 1984 s269(3), this fiduciary constraint did not mean she did not have control of the powers of voting, and he allowed the executors' appeal, i.e. in this case APR was given.

It will, therefore, be necessary to consider carefully who has 'control' of a stud farm company to ensure that APR is obtained where required.

It is necessary to establish what proportion of the value of the shares held by a controlling shareholder can be attributed to the value of the land which forms part of the company's' assets. The process of attribution can involve complex arithmetic. Where control exists before the gift, then gifts of minority holdings may qualify for relief. (As to the meaning of 'control', see IHTA 1984 s269.)

A transfer of qualifying shares will attract APR at 100% of vacant possession value, provided the shareholder has owned the shares and the company has occupied the land for at least two years. This rule is modified where the shares owned on the date of the transfer have not been owned for the two-year period, but replaced other qualifying property, e.g. shares or other property attributable to the underlying property owned by the company. This would apply where there had been a company reconstruction or the incorporation of a business in exchange for shares. Where other eligible property can be established, the period of ownership of the shares transferred must amount to two out of five years ending on the date of transfer. Business property relief for IHT would produce the same result. Shareholders will normally be able to secure

100% business property relief, unless the company is a quoted company, which they do not control.

The stud company owning land – APR Issues

7.33

What is the position where a stud farming company owns 'agricultural' land and lets it out for agricultural purposes including the stud?

The result is generally that the relief is limited to the rate of 50%. However, 100% relief may be available where the agricultural property would carry 100% relief if it were owned by an individual and vacant possession could be recovered within 12 months (or by concession, 24 months) or where the tenancy commenced on or after 1 September 1995.

The controlling shares and the land must have both been respectively owned for seven years and occupied for agricultural purposes by the tenant of the company throughout the seven years immediately before the transfer of the shares.

Where eligible property is involved, the combined ownership period must amount to seven out of ten years ending on the date of transfer. Minority shareholders achieve no IHT relief. This configuration has the additional disadvantage that a disposal of shares will not qualify for capital gains tax holdover relief, because the shares will not be shares in a trading company.

What happens if the shareholder of the Company owns the land and carries out stud farm activities on it?

Asset	*Controlling shareholder*	*Minority shareholder*
Land	Deemed to be occupied by the shareholder (IHTA 1984 s119(1)) and hence	There is no deemed occupation by the shareholder and hence

	relief available after two years occupation by the company. Relief will be at 100% even where the land is let to the company because of the second part of Extra-Statutory Concession F17.	relief is only available after seven years of ownership by the shareholder and seven years occupation of the land for agricultural purposes (IHTA 1984 s117(b)). Relief will be at 100% if the shareholder qualifies under the normal rules or otherwise at 50%.
Shares (agricultural value)	Any agricultural value attributable to the shares will qualify for 100% relief after two years of ownership of the shares.	No agricultural property relief, but business property relief available as for the non-agricultural value.
Shares (non-agricultural)	Will normally qualify for 100% property relief if the company is unquoted.	Will normally qualify for 100% property relief if the company is unquoted.

The opportunity to purchase the original farm to convert to a stud/equine business

7.34

Chapter 5 considers equine VAT in detail, but it seemed appropriate to review the complex position on VAT and the farmhouse in the section on the stud and the interactions with the other taxes surrounding the stud.

With the current elderly profile of farm ownership in the UK, much tax planning is needed around succession and potential sales of the whole farm – or perhaps just the farmhouse – to raise liquid funds. Many UK farms are owned in joint names and this can cause problems on the question of succession or sale. Likewise, many farms have already been on the market and there will be some future sales when one of the joint owners dies. For example, in some cases the beneficiaries cannot afford to 'buy each other out'. If one family member is unable to raise the finances to buy the interests of other members, selling might be the only option. Further, some family members will not want their shares to be bought by other relatives who *can* afford the opportunity due to simple motives such as awkward behaviour. It is essential that such problems are considered well in advance and protected through well-drafted partnership agreements and full, open and honest disclosure of wills and the intentions between the farming partners. Many of these farm sales are being made to buyers who want them to be used for the stud farm and the equine business.

If farms are held jointly by the farming partners, the strategy for what happens after one of them dies must be considered from a practical viewpoint. A key problem that will present itself is what to do with any farmhouses. With the recent apparent uncertainty around the rural property market, the worry of the 'large house' market and how the farmhouse is sold or apportioned can be a problem. However, with the potential tax advantage of only or main residence exemption for capital gains tax, this could be attractive.

Farms are having to be sold after probate as well as during lifetime to realise liquid funds to enable the business to survive. How the farm is owned is important for both capital gains tax and inheritance tax (see **7.17**). There may be disadvantages if houses are lived in individually by brothers and sisters but are owned jointly by them and their siblings. There is much tax planning and legal preparation that needs to be undertaken by the family farming business now. Likewise, this is an excellent opportunity for stud farms and equine businesses to purchase farms from retiring farmers.

Joint ownership can jeopardise only or main residence relief if farming partners live in different jointly owned properties.

VAT planning around the stud farmhouse

7.35

When considering the stud farmhouse and cottages as part of the purchase and overall planning, VAT must be considered. Guidance is given under *VAT Notice 708: building and construction*. Many traditional farmhouses are in a poor state of repair due to recent reductions in farming profits. If the houses are not listed, it might be suggested that the properties could be demolished and rebuilt because this could produce a saving of repair costs and VAT.

The VAT saving arises because the new residential property on a 'knock down' would be a 'new build' and therefore zero rated, providing the various specific conditions are met. On a new build, the contractor will agree to zero-rate the supply of labour and materials because it is a new residential property constructed from bare land. There are many basic problems with knocking down the farmhouse to produce bare land – for example, time delays and the cost of planning permission to rebuild rather than repair. A full cost analysis linked to the assessment of time delay together with tax saving analysis must be produced prior to the start of any such project.

The ability to claim the 20% extra input VAT on the routine repair costs can make a difference on decision-making on the question of whether to demolish or repair. Obviously, some of the input VAT on the repair of the farmhouse can be reclaimed if there is a working farm and a VAT registration. The message is to check the input VAT position as part of the full tax analysis well in advance of the decision-making. Ironically, the VAT position could be the deal-breaker on deciding which route to take regarding the farm repair and improvement strategy ahead of the possible sale or even ahead of the retention.

The 5% reduced rate of VAT is available for many farm residential projects and should be fully reviewed.

Historically, many larger stud farmhouses have had smaller residences connected to them for planning permission purposes or to provide accommodation for family members and suchlike. Therefore, other decision-making considerations around the bare land point can be the small house for staff built alongside an existing stud farmhouse to take advantage of the new build VAT advantage of the additional property. If there is a restriction in the planning consent – for example, that the farmhouse and small house can only be sold together as a single unit, not as separate sales to different buyers, there can be VAT considerations. VATA 1994, Sch 8 Gp 5 Note 2 lists four conditions that must be met for a building to be classed as a separate 'dwelling'.

The key consideration here is that the "separate…disposal of the dwelling is not prohibited by the terms of any covenant, statutory planning consent or similar provision". Since all four conditions must be met to achieve the VAT advantage, an 'and' rather than 'or' situation applies. The advantage of the zero-rate supply of a new build is then lost on the additional property if there is a planning permission restriction of the two houses. The builder is not constructing a new dwelling for VAT purposes and building services and material supplies are standard rated. The dwelling conditions are covered in para 14.2.1 of HMRC *Notice 708*.

If the stud decides to build a small house next to the stud farmhouse all taxes must be considered. The practicalities are that the farmer obtains planning permission for the project and then appoints a builder to do the work. As mentioned, the contractor cannot zero-rate his supply of labour and material if there is a planning permission restriction. Although the additional small house is a new residential property being constructed from bare land, the restriction in the planning consent would require the farmhouse and small house to be sold together as a single unit only, not as separate sales to different buyers.

The 5% VAT rate can apply if farm residences are unoccupied for two years before work starts. This could be helpful if property becomes vacant for some reason, perhaps cashflow. On the other hand, as a planning tool a vacant property has its own drawbacks. For example, what is the effect on inheritance tax relief and what happens if, say, the rules change midway through.

A stud farmhouse could be left empty deliberately simply to achieve the 5% VAT rate on renovation, but this obviously comes with worrying concerns for only or main residence relief (see **1.1**, **2.5** and **2.34**).

Repairs to the stud farmhouse

7.36

As well as being tax-efficient so far as VAT is concerned, if the decision is made to carry out major repairs to the farmhouse income tax efficiency can also be sought. Can the cost of repairs be allowed against profits? Full spreadsheets should be prepared and invoices retained to help with the decision-making.

There must be a clear analysis between expenditure that counts as improvements and repairs to the farmhouse to justify any repair claim for both income tax and VAT. There should also be a forensic analysis of the farmhouse between business and non-business use to ensure the correct allocation of costs.

Tax strategies need to be decided by farming families when they are buying, selling or apportioning properties and it is essential to review the tax consequences of the advice given by land agents on what they consider will achieve the best price in the market. Alternatively, the tax decisions themselves may determine the strategy to maximise sale proceeds. At present, many land agents are reporting a lack of supply of farms due to market uncertainty. However, it is predicted that many new farms and farmhouses will have to be sold to enable the business to survive or to pay out estate beneficiaries. The supply of such properties is therefore likely to increase and many of the buyers will be future stud and equine owners.

In general, the greater VAT and income tax percentage that can be claimed on the stud farmhouse will depend on the level of trading activity. It is usually more tax efficient to maximise trading rather than letting activities. With all the succession dilemmas that face elderly farming families, they must maintain a robust trading activity instead of falling into the trap of letting out property and reducing tax efficiency.

The stud farmhouse and the RNRB

7.37

From 6 April 2017, an additional residence nil-rate band (RNRB) is now available when a residential property that had been the deceased's residence at some point is left, on death, to a direct descendant.

Following the ruling shown by the *Antrobus 2* case, the inheritance tax (IHT) relief on the farmhouse is restricted to agricultural value (AV), i.e. the agricultural property relief (APR) is restricted to AV. The problem with the RNRB is that it does not apply to estates over £2 million (subject to tapering). The RNRB is tapered down by £1 for every £2 that the estate exceeds £2 million. Most farms do exceed £2 million in value on death, so the RNRB might not apply, but the stud farmhouse would qualify for RNRB if the estate is kept below £2 million (subject to tapering). The non-AV of the stud farmhouse (see **7.29**) does qualify for IHT relief from the RNRB, but will such availability be wasted due to the overall value of the estate? Calculations should be carried out with up-to-date values when trying to plan the maximisation of the RNRB.

Direct descendants are children (including step, adopted and foster children) and grandchildren, and the spouse or civil partner of a direct descendant, or surviving spouse or civil partner if they have not remarried or formed another civil partnership. Such identification is complicated, and all wills drafted prior to 6 April 2017 should be refreshed to take into account the RNRB utilisation.

The RNRB is limited to one residential property and cannot be applied over various properties. Where there is more than one residential property in the estate, the executors can nominate which one should qualify for the relief. Such an election puts another pressure on executors. The residential property must have been occupied by the deceased as a residence at some point in time but does not have to have been their main residence. Such leniency regarding properties could be of benefit to farmers who might have moved from the farmhouse to the converted barn, and then to the bungalow with wheelchair access. The additional RNRB will also be available for individuals who downsize or sell their home prior to death and pass assets of an equivalent value onto direct descendants on death, although evidence of the sale of the property will be required in order to claim the relief.

The RNRB will only be available for certain types of trust for qualifying beneficiaries. A will that provides for the estate to pass into a discretionary trust (even if the only potential beneficiaries are direct descendants) would not qualify for the relief. However, if the qualifying residential property passes into a discretionary trust, it is possible for the trustees to make an appointment of the property to direct descendants to ensure the availability of the RNRB. Once again, this is placing more pressure on trustees and farm tax advisers with regard to decision-making.

If a client's estate is worth more than £2 million, equine clients/stud farmers can review whether it is possible to arrange their affairs so that the RNRB can be claimed. If a couple's combined assets exceed £2 million, then they should seek advice to see if their wills can be updated to avoid any 'bunching' effect on the second death – for example, they could revise their wills so that part of the estate of the first to die is inherited by their children.

As mentioned, with equine clients, the lifetime transfers option (see **2.25**), possibly using a holdover election (see **2.26**), is very attractive as part of tax planning. Such an action involves passing part of the farm down to the next generation to reduce the £2 million cap for IHT, so as to maximise the use of the RNRB. Obviously, such a suggestion cannot be looked at in isolation; rather, the tax implications for the whole farm must be considered 'in the round'.

First, the capacity of the donor is something that needs careful thought. A large number of stud farmers are very elderly, and the professional protection that is needed around the mental capacity of the testator can be extended to lifetime gifts. Any tax adviser working in connection with tax planning around lifetime gifts should work with a solicitor, who will have similar responsibilities as to the will in deciding mental capacity on lifetime gifts.

Further, there are reporting considerations to take into account, as a lifetime gift of farm assets is still an effective sale for CGT purposes and must be recorded as such. The beneficiary will have to consider the loss of the tax-free uplift on death on such a gift, i.e. in applying the holdover election, the donee will take on the base cost of the donor and their taxable gain when they themselves come to sell or gift the asset will potentially be much larger.

Notably, for planning purposes it is essential that the updated wills tie into the stud farming partnership (if there is one), and such action signals an excellent time to review the partnership agreement.

While the RNRB is good news for those wishing to pass on the value of their family home to their children or grandchildren, the nil rate band (NRB) itself is now frozen until at least April 2026. Such a freezing means that, for the unmarried, and for those who leave no children or grandchildren, the IHT NRB of £325,000 will remain the same, so more families may be drawn into the IHT net.

The additional NRB was phased in from 2017/18 and from 2020/21 onwards is £175,000.

Clearly, review of all homeowners and stud farmers has to be considered.

Conclusion

The operation of a commercial stud farm represents a superb opportunity for the owner to enjoy very advantageous tax reliefs through inheritance tax relief, the claiming of efficient input VAT and the offsetting of income tax losses. Such inheritance tax relief can incorporate the farmhouse and cottages. However, as stressed throughout the book, each stud operation must be analysed in detail. Tax planning must start at an early stage and each stud must be considered on an individual basis, for example, the origins of the stud could be in an agricultural farm that might have fallen into some decay. All these opportunities need planning, understanding and compliance with the complex array of tax rules. The operation must be proven to be commercial and must be able to evidence such commerciality in order to fall 'within the scope of tax' and to achieve the very favourable tax reliefs.

CHAPTER EIGHT

PLANNING FOR EQUINE TAX LOSSES

Losses are almost inevitable in the early years of an equine related business and must be handled with care. **Chapter 8** explores the need to show the expectation of a commercial profit to support the tax loss. There must be a business plan (see **1.15**) to show potential future profits in order to prove its validity, and the use of a loss against total income. Stud Farms have their own 11-year rule for losses, these are explored in **8.13**. Specifically we look at:

- The various types of loss claims
- The importance of commerciality
- Capping the quantum of the loss
- The role of capital allowances
- Merging equine losses with another trade

Relief for losses

8.1

Equine businesses involve highly individualistic people, so tax planning will often need to be 'tailor made'. Dealing with losses in particular can be problematic and it will generally be advisable to keep a full record on file to control the timing of claims, maximise cash flow and ensure that the claims are fully utilised. Care should be taken in deciding how to claim loss relief and whether to claim or disclaim capital allowances. The consideration of the HMRC attack on equine losses in the context of the need to show 'pursuit of profit' is considered in detail in **Chapter 3**.

Losses from a commercial equine trade are generally allowable for tax purposes while losses from racing are not – unless exceptionally there is a case for the racing to be treated as an extension of the breeding operation.

Where applicable, breeders trading as sole trader or partnerships are able to set the loss from breeding for the tax year (fiscal basis) against other income for that year or, if this is insufficient, against the income of the previous tax year (see **8.3**). If there is insufficient income in the current tax year or the previous year to use up the losses, or no claim is made, the losses can be carried forward and set against profits from the same trade, without time limit. In the first four years of a trade equine trading losses can be carried back and set against the income of the trader of the previous three years.

Careful consideration should always be given to the optimum use of personal allowances and to ensure wherever possible that income is not taxed at higher rates, especially where income is over £100,000. Similarly, accelerating loss relief claims can have useful cash flow consequences especially in the early years of a business.

The ability to claim equine tax losses can affect commercial decisions such as who is formally involved in an equine trading partnership and arrangements for the sharing of profits/losses.

For stud farm losses and the 11-year rule see **8.13**.

The importance of commerciality

8.2

It is fundamental to loss relief claims that the equestrian business can demonstrate that it is being run on a 'commercial basis and with a view to profit' (see **3.1** and **3.9**). If this cannot be established HMRC may seek to restrict any claim for losses.

Perversely, an early claim for losses may actually be of benefit in establishing commerciality. The dispute process may actually help to show that there is a reasonable expectation of profit being earned by the business in future years. Once this is established, it should enable a business to claim other reliefs including capital gains tax (CGT) and inheritance tax (IHT) business reliefs.

There is a basic understanding in the equine world that claims for tax losses are being closely reviewed by HMRC who question their eligibility to be offset against total income. Many equine businesses record large trading losses. It is essential that, to protect the accrued losses, the adviser and client put the following steps in place:

- Business plans (see **1.15**) to show that, from the outset, a profit can be achieved in future years under the proposed structure;

- Revised rolling business plans responding to the actual trading results; and

- Ideally, accounts showing an eventual profit for the operation.

All advisers submitting loss claims on behalf of clients must ask objective questions about potential profit and not just accept in good faith the information provided.

Advisers and taxpayers will have to be prepared to mount a rigorous defence of loss claims, offering evidence to support the ability to achieve future profit. There must also be close scrutiny of the 'derives pleasure' point together with consideration of the badges of trade and the question of whether activities match the definition of a hobby. It is vital to prepare a well thought out business plan before questions are raised by HMRC. If loss claims have already been made, now is the time to collect the robust evidence to support them and ensure clients are warned about the potential vulnerability of the claims.

Closely following the First-tier Tribunal (FTT) case of *Cliff v HMRC* [2019] UKFTT 564 (TC) featuring equine loss claims comes negative findings from the British Horseracing Authority (BHA), which has published *Review of the buying and selling practices of Bloodstock and Racehorses.*

The review presents negative statistics regarding the profitability of breeders. Many would argue that this is bad timing after the decision in *Cliff* to disallow loss claims due to incorrect disclosure and lack of evidence of trading – there were no business plans or business forecasts prepared by Mr Cliff.

A quote from the BHA report: "At the lower end, the Review Team has seen that return on capital for breeders is only 1-3%, which has meant that as many as 66% of breeders are expected to have been unprofitable in 2017 when compared to 45% in 2013." Such generic statistics for the smaller breeder mean not only are there lots of potential loss claims by these breeders, there are also questions on proof of commerciality with a view to a profit. There have been many unsuccessful equine loss claims in the past (e.g. *McMorris* [2014] UKFTT 1116 (TC) and *Thorne* [2014] UKFTT 730 (TC)).

Tax advisers must learn from this information to check the validity of all tax loss claims and to encourage clients to produce evidence to support results and profit potential (e.g. to undertake not just business plans but rolling business plans responding to actual trading results). With the breeding statistics just produced, there is greater need for all breeders and stud farms to look at the structure and profit potential.

The negative cost of production potentially exceeding sales and evidence to show a profit can be produced is key. There is a difference between breeders who board out their mares and stud farms that have their own land.

The latter is farming for tax purposes and the former is not. The stud farm can take advantage of the 'hobby farming' rules, but there must still be evidence that the stud operation is trading commercially with a view to a profit. At the top end of all equine sports (e.g. racing, show jumping, dressage, etc) there are strong profits, but the problems can be at the lower end due to margins and sometimes inexperience. Equine profits can be achieved – there must be full allowance for private usage and a full understanding of the weak areas and rectification action taken.

Choices for claiming losses available to the equine business owner

8.3

The equine taxpayer has a variety of alternatives to select when planning how to claim the trading loss. Reliefs available for companies are set out at **8.18** below. For individuals and partners, income tax loss relief is available as follows:

- set off against other income in current or preceding year (s64 ITA 2007);
- set off against other income in first four years of trade (s72 ITA 2007);
- set off against capital gains on business assets (s71 ITA 2007);
- carry forward against future profits of *same* trade (s83 ITA 2007);
- expenditure in seven years before start of trade set off in first year of trade (pre-trading expenditure) (s57 ITTOIA 2005);
- terminal year loss set off against profits of three preceding years (s89 ITA 207).

In general terms, all the usual rules which apply to income tax trading losses apply equally to equestrian businesses and 'hobby farming' rules don't apply.

For understanding of losses and the interaction of capital allowances see **8.7**.

Setting tax losses against general income (s64)

8.4

Once an equine business is proven to be commercial then the losses will be allowable for tax purposes. HMRC explanations on proof of commerciality are found in s66 (see **8.11**) and are set out below.

Restriction on relief unless trade is commercial

- Trade loss relief against general income for a loss made in a trade in a tax year is not available unless the trade is commercial.
- The trade is commercial if it is carried on throughout the basis period for the tax year:
- On a commercial basis; and
- With a view to the realisation of profits of the trade.
- If at any time a trade is carried on so as to afford a reasonable expectation or profit, it is treated as carried on at that time with a view to the realisation of profits.
- If the trade forms part of a larger undertaking, references to profits of the trade are to be read as references to profits of the undertaking as a whole.
- If there is a change in the basis period in the way in which the trade is carried on, the trade is treated as carried on throughout the basis period in the way in which it is carried on by the end of the basis period.
- The restriction imposed by this section does not apply to a loss made in the exercise of functions conferred by or under an Act.

- This section applies to professions and vocations as it applies to trades.

The legislation provides that a loss from the equestrian business can be set against other income of a tax year or, if this is insufficient, or if the claimant prefers, against other income of the previous tax year.

From 6 April 2013 losses are restricted to 25% of total income (see **8.12**).

This relief can be very beneficial where the business owner has other income from another business, employment income or income from investments. It is not possible to claim only a part of the loss except to that extent that it exceeds available income. Therefore, some careful planning is needed when making a claim so as not to waste personal allowances, but this might not always be possible.

Time limits for claiming the loss

8.5

The time limits for claims are one year for offset against other income in current or future years and five years for the carry forward of losses after 31 January following the tax year of the loss.

These time limits are tight and the taxpayer and adviser must ensure prompt adherence to the deadline. This can also be of importance with regard to the timely registration of a business and assessment of the quantum and nature of the losses.

Opening year losses (s72)

8.6

The provision of ITA 2007 s72 allows losses sustained by an individual in the year of assessment in which he commences a trade and in the three following tax years to be set against his other income in the three tax years before that in which the loss is made, offsetting losses against income for earlier years before that of later years.

Where an individual starts an equestrian business after retiring from some other activity or employment, a high-income source may cease and the facility to offset losses against total income may be very beneficial if there is sufficient total income to absorb the losses, especially if large tax refunds can result. The facility to carry back losses of the first four years of a new business can be extremely useful to maximise loss relief against these high income years.

It is of paramount importance for such loss claims to be able to show that the equine trade is carried on in such a manner that profit can be expected to be realised within a reasonable time. This is of particular importance to the taxpayer who retires from a high-earning business or employment and moves into equine activities. A tough approach is taken by the HMRC in this regard and careful consideration must be given to this when thinking of making claims for losses under the opening year rules.

Losses offset against capital gains

8.7

ITA 2007 s 71 and TCGA 1992 s261B enable trading losses of an individual to be set against capital gains. This provides scope for planning when considering the timing to realise potential disposals likely to give rise to capital gains.

The relief under these acts can only be given after trading losses have first been set against a claimant's other income under ITA 2007 s64. It is not possible to claim trading loss relief against capital gains only, and so it is inevitable that personal allowances for the year could be wasted.

As with claims under ITA 2007 s64, trading losses can only be offset against gains for the same or preceding tax year. Any trading loss which is not offset in this way may be carried forward and set against future trading profits under ITA 2007 s89.

Non-commercial losses do not qualify for relief against capital gains tax.

The maximum amount of any trading loss claim under TCGA 1992 s261B is the amount chargeable to CGT in any year before deducting the annual exemption for CGT. Therefore, the claimant may lose the benefit of the annual exemption from capital gains tax. However, the trading losses are set against the gains of the year before unused capital losses brought forward from earlier years, so this may facilitate these capital losses being used in future years while helping to preserve the annual exemption.

Losses carried forward (s83)

8.8

Where no claim is made under the provisions outlined above, or where such a claim is made but excess losses remain unused, equine trading losses can be carried forward and set against future profits from the same trade (ITA 2007 s83). Such a provision is much more restrictive than other claims where the losses can be set against other income. For this reason and also for cash flow reasons, it is generally preferable, where possible, to avoid carrying forward losses.

On the other hand, there may be times where losses can be used more beneficially in future years where, for example, profits would otherwise be taxed at a higher rate.

A claim to carry forward a loss must be made within five years from 31 January following the year of loss. Since the time limits for s 64 and s 71 ITA 2007 claims are much tighter, this longer time limit is not as relevant because it will be apparent long before the expiry of the time limit whether losses are to be carried forward or not, i.e. whether there is a profit to offset against.

Terminal losses (s89)

8.9

On the permanent discontinuance of any equine business any losses sustained in the twelve months before the date of cessation may be carried back and set against profit of the same trade (ITA 2007 s89). This is subject to the provision that they are NOT relieved elsewhere.

The carry back of losses is restricted to the three tax years prior to the year in which the equine trade ceases. Relief is given first for the latest of those three years. This means that the eligible profits that are available for set off against terminal losses are those for the tax year in which the trade ceases and the three tax years preceding it.

Pre-trading expenditure

8.10

A large proportion of equine businesses take a long time to develop and progress and can incur considerable expenditure before the actual commencement of trading.

Tax relief can be achieved on this expenditure under ITTOIA 2005 s57 if it is incurred in the seven years before commencing to trade. Expenditure may be the subject of such a claim if it would be allowable under normal rules had it been incurred after commencement.

Pre-trading expenditure is treated as incurrent on the day an equine business starts to trade. The relief does not extend to expenditure that would not otherwise be deductible as a trade expense. An example of this is pre-trading purchase of stock of horses which will be shown as opening stock.

Restriction of loss relief for non-commerciality

8.11

Relief is only available for losses which arise from a trade carried out on a commercial basis. HMRC may decide to review claims if the losses continue to be made year after year. If HMRC consider that an activity has not been carried on commercially, they may seek to deny tax relief for the losses of past years.

With HMRC's current enthusiasm to examine equine activities, especially losses, it is not surprising that several cases concerning the eligibility of tax relief in trading loss claims have made their way to the First-tier Tribunal recently. A business must be trading on a commercial basis with a view to making a profit (ITA 2007, s 66) (see **8.4**) if it wishes to claim tax relief on trading losses. The taxpayer has to be able to prove that there is a reasonable expectation of profit from the trading operation. A review of s 66 has already been considered at **8.4**.

The taxpayer in *R Murray* (TC3474) (see **1.14**, **3.20** and **8.11**) was a racehorse breeder and trainer. He began the business in 2005 but did not notify HMRC until he submitted his 2007/08 tax return when he claimed cumulative losses of £51,378. The taxpayer claimed further losses totalling £81,406 for the tax years 2008/09, 2009/10 and 2010/11. The problems associated with racehorse breeding include high infrastructure costs and difficulties achieving targets for sales to ensure a profit. The First-tier Tribunal described as flawed logic the taxpayer's assumption that his breeding and training activities would be sustainable if the tax relief losses were allowable. HMRC enquired into the taxpayer's 2010/11 return and decided the losses were not allowable because he was not trading on a commercial basis with a view to making a profit (ITA 2007, s 66). The judge considered that, although there may have been a reasonable expectation of profit at the start of the taxpayer's business, by 2010/11 the economic downturn, together with the high running costs and consistent losses, led to no hope of profit. The lack of any income supported these concerns, with commerciality therefore also difficult to prove. Although sympathetic to the taxpayer's predicament, the judge considered that the business was not commercial and therefore the losses were not allowable.

The taxpayer lost the case and did not achieve tax relief on the losses.

Cap on the quantum of the loss from 6 April 2013

8.12

Legislation contained in the Finance Act 2013 has created a restriction on the level of income tax reliefs for certain tax deductions where previously there was no cap on the amount of relief that can be claimed. The maximum tax relief that can be claimed will be restricted to the higher of £50,000 or 25% of an individual's adjusted total income as calculated under the relevant tax provisions (ITA 2007 s24A(5). This applied with effect from 6 April 2013.

In addition, since the calculation of 25% of an individual's income is based on their income minus any pension contributions, pension contributions may waste the ability to optimise use of loss reliefs. Please note that gift aid payments to charity are not deducted in calculating the level of income to which the 25% cap applies.

In view of the high repair and infrastructure costs of equine businesses, it is essential to balance costs and income as integrated forecasts. There must be a clear plan regarding the timing of expenditure to structure losses and tax advisers must ensure tax loss memorandums and reconciliations are kept.

Stud farms – the 11-year loss rule

8.13

As losses from farming and breeding often continue for a number of years, specific legislation was brought in during the 1960s to restrict (define and protect) relief for losses in these circumstances. Guidance is found in section 67 ITA 2007 which states that if a tax loss (before taking into account capital allowances) from farming has been made for the past five fiscal years the sideways reliefs against income in the current or prior periods shall not be available for losses sustained in any future year. This is extended to 11 years for stud farms to make a profit, however, losses have to be carried forward once hobby farming status is deemed to apply.

HMRC has been closely reviewing all tax loss claims related to thoroughbred horse breeding, especially when there is no history of profit and the tax relief is at 45%. These are difficult times for the trade, and before conditions improve, it is essential that breeders and studs have protection in place to preserve these claims.

Thoroughbred breeding can be an industry with a slow rate of return. Breeders can't hurry the birth of a foal or its training. Accordingly, there are many breeders who think that they just have to make a profit from the trade by the 11th year when starting off in business, and then every sixth year after that. But though allowances are made for the long-term nature of the trade, to achieve the tax relief that is available there has to be proof of commercial motive in the breeding operation, and clear differences to separate a potentially profit-making business from the hallmarks of a hobby undertaking.

It is worth returning to the 1982 communication from HMRC to the Thoroughbred Breeders' Association (TBA), which stated: '*We have long accepted that the breeding of thoroughbred horses is such a long-term venture, and provided that a stud farming business is potentially profit-making, we would not normally seek to invoke section 397(1) until after 11 years from the start of the business*' (but note that the Income and Corporation Taxes Act, ICTA 1988, s397, is replaced by the Income Tax Act, ITA 2007, s67).

There are a number of clear directions outlined in HMRC's statement. Firstly, the business must be 'potentially profit making'. A recent relevant case, *John Agnew* (TC566), was actually about a beautician's business, but the key factor here was whether, within the existing structure, the business was capable of making a profit (see **3.20**). There are two ways to prove whether potential profit exists: either by achieving an actual profit, or by showing that a profit can and will be made through accurate, well thought out business plans. There has to be a 'financial road map' for the breeding operation showing how the stud farm has learnt from its own specific mistakes, as well as from generic mistakes common in the trade and any problems arising in the bloodstock industry.

The onus is still on the breeders to manage their expectations through financial control, and these valid reservations must be reflected in their business plans (see **1.15**). The breeders' calculation has to ensure that the full production cost, plus overheads, will be exceeded by the anticipated sales price, after allowing for production problems.

The HMRC statement refers specifically to a 'stud farm' (see **7.1**). This involves land ownership and is different from a 'breeding venture', which does not involve land ownership but generally has breeding mares. The key tax point is that stud farming is 'farming' for tax purposes, and therefore can benefit from the various agricultural tax reliefs available to the farming industry.

Caution must be applied to the 'grabbing' of the extended hobby farming rules of 11 years for a breeding business that is not essentially stud farming. Many small studs send their mares away to the stallion to foal down and they send the foals to be prepared for the sales – the lines can be blurred, but the exact nature of the business should be understood. There must be a stud farming operation to meet what are known as the hobby farming rules. When the hobby farming rules were introduced in 1960, the (then) new clause was not designed to debar relief for stud farming, in which there is a view to the overall realisation of profit in the long term, or for any operation run as a serious business.

The tax case *Walls v Livesey* ([1995] STC (SCD) 12) looked at two tests that can be used to prove the commerciality of a business. The first test was that the farmer had neither purpose nor interest in following a course other than the realisation of profit, and the second test that he 'had been blown off course.'

In order to satisfy the second test there must be evidence to show that the problems facing the UK bloodstock industry directly impacted on his increased losses (or failure) to achieve the anticipated profit.

With regard to the first test, there must be evidence to show that there is no motive other than the realisation of profit. There has to be proof of the profit motive as evidence of one of the important 'badges of trade'. With the power of the internet and its potential for revealing contradictory statements through searches of Google or social media, it is essential that there are no quotes anywhere which might suggest otherwise. Indeed it is essential that there are quotes with commercial statements that clarify the desire for profitability as the prime motive. It is important to note that the judgement of profit to meet the 'hobby farming' rules is before capital allowances.

There are also provisions to restrict losses where the involvement in breeding is deemed to be non-active. The tax loss claim will be capped at £25,000. unless there is evidence of 10 hours of active involvement per week. Evidence of the work and involvement should be obtained, especially when the taxpayer making the loss claim has other commercial interests that demand time, making the 10 hours hard to prove. It could actually be easier to pass the 'actively engaged' test with a stud farm operation, as opposed to a breeding operation without land.

Notably, the 11-year loss rule does not apply after a profit occurs. Once a business has made a profit the five-year hobby farming rule applies. This is not too much of a problem if the profit is in, say, year 9, 10 or 11, but if it crops up unexpectedly in year 2 it can cause a lot of problems. No matter how commercial their approach, nor how disciplined, knowledgeable and experienced a stud owner might be, their business is dependent on a large element of luck. Infertility, miscarriages and the loss of foals sometimes cannot be avoided. On the other hand, a surprise superstar foal may arrive without warning. This could cause a profit in, say, year 2 or 3, which would mean that the five-year loss rule comes into play with detrimental effects on the 11-year loss rule. A profit in year 2 will mean that a profit must be achieved again in year 8 just to secure the five years' loss reliefs. If an early profit is achieved the tax practitioner must warn their client of the problem.

Eliminating a loss

8.14

It will at times be desirable to plan to reduce or eliminate a loss in a particular year so as to protect other tax reliefs.

If a partnership has substantial interest payments, consider arranging for the partners to borrow individually and use their new loans to introduce capital into the firm. This will improve the stud farm trading result, and the interest on the personal loans is deductible from other income under ITA 2007 s383. Clients and advisers should, however, be aware that Inspectors are specifically instructed to examine such 'refinancing' tactics carefully to ascertain whether or not they were commercially inspired or undertaken with a view to manipulation of the loss relief rules. HMRC's Manuals specifically warn against obvious manipulations of profits, such as pulling in income into one year, reducing expenses in a particular year or the manipulation of stock valuations etc.

To avoid 11 consecutive years of stud farm losses, planning well in advance to ensure a profit in one particular year may be achievable without running such risks.

Using capital allowances to augment/reduce a loss

8.15

Capital allowance feature in **Chapter 2** (see **2.17**) These allowances are treated in the same way as business expenses and so augment the losses (or reduce profits) in the same way as expenses. If loss relief is denied on the grounds that a business is not run on a commercial basis, it follows that any related capital allowances will not be allowed.

There is scope to reduce losses by restricting the amount of capital allowances claimed. This would be a useful tax planning technique where the equine client could not make good use of the allowances. Some reasons for not claiming capital allowances include:

- the reduction of losses to avoid wasting the benefit of the personal allowance;
- the desire to utilise losses brought forward instead of current year losses;
- the inability to relieve current year losses in a tax-efficient manner;
- wanting to avoid having to carry forward current year losses;
- wanting to carry forward a higher written down value for the capital assets, in particular if an asset is to be sold in the future – increasing the amount of unrelieved capital expenditure would increase a balancing allowance or reduce a balancing charge thus increasing future losses or reducing future profits which otherwise may be taxed at a higher rate.

The restriction for capital allowances does not mean that an exact amount of tax relief can be claimed in a future year but that there will be extra allowances to claim due to the increased amount of the written-down value of the assets carried forward.

Augmentation of losses by capital allowances – a summary

8.16

For certain classes of loss the amount of the loss claim can be increased by including certain qualifying capital allowances. The augmentation of different losses by capital allowances is set out in the table below.

Section	*Class of relief*	*Capital allowances to be included*
ITA 2007 s64	Set off against total income of tax year.	Capital allowances for the year of assessment for which the year of loss is the basis year.
ITA 2007 s83	Carry forward against subsequent profits.	Capital allowances exceeding balancing charges and taxable profits for the relevant year, but allowances brought forward can be applied first against profits and charges.
ITA 2007 s89	Terminal loss relief against earlier profits.	Capital allowances for year in which the trade is permanently discontinued plus the appropriate proportion for the preceding year
ITA 2007 s72	Relief for losses in early years of trade.	Capital allowances for the year of loss so far as not carried back effective for that year.

The trading loss carry back rule will be temporarily extended from one year to three years for losses arising between April 2020 and March 2022. Unincorporated businesses and companies that are not members of a group will be able to obtain relief for up to £2 million of losses in each of 2020/21 and 2021/22. The loss carry back rules will be very beneficial in respect of equine losses.

Trading through a company

8.17

The rate of corporation tax will increase from April 2023 to 25% on profits over £250,000. The rate for small profits under £50,000 will remain at 19% and there will be taper relief for businesses with profits between £50,000 and £250,000 so that their average rate is less than the main rate.

A company carrying on a trade of breeding can claim relief for the loss from breeding against its other income in the period or can carry back the loss against the profits of the preceding period (if the breeding trade was carried on during that period). Alternatively, if the company is part of a group or consortium, the loss can be passed on and set against the profits of the same period of another group or consortium company. As with an individual, any unused losses can be carried forward and used against future profits of the same trade without time limit. As stated above, following the Budget 2021 the trading loss carry back rule will be temporarily extended from one year to three years for losses arising between April 2020 and March 2022. This will be available for both incorporated and unincorporated businesses. Unincorporated businesses and companies that are not members of a group will be able to obtain relief for up to £2 million of losses in each of 2020/21 and 2021/22. Companies that are members of a group will be able to obtain relief for up to £200,000 of losses in each of 2020/21 and 2021/22 without any group limitations. Companies that are members of a group will be able to obtain relief for up to £2 million of losses in each of 2020/21 and 2021/22 but subject to a £2 million cap across the group as a whole.

If an individual or company is carrying back losses to a prior period or a company is passing on losses to another group company, a claim must be made to HMRC. Claims must be made within twelve months from 31 January following the end of the relevant tax year (for individuals) or two years from the end of the relevant accounting period (for companies). No claims are needed where losses are carried forward.

Companies can claim relief for the loss from equestrian businesses as follows:

- against their total profits in the period or against the profits of the preceding period (if the trade was carried on during that period) under CTA 2010 s37(3);
- if the company is part of a group or consortium then the loss can be set against the profits of the same period of another group or consortium company (CTA 2010 s97);
- against future profits of *same* trade under CTA 2010 s45; and
- in the case of terminal losses, against total profits of the preceding three years under CTA 2010 s39.

The hobby farming/non-commercial restrictions apply equally to losses incurred by companies and individuals. The provisions of CTA 2010 s48 will mean that if losses are sustained and restricted, the trading status of the company will be at risk. Losses restricted as non-commercial in this way will not be allowable to be offset against other income of the company, for example, property that is let.

Holistic approach to loss planning

8.18

All farms are 'taxed as one trade' and the distinction between stud farms, farming, and other operations must be understood as there are clear tax planning implications on the impact on the use of loss relief. It is not uncommon for a UK stud owner to have a number of stud farms throughout the UK and overseas (see **Chapter** 7). The impact that this rule has on loss claims, ownership structures and future plans together with other farms and equine businesses (see 8.20) should be considered for tax planning.

The matter is complicated by the fact that stud farms are rarely dedicated studs; they often have other equestrian activities running alongside the stud as well and these must be analysed and evidenced and it is key for all the professionals to work together.

For any equestrian establishment, which has problems of profit making and cash flow, a high earning partner who can introduce capital and utilise some initial tax losses may have considerable tax benefits for tax planning.

The tax planning implications of the use/allocation of profits/losses will have to be reviewed in the light of commerciality. Historically, partnership losses have been allocated to those with the highest income to offset. There is a risk that this may be attacked by HMRC.

If a realistic view is that losses will be incurred in the early years of a business it is imperative to consider in advance how these will best be used.

Active involvement of the traders

8.19

There is a restriction to the amount of losses that 'non-active partners' or sole traders can set against their other income in a particular tax year. Section 103C Income Tax Act (ITA) 2007 set a £25,000 cap on the loss relief that could be claimed and there is an additional restriction being that of the amount of capital introduced by the non-active partner or sole trader, with a non-active partner or sole trader defined as one spending an average of less than ten hours a week personally engaged in the activities of the trade. S74 ITA 2007 extended the loss restriction to non-active sole traders as well as partners.

Thorne – merging equine loss with other trade

8.20

Equine tax losses and HMRC's interest therein has been a feature of the last decade including cases being heard in the tax tribunals. They have become particularly active in challenging claims to set off equine trading losses against other income (see **8.11**).

The facts of the *Thorne* tax tribunal *(Thorne v HMRC [2014] UK FTT 730 (TC))* (see **3.19**) were that in 2004, Mrs Thorne began trading as a horse breeder of event horses to sell. Four years later Mrs Thorne began a new trade of asparagus farming which she anticipated would return substantial profits, although it would be three years before the first crop was harvested.

In Mrs Thorne's 2008-09 self-assessment tax return, she claimed sideways loss relief under ITA 2007, s 64(1) and (2) (see 8.3) for her equestrian and asparagus businesses. HMRC refused the loss claim. Mrs Thorne appealed. The First-tier Tribunal (FTT) dismissed her appeal, saying that the taxpayer was operating two ventures as a single trade but although the asparagus element was run on a commercial basis, the horse breeding one was not.

Many equine businesses are an integral part of another separate business and effectively trade as one operation. Some businesses are merged incorrectly as one trade possibly to 'mask' the poor equine trading results; sometimes the full extent of the equine losses are not realised. This combining of different activities can be a subconscious action on the part of the business owner or deliberate to try and achieve tax efficiency. In this case Mrs Thorne was keen to show the two trades were SEPARATE so that the asparagus loss could still be claimed. It was agreed that the FTT had applied the wrong test for deciding if equine activity and asparagus growing was a single trade. The irony was that horse breeding is farming and asparagus growing could well be defined as market gardening. The Judge stated that: "In our view whether the asparagus business was farming or market gardening was a relevant matter and the failure to consider the question and reach a conclusion on it was an error of law."

The case was reviewed by the Upper Tribunal who stated the FTT had made an error in law in saying there was a single trade. It was therefore necessary to consider whether the asparagus business was market gardening and, if it was, whether as a matter of fact the equestrian trade and the asparagus business constituted a single trade. The judge concluded that there was insufficient information about the relevant factors to decide whether the land on which the asparagus was grown was a market garden. More details were also needed about how the land was cultivated, the use of farming machinery and the skill required to grow it. The Upper Tribunal decided to remit the case to the FTT to reconsider the issue. On that basis, it was not appropriate to judge whether the asparagus growing and horse breeding were a composite single trade.

Many equine businesses are combined with other non-equine businesses and it is essential that there is sufficient detail to decide if they are one trade or if they have more than one trade where the expenses are allocated and the correct preparation of enterprise accounts. This highlights the complexities facing equine businesses – there must be enterprise accounts to define the different activity at the least.

"Forensic analysis" is needed to achieve the loss relief. In addition, there must be legal agreements, good records, and where the equine business does merge with a more profitable activity, it must be possible to 'demerge' the business.

Business plans and enterprise accounts are essential (see **1.15**). ad actually understanding what the business is doing and what is the correct tax treatment is critical. Help is provided by s 996(5) ITA 2007 where market gardening is described as the occupation of land as a garden or nursery for the purposes of growing produce for sale.

Conclusion

In summary, care should always be taken in deciding whether to claim a tax loss against other income etc and whether any claim should be augmented by the relevant capital allowances. As in any situation, the interaction of personal income tax allowances and basic rate bands for income tax should be considered. Likewise, the cash flow considerations of the claim for losses to reduce tax as soon as possible should be reviewed including the carry back of losses. The ability to claim equine tax losses might affect commercial decisions, such as who is formally involved in the equine trading partnership and what the profit/loss share provisions are.

It is fair to say that HMRC have been vicious in their review of tax losses and equine tax losses. The supporting factors must be evidence, documentation, business plans, loss memorandums and the need to prove commercial intent. With loss claims the tax adviser must not just understand the commercial operation business and business plans but the full interaction of such information with the taxpayer's individual circumstances.

CHAPTER NINE

THE EQUESTRIAN LANDLORD – LEGAL ASPECTS BY MARK CHARTER

In this chapter we examine the possible legal structures for the occupation of land with horses. We do so however with particular reference to the position of the landowner who allows his or her land to be occupied with horses, and how that landowner can guard against the risk of the occupier gaining long-term security of tenure. If an occupier gains long term security of tenure (that was never originally intended by the landowner) that may prevent the landowner recovering the land for his or her own use, or developing the land for another purpose. That scenario can enable the occupier to "ransom" the landowner to procure a release of the land from the rights the occupier has secured.

The occupation of land with horses

9.1

The author's experience in practising in this area, and anecdotal evidence would suggest that a large section of horse owners and proprietors of equestrian businesses keep their horses on land they do not own. The arrangements under which horses are kept on land belonging to someone other than the horse owner are many and varied. Unfortunately, these arrangements are frequently entered into without prior professional advice, and without the landowner or horse owner fully appreciating the full legal context and potential consequences of the arrangement. Problems with the 'horsey' occupation of land regrettably are not unusual. This may be partly attributable to the tradition in the countryside of transactions being conducted by verbal agreement – this is problematic because the law is complex, and the only record of the agreement will be individuals' recollection which may have become hazy over time.

There is also a danger that 'one thing leads to another'; for example, a farmer allows a teenage girl to graze her pony on a field. Over time, the girl puts up stables, keeps a number of horses on the land, and expands her equine activities onto adjoining fields. The farmer dies, leaving the farm to his son. The son has plans to increase revenue from the farm which entail recovering possession of the land used for horses. When he approaches the 'tenant' to discuss the handing back of the land she claims she has a business tenancy. The farmer's son then faces the daunting prospect of potentially lengthy and expensive litigation, in which he is at a disadvantage because he was not party to the original agreement (the first-hand knowledge and evidence as to the terms of the agreement from the landlord's perspective having died with his father). It is, therefore, important to make sure the arrangements for the occupation of land by horses are thought out and correct from the outset, failure to do so may result in:

- an inability for the landowner to recover possession of the land when he wants to;
- adverse or unexpected tax effects;
- the occupant claiming compensation from the landowner;
- devaluation of the landowner's property;
- considerable expense in recovering possession or resolving problems; and
- stress and worry.

However, before the reader despairs, provided the appropriate arrangement is identified in the first place, potential problems can be obviated. It should be said that any freehold landowner whose land is mortgaged, before entering into any of the arrangements mentioned below, should first obtain his mortgagee's consent to do so. The terms of modern mortgage deeds are invariably such that failure to obtain the mortgagee's consent would constitute a breach of the landowner's covenants or obligations as mortgagor under the mortgage. Similarly, if the person permitting someone else to use his land for horses, is a tenant himself, he should first check the terms of his lease to see if the proposed arrangement would be permitted, and indeed whether his landlord's express prior consent is required. Failure to comply strictly with the terms of his lease may be disastrous for a tenant, not least because it may lead to the early termination of the lease. A tenant in this situation would also be prudent to take professional advice as to whether there are any other ramifications of the proposed arrangements with the horse owner or proprietor of an equestrian business to be established on the land (for example, could it result in an increase in the rent on a rent review)? In this chapter reference to the 'landowner' is shorthand for either the freehold owner of land, or an existing tenant of the land, looking to allow another to make use of the land under the landowner's control.

The landowner must also consider whether the proposed arrangement will be such that planning consent is first required from the local planning authority. A common misconception is that equine or equestrian activities for town and country planning purposes are synonymous with agricultural use, and consequently the necessity for a planning consent is often overlooked. Consideration of the town and country planning regime is outside the ambit of this chapter, suffice to say, however, that the circumstances in which an equine use will qualify as an agricultural one for planning purposes are extremely limited.

In essence, the possible arrangements can be categorised as follows:

(1) livery agreements;

(2) licences;

(3) profit à prendre;

(4) agistment;

(5) common law lettings;

(6) Farm Business Tenancy agreements;

(7) business tenancies (within the Landlord and Tenant Act 1954).

We shall look at each of these arrangements in turn.

Licences

9.2

A licence is a simple form of agreement between landowner and horse owner, and is used typically to permit the horse owner (non-exclusive) use of land for grazing. In the author's opinion, the use of simple licences (and profit à prendre) are, in most cases, better limited to situations where the proposed arrangement is of short duration and relates to grazing only for private recreational horses.

If the licence purports to grant the horse owner exclusive occupation of the land, that will be fatal to it being construed as a licence (it is of the essence to a licence that the licensee is not granted exclusive rights of occupation). Furthermore, to avoid the risk of a licence being construed as a tenancy by the courts, the licence should not:

- use the language of landlord and tenant (e.g. the use of the expression 'rent'); or

- impose tenant-type obligations (e.g. for hedging and ditching, maintenance and repair).

The danger to the landowner of a licence being construed as a tenancy is that the horse owner may have conferred on him rights which the landowner never intended the horse owner should have the benefit of; this is particularly so if what purports to be a licence, is subsequently determined by the courts to be a business tenancy.

Profit à prendre

9.3

A 'profit à prendre' is a right to take something from the land, which in the case of horses is grass by grazing (a 'profit of pasturage'). It is in the parties' (and particularly the landowner's) interest that the granting of a profit of pasturage should be documented by deed. A profit of pasturage comprises an incorporeal rather than a corporeal hereditament and, accordingly, no tenancy of land arises. The horse owner does not acquire exclusive possession of the land and, indeed, the landowner is treated as remaining in possession of the land, and remains free to exercise all rights over the land (including granting rights to third parties), which are not inconsistent with the right of pasturage granted to the horse owner.

This arrangement can be attractive to landowners who wish to be treated (commonly for tax reasons) as continuing to farm the land (i.e. by growing a crop of grass on the land). As with licences, the deed granting the profit à prendre (to be treated as such) must avoid language or terms which infers any exclusivity of occupation on the part of the horse owner, or seeks to impose tenant type obligations on the horse owner. Again, as with licences, all responsibility for care of the horse will lie with the horse owner (although the prudent landowner will maintain public liability insurance in respect of his land).

Agistment

9.4

A 'contract of agistment' is an agreement whereby the landowner (in this context referred to as 'the agister') agrees to take in someone else's animals to graze on the agister's land for a fee. The horse owner in such an arrangement obtains no tenancy or interest whatsoever in the agister's land, and no part of the agister's land is designated for the purpose of the arrangement. Under such arrangements, the horse(s) are returnable to the horse owner on demand; it is important the contract of agistment expressly provides that the agister will have a lien on the horse(s) until any monies owing under the contract are paid, otherwise the agister will not be entitled to retain a horse until the horse owner has paid his debt to the agister.

Common law lettings

9.5

The conventional grazing agreement to an individual or individuals in respect of ponies or horses kept for private recreational use, will usually be a tenancy under common law. It is essential (for the tenancy to be treated as a common law letting) that the proposed tenancy is not for a horse owner's use in connection with a trade or business. There is, however, a catch for the unwary in that a landowner granting a tenancy to a group of people, such as a riding club, may unwittingly create a business tenancy. The definition of business in the Landlord and Tenant Act 1954 s23(2) includes 'any activity carried on by a body of persons, whether corporate or unincorporate'.

A common law letting for a fixed period will simply expire at the end of its contractual term without any special notice provisions. Periodic common law tenancies, however, require termination by notice, the relevant period of notice being dependent on the type of periodic tenancy:

Type of periodic tenancy	*Notice required*
Weekly	One week
Monthly	One month
Quarterly	One quarter

Year to year	At least 6 months (the expiry of the notice period to coincide with the end of the tenancy year)

It is worth noting that a common law tenant has no right to compensation for improvements to the property let, unless provision for such is written into the tenancy agreement.

Farm business tenancies

9.6

The Agriculture Tenancies Act 1995 introduced a new regime for agricultural tenancies by the introduction of Farm Business Tenancies (FBTs). There was a recognition that increasingly there was a need in the agricultural industry for a more adaptable form of tenancy that could accommodate farmers wishes (or indeed economic need in many cases) to diversify farm activities into areas outside traditional farming ones.

The essential elements of an FBT are that it:

- must have commenced after August 1995, and the property the subject of the FBT used for business;
- the character of the property must be wholly or primarily agricultural – or notices must have been exchanged between landlord and tenant before the tenancy is entered into, stating it is intended to be an FBT;
- FBTs for fixed terms of two years or less expire at the end of their contractual term (without the need for service of notices);
- FBTs from year to year or fixed terms longer than two years run on until either the landlord or tenant serves notice to terminate (of at least 12 months). In practice, this may mean that a notice

with a notice period of between 12 and 24 months has to be served, as the expiry of the notice must coincide with expiration of the relevant tenancy year.

Subject to complying with the requirements of Part III of the 1995 Act (which relates to landlords consent to improvements) tenants' improvements can qualify for compensation. Improvements in this context can be both tangible ones and intangible ones, for example, a planning permission. In essence, the compensation the landowner may have to pay for qualifying improvements equates to the increase in the letting value of the property at the end of the tenancy as a result of the improvements.

FBTs may be suitable where, for example, the land in question is to be used as grazing ancillary to an equestrian business (e.g. a riding school) or where the land use is diversifying out of an agricultural use. At the moment, there is no substantive body of case law to give guidance as to the extent to which land use can diversify out of an agricultural use, and the tenancy remain an FBT within the ambit of the 1995 Act. Accordingly, in the equine context the terms of an FBT need to be very carefully thought out, and in many cases the preferred route may be the creation of a business tenancy contracted out of the provisions of the Landlord and Tenant Act 1954 ss24–28.

Business tenancies under the Landlord And Tenant Act 1954

9.7

Where an equestrian business is to be carried out on the land, a business tenancy, governed by the provisions of the Landlord and Tenant Act 1954, will often be the most suitable form of tenancy.

A wide range of activities can fall within the Act's definition of business (as mentioned at **9.5** above). The 1954 Act potentially:

- gives the tenant long-term security of tenure (as, subject to what is said below, the tenant at the expiry of his tenancy has a statutory right to apply for a new tenancy through the courts, which in turn the landlord can only resist on certain statutory grounds);

- provides for an outgoing tenant to be paid compensation in certain circumstances.

There are, therefore, real dangers for landowners who unwittingly create a 1954 Act business tenancy, particularly where the landowner had only intended the tenancy arrangement to be of relatively short duration before the landowner taking the property back in hand. However, professionally drawn business tenancy agreements will avoid traps for the landowner and provide a good structure for regulating the relationship between landlord and tenant.

Furthermore, the tenant's statutory right to apply for a new tenancy at the expiry of a current tenancy can be removed, if before the grant of such tenancy the necessary steps are taken to "contract out" of the relevant provisions (i.e. sections 24 to 28) of the Landlord and Tenant Act 1954. These steps are essentially once the exact form of the proposed new lease is agreed between the landowner and tenant (but not signed):

- that the landowner serves a notice in a prescribed form giving the tenant formal notice that the provisions of sections 24-28 Landlord and Tenant Act 1954 will be excluded from the new lease/tenancy, and

- the tenant makes and gives to the landowner a declaration/ statement, again in prescribed form, acknowledging the above. (In the event the landowner and the tenant want to complete the new lease or tenancy in less than 14 days from the giving of the landowner's notice, the tenant's response must be in the form of a statutory declaration i.e. a declaration made before a solicitor, commissioner for oaths or notary public).

- – -

This chapter was provided by Mark Charter, a highly experienced agricultural Partner, at Things LLP.

Mark acts on behalf of individuals, families, trusts, partnerships, companies and even government departments on a range of agricultural cases. He advises farmers, estate owners and the wider landowner community across south England and beyond. He can be contacted at mcharter@thrings.com.

MORE BOOKS BY LAW BRIEF PUBLISHING

A selection of our other titles available now:-

'Covid-19, Homeworking and the Law – The Essential Guide to Employment and GDPR Issues' by Forbes Solicitors
'Covid-19, Force Majeure and Frustration of Contracts – The Essential Guide' by Keith Markham
'Covid-19 and Criminal Law – The Essential Guide' by Ramya Nagesh
'Covid-19 and Family Law in England and Wales – The Essential Guide' by Safda Mahmood
'A Practical Guide to the Law of Unlawful Eviction and Harassment – 2nd Edition' by Stephanie Lovegrove
'Covid-19, Residential Property, Equity Release and Enfranchisement – The Essential Guide' by Paul Sams and Louise Uphill
'Covid-19, Brexit and the Law of Commercial Leases – The Essential Guide' by Mark Shelton
'A Practical Guide to Costs in Personal Injury Claims – 2nd Edition' by Matthew Hoe
'A Practical Guide to the General Data Protection Regulation (GDPR) – 2nd Edition' by Keith Markham
'Ellis on Credit Hire – Sixth Edition' by Aidan Ellis & Tim Kevan
'A Practical Guide to Working with Litigants in Person and McKenzie Friends in Family Cases' by Stuart Barlow
'Protecting Unregistered Brands: A Practical Guide to the Law of Passing Off' by Lorna Brazell
'A Practical Guide to Secondary Liability and Joint Enterprise Post-Jogee' by Joanne Cecil & James Mehigan
'A Practical Guide to the Pre-Action RTA Claims Protocol for Personal Injury Lawyers' by Antonia Ford
'A Practical Guide to Neighbour Disputes and the Law' by Alexander Walsh
'A Practical Guide to Forfeiture of Leases' by Mark Shelton
'A Practical Guide to Coercive Control for Legal Practitioners and Victims' by Rachel Horman

'A Practical Guide to Rights Over Airspace and Subsoil' by Daniel Gatty
'Tackling Disclosure in the Criminal Courts – A Practitioner's Guide' by Narita Bahra QC & Don Ramble
'A Practical Guide to the Law of Driverless Cars – Second Edition' by Alex Glassbrook, Emma Northey & Scarlett Milligan
'A Practical Guide to TOLATA Claims' by Greg Williams
'Artificial Intelligence – The Practical Legal Issues' by John Buyers
'A Practical Guide to the Law of Prescription in Scotland' by Andrew Foyle
'A Practical Guide to the Construction and Rectification of Wills and Trust Instruments' by Edward Hewitt
'A Practical Guide to the Law of Bullying and Harassment in the Workplace' by Philip Hyland
'How to Be a Freelance Solicitor: A Practical Guide to the SRA-Regulated Freelance Solicitor Model' by Paul Bennett
'A Practical Guide to Prison Injury Claims' by Malcolm Johnson
'A Practical Guide to the Small Claims Track' by Dominic Bright
'A Practical Guide to Advising Clients at the Police Station' by Colin Stephen McKeown-Beaumont
'A Practical Guide to Antisocial Behaviour Injunctions' by Iain Wightwick
'Practical Mediation: A Guide for Mediators, Advocates, Advisers, Lawyers, and Students in Civil, Commercial, Business, Property, Workplace, and Employment Cases' by Jonathan Dingle with John Sephton
'The Mini-Pupillage Workbook' by David Boyle
'A Practical Guide to Crofting Law' by Brian Inkster
'A Practical Guide to Spousal Maintenance' by Liz Cowell
'A Practical Guide to the Law of Domain Names and Cybersquatting' by Andrew Clemson
'A Practical Guide to the Law of Gender Pay Gap Reporting' by Harini Iyengar

'A Practical Guide to the Rights of Grandparents in Children Proceedings' by Stuart Barlow
'NHS Whistleblowing and the Law' by Joseph England
'Employment Law and the Gig Economy' by Nigel Mackay & Annie Powell
'A Practical Guide to Noise Induced Hearing Loss (NIHL) Claims' by Andrew Mckie, Ian Skeate, Gareth McAloon
'An Introduction to Beauty Negligence Claims – A Practical Guide for the Personal Injury Practitioner' by Greg Almond
'Intercompany Agreements for Transfer Pricing Compliance' by Paul Sutton
'Zen and the Art of Mediation' by Martin Plowman
'A Practical Guide to the SRA Principles, Individual and Law Firm Codes of Conduct 2019 – What Every Law Firm Needs to Know' by Paul Bennett
'A Practical Guide to Adoption for Family Lawyers' by Graham Pegg
'A Practical Guide to Industrial Disease Claims' by Andrew Mckie & Ian Skeate
'A Practical Guide to Redundancy' by Philip Hyland
'A Practical Guide to Vicarious Liability' by Mariel Irvine
'A Practical Guide to Applications for Landlord's Consent and Variation of Leases' by Mark Shelton
'A Practical Guide to Relief from Sanctions Post-Mitchell and Denton' by Peter Causton
'A Practical Guide to Equity Release for Advisors' by Paul Sams
'A Practical Guide to the Law Relating to Food' by Ian Thomas
'A Practical Guide to Financial Services Claims' by Chris Hegarty
'The Law of Houses in Multiple Occupation: A Practical Guide to HMO Proceedings' by Julian Hunt
'A Practical Guide to Unlawful Eviction and Harassment' by Stephanie Lovegrove
'Occupiers, Highways and Defective Premises Claims: A Practical Guide Post-Jackson – 2nd Edition' by Andrew Mckie

www.ingramcontent.com/pod-product-compliance
Lightning Source LLC
LaVergne TN
LVHW052255200926
848481LV00002B/374
9781914608001